Prentice-Hall
Contemporary Topics in Accounting Series
ALFRED RAPPAPORT, SERIES EDITOR

IONA COLLEGE

BEDFORD, *Extensions in Accounting Disclosure*

JAEDICKE AND SPROUSE, *Fund Flows, 2nd ed.*

KELLER, *The Uniformity-Flexibility Issue in Accounting*

LEV, *Financial Statement Analysis: A New Approach*

PALMER, *Analytical Foundations of Planning, Programming, Budgeting Systems*

REVSINE, *Replacement Cost Accounting*

SHANK, *Accounting for Intercorporate Investments*

WAGNER, *Auditing and the Computer*

ZEFF, *A Critical Analysis of the Accounting Principles Board*

**Prentice-Hall
Foundations of Finance Series**

EZRA SOLOMON, SERIES EDITOR

IONA COLLEGE

FINANCIAL
STATEMENT
ANALYSIS

FINANCIAL STATEMENT ANALYSIS
A NEW APPROACH

BARUCH LEV
University of Chicago and Tel-Aviv University

PRENTICE-HALL, INC., ENGLEWOOD CLIFFS, NEW JERSEY

Library of Congress Cataloging in Publication Data

LEV, BARUCH.
  Financial statement analysis.

  (Contemporary topics in accounting)   (Foundations
of finance series)
  Includes bibliographical references.
  1. Financial statements.   I. Title.
HF5681.B2L56   657'.3   74-3287
ISBN   0-13-316265-6
ISBN   0-13-316257-5 (pbk.)

PRINTED IN THE UNITED STATES OF AMERICA

10 9 8 7 6 5 4 3 2 1

Prentice-Hall International, Inc., LONDON

Prentice-Hall of Australia, Pty. Ltd., SYDNEY

Prentice-Hall of Canada, Ltd., TORONTO

Prentice-Hall of India Private Limited, NEW DELHI

Prentice-Hall of Japan, Inc., TOKYO

To
ILANA

Contents

Foreword

Accounting, broadly conceived as the measurement and communication of economic information relevant to decision makers, has undergone dramatic changes during the past decade. Recent advances in quantitative methods, the behavioral sciences, and information technology are influencing current thinking in financial as well as managerial accounting. Leasing, pension plans, the use of convertible securities and warrants in mergers and acquisitions, inflation, and corporate diversification are but a few of the challenging problems facing the accountant.

These developments and the very pervasiveness of accounting activity make it difficult for teachers, students, public accountants, and financial executives to gain convenient access to current thinking on key topics in the field. Journal articles, while current, must often of necessity give only cursory treatment or present a single point of view. Many of the important developments in the field have not crystalized to a point where they can be easily incorporated into textbooks. Further, because textbooks must necessarily limit the space devoted to any one topic, key topics often do not get the attention they properly deserve.

The Contemporary Topics series attempts to fill this gap by covering significant contemporary developments in accounting through brief, but self-contained, studies. These independent studies provide the reader with up-to-date coverage of key topics. For the practitioner, the series offers a succinct overview of developments in research and practice in areas of special interest to him. The series enables the teacher to design courses with maximum flexibility and to expose his students to authoritative analysis of controversial problems.

ALFRED RAPPAPORT

Preface

The major purpose of *Financial Statement Analysis: A New Approach* is to bridge the wide gap between traditional financial statement analysis and modern economic and finance theories. Nowhere is this gap more evident than in the literature relating to the respective areas; texts and articles on financial statement analysis are still basically concerned with financial ratios as they were at the beginning of the century, while microeconomic and finance studies of firm and investor behavior are generally devoid of any reference to the information contained in financial statements. This gap is being bridged by the new approach to financial statement analysis presented in the following chapters, in which financial statement analysis is viewed as an information-processing system designed to provide firm-related data for decision makers. Financial statement analysis is thus considered an integral part of economic and finance decision theories.

The new approach is presented by bringing together the major contributions in finance, accounting, and economics related to financial statement analysis. These studies can be classified into two groups: (a) Descriptive studies, which are concerned with identifying the major determinants of business phenomena in order to *explain* and *predict* individual and corporate decisions. This group includes studies on the behavior of corporate earnings, the determinants of corporate solvency and bond risk premiums, and the effect of financial data and changes in accounting techniques on investor behavior. (b) Prescriptive studies, which are intended to *improve* upon current decisions. The studies in this group are concerned with the optimal prediction of earnings, corporate bankruptcy and bond ratings, the improvement of bank lending decisions, the usefulness of financial data in estimating portfolio model parameters, and financial analysis in efficient capital markets. All these studies share a common characteristic—they are concerned with the role of financial data in decision making—and they thus constitute the new approach to financial statement analysis.

This book is intended for various groups of users. Practitioners, such as financial analysts and accountants, will find both traditional and new financial analysis methods and techniques and will hopefully benefit from the discussion of various related issues in finance, statistics, and accounting. Researchers in finance and accounting will find a detailed inventory of available research and guidelines for future research. Last, but definitely not least, the book can be used as a main or supplementary text in various finance and accounting courses.

This book was developed over several years from notes provided in financial statement analysis courses at the Graduate School of Business of the University of Chicago. The notes were also used as supplementary readings in an advanced financial accounting course (undergraduate level) and a graduate course in financial management and security analysis at Tel-Aviv University.

The reader is assumed to have no special knowledge except for some familiarity with basic principles of financial accounting. The mathematics was deliberately reduced to a minimum, a statistical appendix in Chapter 12 presents the basic concepts needed, and the principles of the portfolio and efficient capital markets theories are provided in an intuitive, nonmathematical way. Thus, it is expected that persons with diverse backgrounds and different levels of expertise will benefit from this book.

Valuable comments and suggestions for improvements were provided by Sidney Davidson, Nicholas Dopuch, Eugene Fama, Nicholas J. Gonedes, Charles R. Nelson, and Harry V. Roberts, all at the University of Chicago; by Ray Ball, University of Queensland; William H. Beaver, Stanford University; and Alfred Rappaport, Northwestern University. Assistance was also obtained from Messrs. Barton J. Cohen and Sergius Kunitzky and Ms. Katherine A. Schipper. The style was considerably improved by Ms. Pat Mackay, and Mss. Ilene Haniotis and Raymonde Rousselot were in charge of typing and proofing the manuscript. I am gratefully indebted to all.

FINANCIAL
STATEMENT
ANALYSIS

CHAPTER ONE

Introduction:
The New Versus
the Traditional Approach to
Financial Statement Analysis

Financial statement analysis is an information-processing system designed to provide data for decision makers. The information is basically derived from published financial statements, but in the process of analysis use is also made of nonaccounting data, such as stock prices and aggregate economic indicators. Users of the financial statement information system are decision makers concerned with evaluating the economic situation of the firm and predicting its future course. The major groups of users are investors, for making portfolio decisions; management, for evaluating the operational and financial efficiency of the firm as a whole and of subunits (e.g., departments); lenders, for determining the credit worthiness of loan applicants; labor unions, for establishing an economic basis for collective bargaining; regulatory agencies (e.g., FPC, SEC, etc.), for controlling the activities of subordinated units; and researchers in economics and business administration, for studying firm and individual behavior. Given these varied uses and motives, it is obvious that no single information system will satisfy all the requirements. Rather, financial statement analysis should be sufficiently general and flexible to accommodate differing user needs.

The present chapter provides a brief survey of the historical development of financial statement analysis and an evaluation of the state of traditional analysis. Discussion then focuses on the new approach to financial statement analysis, which is the main subject of this book.

1

HISTORICAL DEVELOPMENT

The origins of financial statement analysis in the United States can be traced to the second half of the nineteenth century.[1] Two major economic developments created the need for a systematic analysis of firms' financial data: (a) the emergence of the corporation as the main organizational form of business enterprises, resulting in a separation of management from ownership, and (b) the fast-increasing role of financial institutions (e.g., banks, investment and insurance companies, etc.) as the major suppliers of capital for business expansion, requiring a formal evaluation system of borrowers' credit worthiness. Consequently, both investors and lenders began systematically analyzing corporate financial data; the former to evaluate operational performance (investment analysis) and the latter to determine solvency status (credit analysis). The credit analysis function initially dominated the development of financial statement analysis as banks began using financial data on a large scale. Thus, for example, by 1890 it was a routine procedure for commercial banks to request the balance sheets of prospective borrowers for credit evaluation.

The next stage in the development of financial analysis (first decade of the twentieth century) was marked by the use of *financial ratios*. This signified the beginning of the "scientific approach" to the analysis of financial data. Since credit evaluation was still the major function of financial analysis, the indicator most frequently used was the current ratio (current assets divided by current liabilities), which was believed to indicate the firm's solvency position. However, the limitations of this ratio were soon realized, and additional indicators intended to provide a more comprehensive view of the firm's economic situation were developed. Concurrently, *ratio criteria,* such as the well-known 2:1 standard for the current ratio, were established. The scope of analysis was further extended by the use of interfirm comparisons of ratios and the acceptance of the industry average as the major standard for ratio evaluation. The first Federal Income Tax Code, passed in 1913, substantially increased the demand for reliable financial data and analysis.

In the 1920s the development of financial statement analysis was marked by a massive compilation of real data by analysts, credit agencies, trade associations, financial enterprises, and academic institutions. The data usually consisted of industry averages (or medians) of various ratios intended to serve as standards for interfirm analysis.[2] Financial analyst

---

[1] For a detailed history of financial analysis, see J. O. Horrigan, "A Short History of Financial Ratio Analysis," *The Accounting Review*, 43 (April 1968), 284–94; and R. A. Foulke, *Practical Financial Statement Analysis*, 6th ed. (New York: McGraw-Hill Book Company, 1968), Chap. 1.

[2] The most influential publication of the time was A. Wall's "Study of Credit Barometrics," *Federal Reserve Bulletin* (March 1919), pp. 229–43. This was a compilation of seven ratios for 981 firms stratified by industry and geographical location. Wall

firms, such as Dun and Bradstreet, began publishing periodic evaluations of corporate operational performance and statistics on industry average ratios. The formation of the Securities and Exchange Commission in the 1930s substantially increased the demand for detailed and dependable financial data. Thus, the development of financial statement analysis in the 1920s and 1930s was characterized by extensive data collection and by the proliferation of new ratios. This situation continued until recently without any major development: ". . . virtually everything that has been started in ratio analysis is still going on today somewhere." [3]

THE STATE OF TRADITIONAL FINANCIAL STATEMENT ANALYSIS

The major objective of financial statement analysis is to provide decision makers with firm-related data required in the process of decision making. One would therefore expect financial statement analysis to be an integral part of the various disciplines concerned with decision making, such as the microeconomic theories of investment and capital asset valuation and the finance theories of security analysis and portfolio management. This, however, is not the case, since financial statement analysis is almost completely alienated from decision theories. Microeconomic models of individual and firm behavior are usually devoid of any reference to financial analysis, and to the extent that economists discuss the usefulness of financial data they usually conclude that the reported information is irrelevant to decision makers because of the serious inconsistencies between accounting and economic valuation concepts.[4] The theory of finance, both on the corporate and on the individual investor level, also largely ignores financial statement analysis. For example, the extensive portfolio theory literature is practically devoid of studies integrating financial statement information with the input requirements of the portfolio model.[5] Moreover, the recently de-

---

was among the first to systematically use several ratios for financial analysis and to employ empirically determined ratio criteria.

[3] Horrigan, *op. cit.,* p. 248.

[4] See Chapter 6 for elaboration.

[5] W. Sharpe, one of the major contributors to portfolio theory, provides in his recent book, *Portfolio Theory and Capital Markets* (New York: McGraw-Hill Book Company, 1970), a bibliographical list of over 150 related books and articles, none of which deals with financial analysis. It is also interesting to note that reading collections on the theory of finance usually do not include studies related to financial statement analysis; see, for example, S. H. Archer and C. A. D'Ambrosio, *The Theory of Business Finance: A Book of Readings* (New York: The Macmillan Company, 1969).

veloped efficient capital markets theory is sometimes interpreted as implying the uselessness of financial statement analysis.[6] Specifically, prices in efficient capital markets reflect all publicly available information concerning the value of securities. Financial statement data are obviously publicly available; therefore, it is argued, the relevant information will be immediately reflected in security prices upon the release of financial reports and nothing is to be gained from the analysis of such data.[7]

Why do academicians shy away from traditional financial statement analysis?[8] The major reason seems to be the failure of financial analysis to keep pace with the developments in economics and finance. The historical survey of the preceding section clearly indicates that financial statement analysis still remains in the initial stage of the development of a science. A large amount of data and numerous financial ratios are available, yet the usefulness of the traditional tools and techniques has not been established.[9] To establish usefulness, research in financial analysis must proceed to the more advanced stages of science development—those involving model construction and verification. Systematic efforts must be made to design appropriate financial information systems and to test their usefulness for decision makers. Traditional financial statement analysis evidently did not reach this advanced stage of development, and hence the alienation from economic and finance theories.

THE NEW APPROACH TO FINANCIAL STATEMENT ANALYSIS

The long stalemate in the development of financial statement analysis appears to be over. Recent research in the area signifies the

[6] See Chapter 14 for elaboration on this theory.

[7] See, for example, F. Black, "Implications of the Random Walk Hypothesis for Portfolio Management," *Financial Analysts Journal*, 27 (March–April 1971), 16–22.

[8] Although no dependable data are available, financial statement analysis is probably extensively used in practice. The Financial Analysts Federation presently incorporates about fourteen thousand members (not all, of course, actively engaged in financial statement analysis); financial analysis firms, such as Dun and Bradstreet, are fast growing; financial institutions, such as banks and investment houses, employ a large number of financial analysts; regulatory agencies, such as the SEC and public utility commissions, are extensively engaged in financial analysis; etc.

[9] Horrigan, *op. cit.*, p. 294, notes: "From a negative viewpoint, the most striking aspect of ratio analysis is the absence of an explicit theoretical structure. Under the dominant approach of 'pragmatical empiricism,' the user of ratios is required to rely upon the authority of an author's experience. As a result, the subject of ratio analysis is replete with untested assertions about which ratios should be used and what their proper levels should be."

beginning of a new approach, which is mainly characterized by the emphasis on developing financial analysis techniques *within* the context of formal decision models. Financial statement analysis is thus viewed as an information-processing system designed to provide data for decision-making models, such as the portfolio selection model, bank-lending decision models, and corporate financial management models. The development of modern financial analysis is fused with decision model construction and verification; in areas where formal, well-specified models exist, such as the portfolio model for investment in securities, the purpose of financial statement analysis is to provide the data required by the model (e.g., predictions of future returns) in the most efficient (less costly) way. In decision areas where no formal models exist, such as bank-lending operations, the role of financial analysis is even broader; it must provide part or all of the information required for the construction and verification of decision models.

The major difference between the new and the traditional approach to financial statement analysis is therefore the framework within which analytical methods and techniques are developed. In the traditional approach this framework was never defined appropriately, resulting in the lack of direction and progress described in the preceding section. As to the new approach, financial statement tools and techniques are developed and tested within the well-defined framework of decision theory. The information users (i.e., decision makers) thus direct the development of financial analysis. The strong orientation of modern financial analysis toward decision making is reflected in the following characteristics:

1. Financial statement analysis is no longer detached from economic theories and models. The production of information (financial analysis) is now an integral part of the information use (economic and finance models).

2. The construction and verification of financial analysis systems require considerable analytical sophistication. The informational demands of modern decision models, such as those derived from portfolio theory, cannot be satisfied by simple financial ratios. Accordingly, advanced statistical techniques, such as regression analysis, are used to develop and verify the financial statement information systems.

3. Modern financial analysis is no longer restricted to the accounting data conventionally reported in financial statements. Use is made of unreported data, such as market values of assets and management's forecasts of future earnings. The analysis also encompasses nonaccounting data, such as security prices and bond ratings.

It should be noted at the outset that the new approach to financial statement analysis is still in the embryonic stage. The scope of research is limited to a few phenomena, such as bankruptcy, earnings growth, and bond ratings, and the studies often suffer from serious conceptual and methodological shortcomings. This is, in part, the fault of researchers in financial analysis, but it is also a reflection on the unsatisfactory state of decision theory under conditions of uncertainty. The imperfect knowledge of decision makers' behavior and informational needs obviously hinders the progress of financial statement analysis. However, despite the various shortcomings, it seems that the right course for the development of financial statement analysis has been found and is being pursued.

BOOK OUTLINE

This book focuses on the new approach to financial statement analysis. Its major objectives are to determine the state of this approach by evaluating the usefulness of available techniques, to indicate systematic deficiencies and shortcomings of current research, and to suggest changes and modifications required for further progress. The book consists of the following three main parts:

1. *The mechanics of financial statement analysis* (Chapters 2–6). The major objective of this part is to bridge the gap between the traditional and the new approach and to provide the reader with the necessary tools and concepts required for the application of financial statement analysis. It includes a presentation and an evaluation of traditional ratio analysis, the introduction of new indicators—decomposition measures—designed to increase the efficiency of analysis, a discussion of various related statistical issues, and an evaluation of accounting measurement and reporting principles affecting the usefulness of financial analysis.

2. *Application of financial statement analysis* (Chapters 7–11). The objective is to present and evaluate the usefulness of various models and information systems based mainly on financial statement data. Accordingly, this part of the book opens with a general discussion of the role of financial analysis in decision making. Attention is then turned to the various applications of financial statement information systems, particularly the description and prediction of economic phenomena such as earnings growth rates, corporate bankruptcy, bond ratings and risk premiums, and bank-lending decisions.

3. *Relationship with modern finance theories* (Chapters 12–15). Given that the major purpose of financial statement analysis is to provide data for investment decisions, it is imperative to investigate the relationship between financial analysis and the theories concerned with investment decisions—the portfolio theory and the efficient capital markets theory. Accordingly, this part includes a discussion of the basic principles underlying these theories, the supporting evidence, and the implications for financial statement analysis.

The synthesis in Chapter 16 highlights the main conclusions drawn throughout the book and indicates the desired course of development for financial statement analysis. Discussion in this chapter is directed to the main groups concerned with financial analysis: practitioners, accountants, and researchers.

PART ONE

THE MECHANICS OF FINANCIAL STATEMENT ANALYSIS

CHAPTER TWO

Financial Ratio Analysis

Since the late 1800s, ratio analysis has been the major tool used in the interpretation and evaluation of financial statements for investment decision making. Generally, such an analysis involves the breakdown of the examined financial reports into component parts (e.g., fixed and current assets), which are then evaluated in relation to each other and to exogenous standards. Ratios, rates, and percentages expedite the analysis by reducing the large number of items involved to a relatively small set of readily comprehended and economically meaningful indicators. Thus, for example, the large number of current assets and liability items may be compressed into one ratio—current assets over current liabilities—to yield an indicator of the firm's short-term liquidity position.

Financial ratios may be classified by the source of data as follows:

1. Balance sheet ratios
2. Income statement ratios
3. Fund statement ratios
4. Mixed ratios

The fourth ratio category consists of measures whose numerator and denominator are derived from different sources (e.g., net income to total assets).

Ratios can also be classified according to the different economic aspects of the firm's operations:

1. Profitability ratios
2. Short-term solvency (liquidity) ratios
3. Long-term solvency ratios
4. Efficiency (turnover) ratios

This classification is oriented to the needs of users; investors will be mainly concerned with profitability ratios, lenders with solvency ratios, and so forth.

The discussion in this chapter is concerned with the computation and interpretation of various ratios currently used in the analysis of financial statements. Special issues involved in ratio analysis, such as the statistical and accounting problems encountered, are discussed in subsequent chapters. The order of presentation is according to the preceding classification—needs of users. The published financial statements of Lockheed Aircraft Corporation (henceforth Lockheed) are used throughout this chapter for demonstration purposes. A summary of these statements is presented in Tables 2.1 and 2.2.

Lockheed is a major designer and producer of advanced defense systems and defense equipment. It also engages in commercial and military aircraft design and production, military and commercial shipbuilding and repair, propulsion and electronic products and services, and ocean and aircraft systems, and it participates in various space programs. In 1969, sales to the U.S. government accounted for 89 percent of total sales, while sales to foreign governments and commercial customers amounted to 5 and 6 percent of the total, respectively. Various major contracts with the Army and the Air Force were canceled in 1968 and 1969, resulting in a marked deterioration in the company's operating performance. Some of these contracts are still under dispute,[1] but the company wrote off $140 million in 1968 and $150 million in 1969 to provide for estimated losses on the disputed contracts. In 1969 and 1970, Lockheed encountered serious financial problems, mainly because of the disputed contracts, and appealed to the Department of Defense for assistance.

Each ratio will be analyzed in two ways: (*a*) a time-series analysis, in which the historical behavior of the ratio is examined, and (*b*) a cross-sectional analysis, in which the ratio is evaluated in relation to a representative ratio of other firms in the industry for the same time

[1] As of the end of 1970.

TABLE 2.1

Lockheed Aircraft Corporation
Summary of Operating Financial Data for the Years 1965–1970
(THOUSANDS OF DOLLARS)

Operations for the Year	1965	1966	1967	1968	1969	1970
Net Sales	1,814,085	2,084,759	2,335,456	2,217,366	2,074,639	2,535,603
Operating Expenses	1,715,485	1,977,368	2,234,573	2,140,586	2,145,895	2,675,721
Net Earnings	98,600	107,391	100,883	76,780	71,256 D	140,118 D
Other Income	3,963	2,391	5,342	8,355	7,592	12,377
Total Income	102,563	109,782	106,225	85,135	63,664 D	127,741 D
Interest Expenses	1,484	2,499	6,806	6,869	13,158	32,261
Federal Income Tax	47,390	48,400	45,060	33,790	44,180 C	73,720 C
Net Income	53,689	58,883	54,359	44,476	32,642 D	86,282 D
Supplementary Data						
Cash Dividends	22,024	24,478	24,631	24,731	19,139	—
Depreciation	21,196	25,350	30,993	38,086	43,939	56,355
Common Stock Prices { High	69 5/8	73	73 7/8	60 5/8	50	21 3/8
Low	36 5/8	49	48 7/8	40 1/2	17	7
Number of Shares	11,078,000	11,153,000	11,221,000	11,252,000	11,359,000	11,359,000

Source: Moody's Industrial Manual, 1971, p. 2507.
D Debit.
C Credit.

TABLE 2.2

Lockheed Aircraft Corporation
Summary Consolidated Balance Sheet Data for the End of Years 1965–1970
(THOUSANDS OF DOLLARS)

	1965	1966	1967	1968	1969	1970
Assets						
Cash [a]	42,599	25,183	91,684	106,654	52,062	79,497
Receivables	192,183	206,468	264,238	236,552	244,775	179,087
Inventories	246,228	285,543	274,714	285,707	500,417	693,920
Prepaid Expenses [b]	14,026	29,559	29,599	34,324	129,643	19,407
Total Current Assets	495,036	546,753	660,235	663,237	926,897	971,911
Investment in Affiliates	4,319	4,783	5,165	4,459	4,277	4,184
Net Property, Plant and Equipment	129,392	175,126	213,517	266,454	337,849	343,446
Other Deferred Charges	642	353	2,113	2,633	2,421	3,088
Total Assets	629,389	727,015	881,030	936,783	1,271,444	1,322,629
Liabilities and Equity						
Total Current Liabilities	314,782	377,024	367,212	427,970	614,153	503,495
Long-Term Debt	16,865	16,865	140,000	138,125	336,250	584,375
Total Stockholders' Equity	297,742	333,126	373,818	370,688	321,041	234,759
Total Liabilities and Equities	629,389	727,015	881,030	936,783	1,271,444	1,322,629

Source: Moody's Industrial Manual, 1971, p. 2508.
[a] Including short-term commercial papers.
[b] Including anticipated refund of federal income tax.

14

period. For the cross-sectional analysis of Lockheed's data, average ratios were calculated for the aerospace industry.[2]

PROFITABILITY RATIOS

Profitability ratios are designed for the evaluation of the firm's operational performance. The numerator of the ratios consists of periodic profits according to a specific definition, while the denominator represents the relevant investment base. The ratios thus yield an indicator of the firm's efficiency in using the capital committed by stockholders and lenders. Following are some widely used profitability ratios:

1. Net income to total assets

This is a measure for the average profitability of the firm's assets, designed to indicate the efficiency of capital employment.[3] To concentrate on operational (business) efficiency, as distinct from financial efficiency, the numerator of the ratio usually includes income tax expenses but excludes interest charges and dividends.[4] The exclusion of financing charges allows, among other things, a more appropriate interfirm comparison because differences among firms in capital structure, reflected in different interest charges, will not affect the ratio. Since the numerator of the ratio represents a *flow* over the entire period while the denominator reflects the *stock* of assets at a given point in time, it seems preferable to measure total assets as the average balance outstanding during the examined period. In most cases, the average of the beginning and ending balances of total assets would suffice; however, if significant asset changes occurred during the period, a weighted average would be appropriate.

It should be noted that the historical valuation of assets in the balance sheet will bias this profitability measure upward during periods of rising price levels. While the numerator of the ratio (net income)

---

2 The following firms were included in the aerospace industry: Aerojet-General, Avco, Bendix, Boeing, Curtiss-Wright, General Dynamics, Grumman Aircraft Engineering, Martin-Marietta, McDonnell-Douglas, North-American Rockwell, Northrop, TRW, Thiokol Chemical, and United Aircraft. The aerospace industry is thus comprised of fourteen firms whose financial data were derived from *Moody's Industrial Manual.*

3 For elaboration on the managerial usefulness of this ratio, see *Experience with Return on Capital to Appraise Management Performance* (Accounting Practice Report, No. 14, National Association of Accountants, 1962).

4 Note that the tax expense should be corrected for the appropriate amount of tax savings attributed to the interest charges excluded from net income. Specifically, the numerator of the ratio should be measured as

$$X - (T + t \cdot R), \tag{2.1}$$

where X = reported income *before* interest, dividends, and taxes; T = total income tax expense; t = income tax rate; and R = total interest charges.

is, to a large extent, measured in current values,[5] the denominator (total assets) is measured in historical prices which are usually lower than current prices. Care should therefore be exercised when profitability ratios of firms with different asset ages are compared.[6]

The net income to total assets ratios of Lockheed and the industry averages for the period 1965–70 are presented in Table 2.3. Lockheed's profitability of assets deteriorated steadily during 1965–68 and plunged

TABLE 2.3

Profitability Ratios [a]

Ratio		1965	1966	1967	1968	1969	1970
1. Net income / Total assets	L [b]	.0865	.0828	.0657	.0513	−.0203	−.0526
	I [b]	.0754	.0701	.0540	.0665	.0589	.0519
2. Income available for common / Common stockholder's equity	L	.1803	.1768	.1454	.1200	−.1017	−.3675
	I	.1283	.1252	.0991	.1120	.0889	.0652
3. Earnings per share ($)	L	4.86	5.28	4.84	3.95	−2.87	−7.60
	I	3.64	3.06	2.52	2.81	2.36	1.76
4. Price-earnings ratio	L	10.93	11.55	12.63	12.77	deficit	deficit
	I [c]	13.56	12.60	15.63	15.92	12.54	11.46
5. Dividends / Net income	L	.4102	.4157	.4531	.5561	−.5863	0 [d]
	I [e]	.4362	.3936	.3535	.4311	.4743	.6442
6. Operating income / Operating assets	L	.1577	.1487	.1152	.0824	−.0562	−.1063
	I	.1370	.1213	.0827	.1360	.1146	.4460

[a] The explicit computation of the 1965 ratios for Lockheed is presented in the Appendix.

[b] L and I indicate the ratios for Lockheed and the industry means, respectively.

[c] Several firms with unusually large price-earnings ratios were excluded from the industry averages to keep the means representative: McDonnell-Douglas in 1966 and 1967 (PE ratios of 35.57 and 1,408.33, respectively); Aerojet-General, Boeing, and General Dynamics in 1969 (PE ratios of 34.56, 94.02, and 151.04, respectively); and Avco in 1970 (PE ratio of 42.81).

[d] No dividends were paid in 1970.

[e] Several firms were excluded from these measures in order to keep the industry means representative: McDonnell-Douglas in 1967 (payout ratio of 10.8358); Aerojet-General, Boeing, and General Dynamics in 1969 (payout ratios of 1.2024, 2.9323, and 4.1632, respectively).

[5] The main exception is the depreciation charge.

[6] More on the effects of price-level changes in Chapter 6.

sharply to losses in 1969 and 1970. Note that the industry's profitability also declined during the same period, yet at a substantially slower rate than Lockheed's. The deterioration in Lockheed's profitability is even more striking given that in the first three years its ratios were above the industry averages (in 1965, for example, 8.65 vs. 7.54 percent), which indicates a higher-than-average assets' profitability for Lockheed. Therefore, it can be concluded that while the assets' profitability of the aerospace industry declined continuously between 1965 and 1970, Lockheed's profitability decreased much more sharply in the latter half of the period, as a result of increases in operating expenses unmatched by sales increases.

2. Income available for common stockholders to stockholders' equity

This ratio indicates the profitability of the capital supplied by common stockholders.[7] The numerator is defined as reported net income after taxes, interest, and preferred dividends, but before common stock dividends. The denominator can be defined as the year-end balance of stockholders' equity, or, in the case of substantial capital changes, an average of the outstanding equity balance during the period.

It should be noted that this stockholders' profitability measure will usually differ from the *market* yield on common stocks. The latter is defined as the ratio of dividends plus capital gains to the beginning-of-period price of the stock.[8] The main source of difference is the *expectations* of investors regarding the future economic conditions of the firm. These expectations are reflected (via stock prices) in the market yield measure but, of course, do not affect the accounting values. An evaluation of the usefulness of accounting-based versus market-based measures is provided in Part III of the book.

The income available for common to common equity ratios for Lockheed and the industry averages are presented in Table 2.3. The behavior of this ratio over time and relative to the industry means

---

[7] This capital includes, of course, retained earnings, since ". . . as long as management is presumed to be acting in the best interest of the stockholders, retained earnings can be regarded as equivalent to a fully subscribed, preemptive issue of common stock." F. Modigliani and M. H. Miller, "The Cost of Capital, Corporation Finance, and the Theory of Investment," *American Economic Review*, 48 (June 1958), 266.

[8] Specifically:

$$i_{k,t} = (d_{k,t} + p_{k,t+1} - p_{k,t})/p_{k,t} , \qquad (2.2)$$

where

$i_{k,t}$ = yield on stock k during period t,

$d_{k,t}$ = cash dividends received during t,

$p_{k,t}$ and $p_{k,t+1}$ = prices of stock k at the beginning and the end of period t, respectively.

resembles closely that of its predecessor—net income to total assets. The one exception occurred in 1968—Lockheed's profitability of total assets was already lower than that of the industry (5.13 vs. 6.65 percent), while the profitability of Lockheed's common equity was still slightly higher than the industry average (12.00 vs. 11.20 percent). The income to total assets ratio thus provided an earlier warning regarding the subsequent deterioration in Lockheed's profitability.

3. Earnings-per-share

This is a well known and widely used indicator of the performance of a business enterprise. The numerator is defined as net income after interest, taxes, and preferred dividends (i.e., available for common), while the denominator represents the number of common shares outstanding (at year-end or as a yearly average). The earnings-per-share (EPS) figure plays a prominent role in practical investment analysis.[9] Straightforwardly interpreted, it represents the amount of earnings allocated to one share of common stock. However, more importance is often imputed to this measure, for example:

> The amount of net income remaining after allowing for the fixed obligation of dividend distributions to preferred shareholders is a crude but indispensable measure of the increase in well-being of common shareholders. Earnings per share is used as a basis for predicting dividends and growth and hence future market values of common shares. . . . Indeed, corporate managers often define their policy goals in terms of earnings per share of common stocks.[10]

Despite its wide use in practice, the EPS figure is often an ambiguous measure of performance because of the earnings retention phenomenon. Specifically, since most firms periodically retain a portion of their earnings, the amount of equity per share of these firms tends to increase over time. Consequently, EPS will increase even though the firm's profitability of operations has not changed, or even decreased. Suppose, for example, that a firm's equity at end of period t was $10,000 and net income for t was $2,000, of which $500 was distributed as dividends. Suppose further that the firm has one thousand shares outstanding, yielding a $2.00 EPS for period t. In the following period, the

[9] "In Wall Street it is customary to sum up the statistical data about a common stock in three salient figures. These are the earnings per share, the dividend rate and the price." B. Graham, D. L. Dodd, and S. Cottle, *Security Analysis*, 4th ed. (New York: McGraw-Hill Book Company, 1962), p. 224.

[10] R. K. Jaedicke and R. T. Sprouse, *Accounting Flows: Income, Funds and Cash*, Foundations of Finance Series (Englewood Cliffs, N.J.: Prentice-Hall, Inc., 1965), p. 150

profitability of operations decreased from 20 percent on equity during t to 18 percent, yielding a net income of \$2,070 (i.e., .18 × 11,500). However, EPS for $t + 1$ will increase from \$2.00 to \$2.07. Given the retention phenomenon, EPS changes cannot be directly attributed to changes in the firm's performance.[11]

An adjustment sometimes suggested to account for the earnings retention effect is to divide the EPS figure by common equity per share. Accordingly, EPS is adjusted for changes in the investment base per share. Note, however, that the EPS figure is transformed by this adjustment to the ratio of income available for common stockholders to stockholders' equity, discussed above.

Additional problems are involved in the computation and interpretation of EPS. Convertible securities, stock options, or stock warrants complicate the computation considerably.[12] Changes in the number of shares resulting from stock dividends and/or stock splits require an adjustment to a common base (constant number of shares) if EPS time series are to be examined.[13] Finally, the comparison of EPS for different firms may be misleading because of the economic meaninglessness of the *number* of shares. Two firms may be identical in all economic respects (e.g., size, profitability, growth, etc.) yet have a different number of shares outstanding. The different EPS values for these firms obviously have no economic meaning. Considering all the problems discussed above, the EPS figure seems to be a dubious measure of performance.

The EPS figures for Lockheed are presented in Table 2.3.[14] Lockheed's figures are relatively stable for the period 1965–67 and drop sharply thereafter, while the industry averages decline continuously over the entire period 1965–70. Lockheed's EPS outperformed the industry averages during the period 1965–68. The general pattern is thus similar to that of the profitability ratios discussed earlier.

[11] A recent empirical example of the possible misinterpretation of EPS changes was provided in B. Lev and G. Mandelker, "The Micro-Economic Consequences of Corporate Mergers," *Journal of Business*, 45 (January 1972), 101. The eleven-year series of average EPS for merged firms was monotonically increasing, while all other measures of profitability (including the market rate of return) were decreasing. The increase in EPS was probably the result of the earnings retention phenomenon.

[12] Some of these computational problems are discussed in APB Opinion No. 15 (New York: American Institute of Certified Public Accountants, 1969). An example of a possible misinterpretation is provided in Lytton Industries' 1967 annual report. The reported \$2.25 EPS figure was based on present common stocks plus those that would have been outstanding if one of the convertible preferred stock issues had been entirely converted. However, one more issue of convertible preferred stock and three issues of convertible debentures were outstanding, but not included in the EPS computation.

[13] For elaboration on such adjustments, see H. Levy and M. Sarnat, *Investment and Portfolio Analysis* (New York: John Wiley & Sons, Inc., 1972), pp. 32–49.

[14] These figures and the industry averages were derived from the firms' financial statements and from *Moody's Industrial Manual,* 1971.

4. Price-earnings ratio

This measure is defined as the ratio of the market price of a common stock (usually computed as an average price for the period) to its earnings-per-share. This ratio is a natural extension of the EPS measure, relating the firm's earnings to stock prices in order to answer the question: How much is the investor paying for the EPS? The belief in the existence of a close relationship between the firm's earnings and its stock prices is firmly rooted in investment theory and practice. It derives from the classic economic approach to assets valuation under conditions of certainty where the value of an asset (e.g., a building, a pension plan, or a security) is determined by the present value of the net earnings stream to be generated by the asset. Accordingly, the value of a share will be related to the expected stream of the firm's earnings and will change when these expectations change. However, the exact form and extent of this relationship, in a world of uncertainty, is still largely unknown.[15]

Since stock prices generally reflect investors' expectations regarding future earnings of the firm, the price-earnings (PE) ratios of companies with prospects of a high earnings growth will be higher (other things equal) than those of companies with lower growth prospects.[16] Differences in PE ratios (for a given firm over time, and/or across firms) will therefore reflect differences in investors' expectations regarding the future earnings growth of firms:

> A strong, successful, and promising company usually sells at a higher multiplier of current or average earnings than one that is less strong, less successful, and less promising.[17]

The PE ratio as conventionally calculated (i.e., using past earnings) is thus an indicator of the future earnings prospects of the firm, as anticipated by the market.[18]

When *anticipated* earnings are substituted for past earnings, the PE ratio will indicate the aggregate discount rate applied by investors

---

[15] More on this subject in Chapter 8.

[16] It should be noted that cross-sectional comparisons of PE ratios are, unlike those of EPS, economically meaningful, since the arbitrary figure of the number of shares is canceled in the PE ratio calculation.

[17] Graham, Dodd, and Cottle, *op. cit.*, p. 230.

[18] Indeed, anticipated earnings growth rates have been empirically found to account for a large portion of the differences among PE ratios of firms; see R. A. Brealey, *An Introduction to Risk and Return from Common Stocks* (Cambridge, Mass.: M.I.T. Press, 1969), pp. 78–81.

to the firm's future earnings.[19] This rate may be an approximation to the firm's cost of capital, reflecting, among other things, the riskiness of the firm's operations as perceived by the market. However, operational use of this modified PE ratio is limited, since it requires information about the market's expectation with respect to the firm's future earnings, which is generally unavailable.

Lockheed's PE ratios along with the industry averages are presented in Table 2.3.[20] Note that Lockheed's ratios are lower than the industry averages throughout the entire period 1965–70, while, as we saw above, other profitability measures indicated that Lockheed outperformed the industry averages during the period 1965–68. This inconsistency may be explained by the fact that the PE ratio incorporated market expectations regarding Lockheed's future profitability, whereas the preceding measures were exclusively based on accounting data. Lockheed's lower-than-average PE ratios thus indicate that investors predicted the decrease in earnings growth at least as early as 1965.

5. Other profitability ratios

In addition to the ratios discussed above, the following profitability measures are sometimes suggested in the literature: (a) *Dividends to net income,* or "payout ratio," which measures the percentage of net income distributed to stockholders. This ratio is an indicator of the firm's dividend policy and is supposed to reflect management's perceptions regarding the uncertainty associated with future earnings.[21] (b) *Operating income to operating assets,* which indicates management's efficiency in using the operating assets (i.e., total assets excluding investments in subsidiaries, etc.). As compared with the net income to total assets ratio, the exclusion of nonoperating income from the numerator and nonoperating assets from the denominator is intended to focus on management's performance in the main line of business. This ratio therefore seems more suitable for firms with a relatively large amount of nonoperating assets, such as holding companies.

[19] This statement is obvious in a world of certainty and a perpetual EPS stream of $x per period. The current price of a share, p, will equal the discounted value of the future earnings-per-share series:

$$p = x/i , \qquad (2.3)$$

where i is the discount rate. Accordingly, i, the discount rate, equals x/p, the reciprocal of the PE ratio. In a world of uncertainty, the relationship between stock prices and anticipated earnings is, of course, much more complicated, yet the PE ratio may still provide an indication of the discount rate, applied by the market to the specific stock.

[20] These data were computed by dividing the average of the highest and the lowest price during the year by earnings-per-share.

[21] This association between the payout ratio and the firm's risk is discussed in Chapter 13.

SHORT-TERM SOLVENCY (LIQUIDITY) RATIOS

The general objective of short-term solvency (liquidity) ratios is to indicate the firm's ability to meet its short-term financial obligations. Accordingly, attention is focused on the size of the firm's reservoir of liquid assets relative to its maturing liabilities. Liquidity measures are believed to be of prime interest to short-term lenders such as banks and merchandise suppliers.

1. Current (working capital) ratio

This measure is defined as the ratio of current assets to current liabilities.[22] Since current assets are generally regarded as the reservoir from which maturing obligations can be paid, it seems reasonable to assume that the larger the current ratio, the larger the safety margin of short-term creditors.

The attitude of analysts toward the current ratio has changed considerably over time. In the early days of financial statement analysis, it was often the only ratio used in the evaluation of credit worthiness. Strict standards such as the "two for one" (i.e., current assets should be at least twice as large as current liabilities) are alleged to have been employed by lenders. However, with the development of financial analysis it became clear that information additional to that provided by the current ratio, particularly on the flow of funds, was required for solvency evaluation. This shifted analysts' attention to more economically meaningful indicators.[23]

Lockheed's current ratios and the industry averages are presented in Table 2.4. Lockheed's ratios were relatively stable up to 1969 and increased in 1970, while the industry averages were relatively stable and close to the 2:1 standard. Lockheed's ratios were lower than the industry means throughout the period 1965–69. It is interesting to note that while Lockheed sustained substantial losses during 1969 and 1970, its current position improved, mainly as a result of a substantial decrease in current liabilities during 1970. Thus, the deterioration in Lockheed's operating performance did not affect its liquidity position as measured by the current ratio.

2. Quick (acid-test) ratio

It is often argued that inventories and prepaid expenses, included in the numerator of the current ratio, can hardly be regarded as liquid

---

[22] The *difference* between current assets and current liabilities is defined as working capital.

[23] For a critical appraisal of conventional solvency (liquidity) analysis, see J. E. Walter, "Determination of Technical Solvency," *Journal of Business*, 31 (January 1957), 30–43.

assets and hence should be excluded from liquidity measures. Accordingly, the quick ratio was suggested to focus on assets that can readily be used to redeem obligations. The quick ratio includes in the numerator cash, marketable securities, and receivables, while the denominator consists of current liabilities. This ratio therefore provides a stricter test of liquidity than the current ratio.

Lockheed's quick ratios are presented in Table 2.4. They fluctuate considerably during the period 1965–68 and drop sharply thereafter, reflecting the substantial decrease in cash and receivables during 1969 and 1970. The ratios for 1969 and 1970 are substantially below the industry means, reflecting an unusually strained liquidity position. Recall that the current ratio, discussed above, revealed a different pattern. This difference is explained by the fact that the cash and receivables decreases in 1969 and 1970 were more than offset by inventory increases. The earlier conclusions regarding the improvement in Lockheed's liquidity position should therefore be modified: Lockheed's liquidity, as measured by the quick assets, actually deteriorated during 1969 and 1970, an event that was coupled with a substantial increase in inventories.

3. Flows-of-funds ratios

Conventional liquidity indicators, such as the current and quick ratios, suffer from a major shortcoming which stems from their static structure. Specifically, these ratios reflect the situation prevailing on the balance sheet date, thereby limiting consideration to the surplus of current assets over current liabilities at a point in time. However, the sufficiency of the liquid assets reservoir at a point in time reflects only one aspect of the solvency situation; another, potentially more im-

TABLE 2.4

Short-Term Solvency Ratios [a]

	Ratio		1965	1966	1967	1968	1969	1970
1.	Current assets	L [b]	1.5726	1.4502	1.7980	1.5497	1.5092	1.9303
	Current liabilities (current ratio)	I [b]	2.0462	1.9359	2.1578	1.9741	1.8014	1.8962
2.	Quick ratio	L	.7459	.6144	.9693	.8019	.4833	.5136
		I	1.1766	.9882	1.1549	.9450	.8775	.9423

[a] See Appendix for the computation of Lockheed's 1965 ratios.
[b] L and I indicate ratios for Lockheed and the industry means, respectively.

portant, solvency aspect is the extent of matching between periodic cash inflows and outflows. The maintenance of adequate liquidity (and, of course, solvency) obviously requires a close matching or synchronization of cash flows.[24] A general approach to solvency evaluation should therefore consider the relationship between cash inflows and outflows throughout the period, as well as the size of the existing liquid assets reservoir.[25]

Various measures reflecting some aspects of fund flows were suggested for such liquidity evaluation. For example, the "interval measure," which compares the quick assets (cash, marketable securities, and receivables) with the average daily flow of cash expenditures for operations; [26] the ratio of net working capital to funds provided by operations (the latter defined as net earnings plus depreciation and other noncash charges); [27] the ratio of funds provided by operations to current debt; [28] and a liquidity index based on projected funds flows.[29] These various flow-of-funds measures express in different ways the basic notion that for solvency to prevail, the existing reservoir of liquid assets plus periodic cash inflows should cover the cash outflows by a sufficient margin to protect against possible reductions in inflows or increments in outflows.[30] These measures thus incorporate a dynamic element in liquidity evaluation.

LONG-TERM SOLVENCY RATIOS

The main objective of long-term solvency ratios is to indicate the firm's ability to meet both the principal and interest payments on long-

---

[24] This point is emphasized in advanced cash management models where the optimal cash balance is a function of, among other things, the lack of synchronization between inflows and outflows (measured, say, by the variance of the cash balance). See M. H. Miller and D. Orr, "A Model of the Demand for Money by Firms," *Quarterly Journal of Economics*, 80 (1966), 413–35.

[25] Indeed, empirical evidence, presented in Chapter 9, suggests that ratios reflecting flows of funds are superior to the static liquidity ratios in predicting corporate bankruptcy.

[26] G. Sorter and G. Benston, "Appraising the Defensive Position of a Firm: The Interval Measure," *The Accounting Review*, 35 (October 1960), 633–40.

[27] H. Bierman, Jr., "Measuring Financial Liquidity," *The Accounting Review*, 35 (October 1960), 628–32.

[28] Walter, *op. cit.*

[29] K. W. Lemke, "The Evaluation of Liquidity: An Analytical Study," *Journal of Accounting Research*, 8 (Spring 1970), 47–77. A critique of the current ratio as a liquidity measure is provided in this article.

[30] A comprehensive discussion and demonstration of flow-of-funds measures is presented in Jaedicke and Sprouse, *op. cit.*

term obligations. As opposed to the short-term liquidity ratios, these measures stress the long-run financial and operating structure of the firm.

1. Debt to equity ratio

The numerator of this ratio consists of short-term as well as long-term liabilities (sometimes even preferred stock), while the denominator consists of stockholders' equity. This measure of solvency is based on the notion that the larger the ratio of debt to equity, the lower the protection of lenders. This is, of course, an oversimplified approach to the measurement of lenders' protection, since, in periods of price increases, the historical value of assets will usually be understated relative to their current (liquidation) value. Accordingly, the reservoir from which debt can be paid in liquidation may be larger than that indicated by the equity figure.[31] Moreover, some forms of long-term debt (e.g., bonds) are usually protected by specific collateral and are therefore superior in protection to other kinds of debt. The debt to equity ratio obviously does not distinguish between the different degrees of debt protection. However, despite these shortcomings, this ratio is widely used as an indicator of lenders' risk.

The debt to equity ratio, indicating the firm's capital structure (leverage), is also a measure of the *financial risk* associated with the common stocks. Financial risk is usually defined in terms of the volatility of the earnings stream that accrues to common stockholders. It is obvious that for a given, fluctuating stream of operating earnings (i.e., earnings before interest), the larger the fixed amount of interest charges, the higher the volatility of the residual—net earnings to stockholders. Suppose, for example, that a firm's operating earnings, amounting to $1 million during year t, decreased by 10 percent in the following year, $t + 1$. In the absence of interest charges (i.e., an all-equity firm), the decrease in net earnings accruing to stockholders will also be 10 percent. However, when interest charges exist, the decrease in net earnings will be *larger* than 10 percent (e.g., when the interest payments amount to $500,000, the decrease in net earnings will be 20 percent [32]). Increases in operating earnings will obviously result in larger relative increases in net earnings to stockholders when interest-bearing debt exists as compared with an all-equity firm. Generally, the higher the relative amount of debt in the firm's capital, the larger the volatility of net earnings, and therefore the higher the financial risk associated with

---

[31] It may, of course, also be smaller as a result of capital losses in liquidation.

[32] Net earnings in t: $1,000,000 − $500,000 = $500,000, while net earnings in $t + 1$: $900,000 − $500,000 = $400,000—a decrease of 20 percent.

the common stocks.[33] The ratio of debt to equity thus indicates some risk aspects associated with both lenders and stockholders.[34]

The debt to equity ratios of Lockheed and the industry averages are presented in Table 2.5. Lockheed's ratios are continuously increasing; in 1970, over 82 percent of the firm's capital was provided by lenders—an unusually high leverage. This is a result of the constant increase in long-term debt and the heavy losses incurred during 1969–70. In contrast, the industry's degree of leverage reveals only a moderate increase during the examined period. Lockheed's financial structure in 1969 and 1970 clearly indicates a substantially higher-than-average risk for both lenders and stockholders.

2. Times interest earned

This is the ratio of income before interest to periodic interest charges.[35] It is supposed to indicate the safety margin of the fixed payments to lenders; the higher the ratio, the larger the safety margin. Since ability to *pay* interest is examined here, it seems more appropriate to define the numerator as cash flows (i.e., income plus depreciation) rather than as income.

The ratios for Lockheed are presented in Table 2.5. The fast deterioration in Lockheed's ratios is the combined result of Lockheed's earnings decreases and interest payment increases. A marked decrease is also evident for the industry averages resulting from similar reasons. Note that Lockheed's ratios during the period 1965–68 were still higher than the industry averages.

3. Other ratios

Capital structure, or degree of leverage, is sometimes measured in alternative ways, such as *stockholders' equity to total capital* and *total debt to total capital*. The specific choice of leverage measure is a matter of convenience, since they all perfectly correspond to each other. It should be noted that in the finance literature, degree of leverage is often

---

[33] Financial risk should be distinguished from the business risk that is caused by nonfinancial factors, such as line of business and size. This distinction was already pointed out by Alfred Marshall: "Let us suppose that two men are carrying on similar businesses, the one working with his own, the other chiefly with borrowed, capital. There is one set of risks which is common to both; which may be described as the *trade risks* of the particular business in which they are engaged. . . . But there is another set of risks, the burden of which has to be borne by the man working with borrowed capital, and not by the other. . . ." A. Marshall, *Principles of Economics*, 8th ed. (New York: The Macmillan Company, 1952), pp. 589–90.

[34] A more comprehensive treatment of risk is presented in Chapters 10 and 12.

[35] The interest in the denominator sometimes includes noninterest fixed items, such as principal payments and payments under noncancelable leases. Income is usually defined on an after-tax basis.

TABLE 2.5

Long-Term Solvency Ratios [a]

	Ratio		1965	1966	1967	1968	1969	1970
1.	Equity	L [b]	1.1137	1.1825	1.3568	1.5272	2.9604	4.6338
	Debt	I [b]	.7915	.9384	1.0231	1.0610	1.1608	1.1204
2.	Times interest	L	37.18	24.56	8.99	7.47	deficit	deficit
	earned	I	10.06	7.64	4.78	5.34	3.99	2.79

[a] See Appendix for the computation of Lockheed's 1965 ratios.
[b] L and I indicate ratios for Lockheed and the industry means, respectively.

measured in terms of *market* rather than accounting values, that is, the total values of stocks and bonds are based on stock market prices. The accounting-based and market-based measures of capital structure will usually differ substantially.

EFFICIENCY (TURNOVER) RATIOS

Efficiency (turnover) ratios usually consist of the sales figure in the numerator and the balance of an asset (e.g., inventory, accounts receivable, etc.) in the denominator. The objective is to indicate various aspects of operational efficiency. Attention is focused here on *specific* assets rather than on the overall efficiency of asset utilization measured by the profitability ratios.

1. Average collection period for accounts receivable

This measure is computed in two stages:

I. Average daily net sales $= \dfrac{\text{Annual net sales }[36]}{360 \text{ days}}$ ✓

II. Average collection period $= \dfrac{\text{Average balance of accounts receivable}}{\text{Average daily net sales (from stage I)}}$

[36] Since accounts receivable are involved, it is desirable to use annual *credit* sales rather than total sales. However, the breakdown of total sales into the cash and credit components is usually unavailable in the published financial statements. With respect to the denominator, a different figure (e.g., 250 working days) is sometimes used. However, as long as consistency (over time and across firms) is maintained, the specific choice of number of days will not affect the evaluation.

This ratio indicates the average collection period of the accounts receivable, or the average duration (from inception to collection) of accounts receivable. It has several important uses for analysts and management. When compared with the firm's policy regarding the credit duration,[37] the ratio indicates the efficiency of the credit department. Suppose, for example, that the firm's policy concerning credit duration is sixty days, yet the computed measure of the average collection period for accounts receivable is eighty days. This difference between the target and the actual credit duration is an indication of (*a*) a deviation of the credit department from management's policy by extending credit for longer periods than intended, and/or (*b*) inefficiency in the collection efforts of accounts receivable.

The average collection period measure also indicates the degree of liquidity of the firm's accounts receivable; the smaller the measure (i.e., the shorter the collection period), the higher the average liquidity. This aspect of the average collection period ratio is relevant to the evaluation of the firm's short-term liquidity position.

The average receivables collection period for Lockheed and the industry means are presented in Table 2.6. Lockheed's collection period

TABLE 2.6

Efficiency (Turnover) Ratios [a]

	Ratio		1965	1966	1967	1968	1969	1970
1.	Collection period for accounts receivable (days)	L [b]	38.14	35.65	40.73	38.41	42.48	25.43
		I [b]	48.95	45.91	43.58	45.19	51.76	56.72
2.	Inventory turnover	L	7.3675	7.3010	8.5014	7.7610	4.1458	3.6540
		I	6.4985	5.5951	5.4812	5.0246	5.0668	5.5471
3.	Net sales / Stockholders' equity	L	6.0928	6.2582	6.2476	5.9818	6.4622	10.8009
		I	4.0763	4.1935	4.1479	4.2898	3.9229	3.5025
4.	Net sales / Net working capital	L	10.0640	12.2829	7.9702	9.4249	6.6337	5.4131
		I	6.9405	7.5802	8.8071	8.5116	7.4643	6.2445

[a] See Appendix for the computation of Lockheed's 1965 ratios.
[b] L and I indicate ratios for Lockheed and the industry means, respectively.

[37] This policy is often publicly announced by the firm. Sometimes conventional terms are used, such as "2/10 n/60," indicating that a credit purchase has to be paid within 60 days, but if paid within 10 days a 2 percent cash discount will be granted.

was relatively stable until 1969 but dropped sharply in 1970. The change in 1970 was mainly a result of a sharp decrease in accounts receivable, which probably reflects management's efforts to improve the hard-pressed liquidity position by restricting credit and increasing the collection efforts. The industry averages increased slightly during 1969 and 1970, probably indicating the improvement in credit terms offered by aerospace firms as demand for aircraft dropped. Lockheed's measures are in all years below the industry averages, a finding to be expected for a firm producing almost exclusively for the government.

2. Inventory turnover ratio

This measure is usually defined as the cost of sales divided by the average inventory balance. Cost of sales is used rather than sales, since the denominator (inventories) is generally valued at cost. The inventory turnover ratio is supposed to indicate the efficiency of the firm's inventory management; the higher the ratio, the more efficient the management of inventories. The underlying reason is the belief that the smaller the inventory level needed to support a given volume of sales (i.e., the higher the turnover ratio), the better the inventory management. This is, of course, an oversimplification, since, as is well known from inventory theory, a lower-than-optimal inventory level may be as costly to the firm (in the form of lost sales, high costs caused by hurried production, etc.) as a higher-than-optimal balance. The objective of inventory management is to maintain an *optimal* inventory level rather than to minimize it. Consequently, a high inventory turnover ratio does not necessarily indicate an optimal inventory management. Nevertheless, substantial changes over time in the inventory turnover ratio and/or systematic deviations from industry standards may indicate to the analyst the desirability of probing deeper into the inventory problem. For example, the existence of slow-moving or "dead" (obsolete) inventory items may be indicated by low or decreasing turnover ratios.

The inventory turnover ratios for Lockheed are presented in Table 2.6. The sharp decrease of the ratios in 1969 and 1970 was caused by a disproportionate increase (to sales) in inventories (from $285,707,000 in 1968 to $500,417,000 and $693,920,000 in 1969 and 1970, respectively). This inventory increase is claimed by Lockheed to have resulted from the disputed contracts that were canceled by the Defense Department. The industry averages were relatively stable and usually (except for 1969 and 1970) lower than Lockheed's ratios.

3. Industry-specific measures

The ratios discussed above were designed for the financial analysis of manufacturing firms. The analysis of nonmanufacturing firms usually requires the use of additional measures reflecting the specific character-istics of the firms' operations. For example, the following ratios reflect important characteristics of airline operations: (*a*) *Passenger load factor,* measured as passenger revenue seat-miles-flown/seat-miles-offered, and indicating the extent of idle or underutilized capacity. Given the rela-tively high fixed costs of airlines, large profits are realized when a carrier exceeds its break-even load factor, while substantial losses occur when it fails to do so. (*b*) *Average miles per plane departure,* indicating, among other things, the profitability of the airlines' routes. Given the high fixed costs per plane departure (ground facilities, maintenance, increased fuel consumption during takeoffs, etc.) and the very low variable costs, it is obvious that the longer the route, the lower the average costs per mile and the higher the profitability of operations. (*c*) *Revenues per passenger mile,* indicating fare policies of the firm.

Airline efficiency of operations measures can be applied to other transportation industries, such as railroads and trucking. The load factor indicators can be used to measure operational efficiency of hotels, restaurants, and convention halls. Other service industries, such as banks and insurance companies, have also developed specific ratios (e.g., the loans to deposits ratio for banks).

4. Other ratios

(*a*) *Inventory holding period*—it is possible to compute a measure indicating the average selling period (in days) of the inventory: 360 (days)/inventory turnover ratio. This measure is similar to the receiv-ables average collection period and indicates the degree of liquidity of inventories; the larger the measure, the lower the liquidity. (*b*) *Net sales to stockholders' equity* indicates the activity level of stockholders' investment in the firm. A higher than normal ratio, for example, may indicate an excessive volume of business on a "thin" margin of invested capital.[38] (*c*) *Net sales to net working capital* is supposed to indicate the adequacy of the working capital reservoir in supporting the firm's vol-ume of trade.

SUMMARY

A survey of ratios currently used in the analysis of financial state-ments was provided above. The ratios were classified into four major categories indicating: (*a*) the profitability of the firm's operations and the efficiency of using its capital, (*b*) the firm's ability to meet its short-

---

[38] In this context, analysts use the terms overtrading and undertrading, refer-ring to the existence of an optimal relationship between sales and stockholders' equity. For elaboration, see R. A. Foulke, *Practical Financial Statement Analysis,* 6th ed. (Hightstown, N.J.: McGraw-Hill Book Company, 1968), pp. 390–91.

term financial obligations, (*c*) the capital structure of the firm and the ability to meet long-term obligations, and (*d*) operational efficiency and the extent of asset utilization.

Financial ratios are indicators of economic phenomena underlying the firm's operations. They rarely provide the analyst with final answers; more often they point to areas where further investigation may be rewarding. Ratio analysis should therefore be regarded as a preliminary stage in the process of investment decision making.

APPENDIX: THE COMPUTATION OF LOCKHEED'S RATIOS FOR 1965 (presented in Tables 2.3 through 2.6)

1. *Net income to total assets.*

Income before interest, dividends, and taxes		$102,563,000
Deduct: Income taxes	$47,390,000	
Tax savings on interest [39] (.50 × 1,484,000)	742,000	48,132,000
Adjusted net income after taxes		$54,431,000

$$\frac{\text{Net income}}{\text{Total assets [40]}} = \frac{54,431,000}{629,389,000} = .0865.$$

2. *Income available for common to common equity.*

$$\frac{53,689,000}{297,742,000} = .1803.$$

3. *Earnings-per-share.*

$$\frac{53,689,000}{11,078,000} = \$4.86.$$

4. *Price-earnings ratio.*

$$\frac{\text{Average (of the high-low) price}}{\text{Earnings-per-share}} = \frac{53.125}{4.86} = 10.93.$$

5. *Dividends to net income.*

$$\frac{22,024,000}{53,689,000} = .4102.$$

6. *Operating income to operating assets.*

$$\frac{98,600,000}{(629,389,000 - 4,319,000)} = .1577.$$

[39] Assuming 50 percent corporate income tax.
[40] End-of-year balance.

7. *Current ratio.*

$$\frac{495,036,000}{314,782,000} = \underline{\underline{1.5726.}}$$

8. *Quick ratio.*

$$\frac{234,782,000}{314,782,000} = \underline{\underline{.7459.}}$$

9. *Debt to equity ratio.*

$$\frac{331,647,000}{297,742,000} = \underline{\underline{1.1137.}}$$

10. *Times interest earned.*

$$\frac{\text{Income before interest}}{\text{Interest charges}} = \frac{55,173,000}{1,484,000} = \underline{\underline{37.18.}}$$

11. *Average collection period for accounts receivable.*

$$\text{Average daily net sales: } \frac{1,814,085,000}{360} = \$5,039,125.$$

$$\text{Average collection period: } \frac{192,183,000}{5,039,125} = 38.14 \text{ days.}$$

12. *Inventory turnover ratio.*

$$\frac{\text{Net sales }^{41}}{\text{Inventories}} = \frac{1,814,085,000}{246,228,000} = \underline{\underline{7.3675.}}$$

[41] Net sales were used, since the cost of sales figure was unavailable.

CHAPTER THREE

Issues in
Financial Ratio Analysis

The mechanics of ratio analysis were discussed and demonstrated in the preceding chapter. We now turn to a discussion of various conceptual as well as practical issues involved in the analysis. An examination of the literature reveals that the principles and postulates available are wholly inadequate for modern analysis, thus emphasizing the need for a construction of a firm conceptual basis for financial analysis. The practical methods of financial analysis and the problems involved in their application are then discussed; particularly, the desirability of a shift from univariate to multivariate financial analysis. Finally, given the unprecedented growth of corporate diversification in recent years, the problems involved in the financial analysis of diversified companies are examined.

PRINCIPLES OF RATIO ANALYSIS

An examination of the literature reveals that the formation and interpretation of ratio analysis are based on the various principles and postulates summarized below.[1]

[1] This section draws on J. O. Horrigan, "An Evaluation of Financial Ratio Analysis" (Ph.D. dissertation, University of Chicago, 1967), Chap. 3.

1. Objectives of ratio analysis

The major objective of ratio analysis is considered to be the facilitation of financial statement interpretation. This is basically achieved by reducing the large number of financial statement items to a relatively small set of ratios.[2] Such ratios relate the absolute values of financial items to common bases (e.g., total assets), allowing a meaningful comparison of financial data both over time and across firms for a given time period.

The financial analysis literature usually views ratios as indicators of firm deficiencies, such as poor liquidity or low profitability. Thus, the negative function of ratios is emphasized; ". . . a favorable ratio may mean nothing . . . an unfavorable ratio is significant." [3] Financial ratios are not intended to provide definite answers; their real value is derived from the questions they provoke. Ratios are therefore symptoms of the firm's economic condition intended to guide the analyst in his financial investigation.

2. Ratio formation

With respect to the formation of ratios, the literature generally argues for some logical relationship between the items in the numerator and the denominator. Three kinds of logical relationships have been suggested: (a) Ratios should relate matching components, such as earnings to the investment base. The test for matching is whether an *economic* relationship exists between the two values. (b) Ratios should be formed only from elements based on common values. Thus, for example, cost of sales should be used in the numerator of the inventory turnover ratio, since the denominator (inventory) is valued at cost. (c) Ratios should be formed only if the components are functionally related, that is, if they vary in some definable manner. For example, the usefulness of the ratio of net earnings to sales was questioned because the fixed expenses do not vary with sales.

These criteria for ratio formation are obviously inadequate. The requirement for an economically meaningful relationship between ratio components is self-evident; the need for a common value-basis of ratio components is logically unsupported; [4] and the restriction of ratios to

---

[2] The number of different ratios that can be computed from financial statement items is, of course, also very large. However, since most of these ratios are economically meaningless (e.g., income tax expense divided by accounts payable), it seems that a large part of the information contained in financial statements could be conveyed by a relatively small number of ratios.

[3] S. Gilman, *Analyzing Financial Statements* (New York: The Ronald Press Company, 1925), p. 44.

[4] It was suggested, for example, that the sales to inventory ratio is a better measure of the firm's ability to recover cash than the cost of sales to inventory ratio;

covariable items is inconsistent with the objective of financial analysis, since the relationship generally sought is not the one between the numerator and the denominator but that between the ratio and some other economic indicator.

3. Ratio interpretation

As expected, the literature on ratio analysis is rather vague regarding the interpretation of ratios. The most elementary approach to ratio interpretation classifies financial statement items into "good" and "bad" categories; the former includes assets, revenues, and equities, while the latter is comprised of liabilities and expenses. This good-bad classification is supposed to provide a framework for ratio interpretation. Thus, for example, a high current ratio is desirable, since it indicates an excess of "good" (assets) over "bad" (liabilities).

However, such a naïve framework for ratio interpretation is obviously unsatisfactory. First, many ratios (e.g., the turnover and profitability ratios) contain "good" items in both the numerator and the denominator, in which case, interpretation by the good-bad criterion is ambiguous. Second, no guidelines are provided with respect to optimal ratio sizes; in other words, are high "good" ratios always good? This is clearly not the case, since high liquidity ratios, for example, may indicate the existence of idle cash resulting in a loss of alternative income, and high turnover ratios may be caused by lower than optimal inventory levels.

Given the inadequacy of the good-bad framework, a need arises for ratio standards against which the firm's observed measures can be compared and inferences drawn. The most frequently advanced standard in the ratio analysis literature is the industry average or some alternative measure of industry central tendency, such as the median. Observed ratios, it is argued, should be compared with industry averages, and inferences should be based on the extent and direction of deviation from the average. However, despite the intuitive appeal of the industry average criterion, some fundamental questions remain unanswered. First, is there a strong common effect operating on ratios within industry classifications, that is, is the industry framework the appropriate one for ratio analysis? [5] Second, why should the industry *average* be regarded as an optimal target with which an examined ratio should be compared? Is it not more reasonable to evaluate the performance of a firm against

---

see I. M. Mackler, "A Suggestion for the Measurement of Solvency," *The Accounting Review*, 17 (October 1942), 351.

[5] For stock prices, it was found that the industry effect is rather marginal relative to the overall market effect. See B. F. King, "Market and Industry Factors in Stock Price Behavior," *Journal of Business*, 39 (January 1966), 134–90.

that of the most successful firms in the industry? Third, should inferences be based on the absolute or relative differences from the standard? Fourth, what measure of central tendency—the mean, mode, or median —should serve as the standard? Fifth, which industry classification is the most appropriate (e.g., the SIC code, etc.), and what degree of homogeneity (e.g., two digits, three digits, etc.) should be chosen? Since no satisfactory answers to these questions are provided in the ratio analysis literature, it must be concluded that the adequacy of an industry standard for ratio interpretation is as yet unverified.

In addition to the industry average standard, the use of absolute ratio criteria is sometimes suggested in the literature. A well-known absolute criterion is the 2:1 value for the current ratio. Other, somewhat less-known, criteria are that both the net worth to fixed assets and the net worth to total debt ratios should at least equal one. Here again, no convincing a priori optimality reasoning or empirical evidence is advanced to support the use of such absolute ratio criteria.

Summarizing, ratio analysis principles concerning both the objectives and the execution of the analysis were shown above to be wholly inadequate. They are surprisingly naïve, often ambiguous, and usually unverified from an empirical point of view.[6]

PRACTICAL METHODS OF RATIO ANALYSIS

Financial ratios are conventionally analyzed in two ways: time-series and cross-sectional analyses. The former is concerned with the behavior of a given ratio over time, while the latter involves comparisons between the investigated firm's ratios and those of related firms. Both the time-series and cross-sectional aspects can be combined into one method—the residual analysis—to be presented below. The preceding analyses are all of the *univariate* mode, that is, the ratios are examined one at a time. A shift toward multivariate ratio analysis, in which several measures are *simultaneously* considered, seems warranted, since it is generally regarded to be superior to the univariate analysis.

1. Time-series (intrafirm) analyses

The major objective of analyzing a time series of financial ratios is to predict future values of the ratios. The general approach to such discrete time-series predictions is to search for systematic patterns in the historic behavior of the series; knowledge of such patterns can then be used in the prediction process. This approach to the prediction of ratios rests on the assumption that the underlying process generating the ratio

[6] A framework for financial statement analysis will be outlined in Chapter 7.

series is *stable* over time, that is, the process continues to operate as it did in the past. Systematic patterns in the behavior of ratio time series can be determined by various statistical techniques, such as plotting the data on scatter diagrams, serial correlation and runs analyses, and various transformations of the original data.[7]

The optimal prediction model to be used depends, of course, on the statistical nature of the process generating the ratio series. However, most processes in business and economics are very complex and, in many cases, not even well understood because of the large number of factors with complex interactions involved. For example, a firm's net income is usually affected by economy-wide factors (e.g., interest rate and price-level fluctuations), by factors specific to the industry in which the firm operates (e.g., a change in demand for the industry's product), and by factors specific to the firm (e.g., firm size and quality of management). Consequently, practicable prediction models are, at best, approximations to local segments of the observed time series. However, the better one understands the basic mechanism governing the process being predicted, the better, on the average, the performance of the prediction model. The technical aspects of time-series forecasting are rather complex and obviously beyond the scope of this book.[8] However, the usefulness of financial data in predicting business events, such as earnings growth and corporate bankruptcy, is the central issue dealt with in Parts II and III of the book.

2. Cross-sectional (interfirm) analysis

The objective of the interfirm mode of analysis is to derive information needed for financial decisions by comparing the investigated ratios with exogenous norms or standards. As mentioned above, such standards are usually based on industry-wide measures of central tendency, and inferences are based on both the direction and the extent of deviation from the standard. Comparison with industry-wide measures is known as the *standard ratios* technique. Data on such standard ratios, that is, industry means or medians, for a large set of industries are periodically published by Dun and Bradstreet, Robert Morris Associates, and other financial institutions.

---

[7] The behavior of a time series can be random, i.e., the observations do not behave in any systematic pattern. Such behavior, statistically defined as "random walk," implies that past observations are of limited or no value for prediction purposes. This subject will be further discussed in Chapter 8.

[8] For a practical text, see R. Brown, *Smoothing, Forecasting and Prediction of Discrete Time Series* (Englewood Cliffs, N.J.: Prentice-Hall, Inc., 1963). A more advanced treatment of forecasting is presented in G. E. P. Box and G. H. Jenkins, *Time Series Analysis* (San Francisco: Holden-Day, Inc., 1970); and in C. Nelson, *Applied Time Series Analysis* (San Francisco: Holden-Day, Inc., 1973).

It is often argued in the financial analysis literature that interfirm ratio analysis should be restricted to "comparable" firms having similar characteristics. Comparability is believed to be enhanced if the firms—

(a) belong to the same industry,
(b) are of similar size,
(c) use similar accounting methods, and
(d) are located in the same geographical area.

However, as will be shown below, there is only little evidence to indicate that violating the comparability criteria will seriously disrupt financial statement analysis.

With respect to the *industry effect,* Chudson found that the liquidity and turnover ratios were significantly different among industry groupings.[9] Horrigan corroborated these findings with respect to the turnover ratios and also reported significant differences among industries for the net income to sales ratio.[10] The evidence regarding the *firm-size effect* on ratios was summarized by Horrigan as follows:

(i) Short-term liquidity ratios are related to size of firm in a positive, parabolic manner. That is, the relationship is positive for smaller firms and negative for larger firms.
(ii) Long-term solvency ratios are also related to size of firm in a positive parabolic manner.
(iii) Capital turnover ratios all vary inversely with size of firm.
(iv) Profit margin ratios vary directly with size of firm.
(v) Return on investment ratios also vary directly with size of firm.[11]

Care should be exercised in the evaluation of the these conclusions, since (*a*) they were based on aggregate data, and (*b*) no attempt has been made to statistically isolate the size effect from other possible effects, such as industry or age of firm. As expected, different accounting methods were found to affect financial ratios;[12] the capitalization of leases, for example, will lower all the long-term solvency ratios, and the sales to fixed assets ratio.

[9] W. A. Chudson, *The Pattern of Corporate Financial Structure: A Cross-Section of Manufacturing, Mining, Trade, and Construction, 1937* (New York: National Bureau of Economic Research, 1945), pp. 68, 118–28, 141–42.

[10] Horrigan, *op. cit.*, p. 112.

[11] *Ibid.*, pp. 109–10. Horrigan provides detailed references to the various empirical studies on which these conclusions are based.

[12] For evidence, see G. C. Holdren, "Lifo and Ratio Analysis," *The Accounting Review*, 39 (January 1964), 70–85; and A. T. Nelson, "Capitalizing Leases: The Effect on Financial Ratios," *Journal of Accountancy*, 116 (July 1963), 49–58.

The widespread belief in the importance of the comparability guidelines to ratio analysis usually led researchers to stratify samples according to the above criteria. Most often, samples were stratified by industry and size of firms (see, for example, the bankruptcy prediction models presented in Chapter 9); samples were sometimes also stratified by accounting method [13] and by geographical location.[14] Since, as was mentioned above, the need for stratification has not been convincingly established, analysts and researchers would do well to exercise more judgment in their stratification decisions.

3. A combination of time-series and cross-sectional analysis: the "residual method"

The residual method suggested here for ratio analysis is widely used by researchers in finance for studying the behavior of stock prices.[15] The basic premise underlying the method is that if the investigated variable (e.g., stock prices) is cross-sectionally correlated, its variability can be decomposed into two parts: that caused by *general* factors affecting all firms and that caused by *specific* factors affecting only the firm under study. For some purposes, the analyst will be interested only in the latter, specific factors. For example, if the effect of earnings announcements on stock prices is investigated, it might be misleading to examine the behavior of the firm's stock prices in the vicinity of its announcement date, since all or part of the observed changes might have been caused by factors affecting all stocks (e.g., an increase in prime interest rates). It is therefore necessary to eliminate the common effects on prices before the reaction to earnings announcements or any other event specific to the firm can be determined.

The practical method used by finance researchers to account for general market changes is to regress the series of rates of return on a specific stock, R_{jt}, on an index representing the returns on all stocks, R_{Mt} (e.g., the Standard and Poor's index), and examine the behavior of the regression residuals, u_{jt}: [16]

$$R_{jt} = a_j + b_j R_{Mt} + u_{jt}. \tag{3.1}$$

[13] For example, Miller and Modigliani mention the within-industry uniformity of accounting practices as one of the reasons for studying the electric utility industry. See M. H. Miller and F. Modigliani, "Some Estimates of the Cost of Capital to the Electric Utility Industry, 1954–57," *American Economic Review*, 56 (June 1966), 335.

[14] See P. A. Meyer and H. W. Pifer, "Prediction of Bank Failures," *Journal of Finance*, 35 (September 1970), 853–68.

[15] See, for example, E. F. Fama, L. Fisher, M. C. Jensen, and R. Roll, "The Adjustment of Stock Prices to New Information," *International Economic Review*, 10 (February 1969), 1–21.

[16] This approach is, of course, based on the strong common effect operating on all stocks—the "market factor"; see King, *op. cit.*

The series of regression residuals, u_{jt}, thus reflects the portion of the return change that was *specific* to stock j.[17]

The residual analysis can obviously be applied to time series of financial ratios in order to account for industry- and economy-wide common effects.[18] Denote a given ratio (e.g., net income to total assets) for firm j in time t by x_{jt}, and the industry- and economy-wide averages of this ratio by x_{It} and x_{Et}, respectively. The residuals, u_{jt}, of the following regression:

$$x_{jt} = a_j + b_j x_{It} + c_j x_{Et} + u_{jt} \qquad (3.2)$$

will thus reflect the deviations over time of firm j's net income to total assets ratio from the industry and economy averages.[19] The residual method therefore combines the time-series with the cross-sectional (i.e., comparison with industry and economy ratio averages) aspects of the analysis.

For demonstration, Lockheed's net income to total assets ratio for the twenty-year period 1952–71 was regressed on the average ratio for the aerospace industry and the average ratio for all firms on Standard and Poor's Compustat tape,[20] in the manner of (3.2). The twenty regression residuals are presented in Table 3.1 and plotted in Figure 3.1. Examination of the residuals' behavior reveals three distinct subperiods: 1952–60—ratios were unstable and generally lower than the averages (evidenced by the negative residuals); 1961–67—generally stable and above-average ratios; and 1968–70—steep decline in profitability discussed in the preceding chapter.

4. Multivariate ratio analysis

Early users of financial ratios emphasized the single-ratio approach which refers to the consideration of only one ratio in the decision. Thus, for example, it is believed that in the late 1800s and early 1900s the credit worthiness of prospective borrowers was determined mainly on the basis of the current ratio. However, the limitations of a financial analysis restricted to one ratio were soon evident and it became recognized that a comprehensive evaluation of the firm's economic situation required an examination of several key ratios each shedding light on a

[17] This method is further discussed in Chapter 13.

[18] For evidence on such effects, see R. Ball and P. Brown, "Some Preliminary Findings on the Association between the Earnings of a Firm, Its Industry and the Economy," *Empirical Research in Accounting: Selected Studies, 1967*, Supplement to Vol. 5, *Journal of Accounting Research*, 55–77.

[19] It is, of course, assumed here that the data satisfy the basic assumptions of the linear regression model (e.g., that a linear relationship exists between the firm's ratios and those of the industry and the economy).

[20] Both averages excluded Lockheed's data.

TABLE 3.1

Residuals from a Regression of Lockheed's Net Income to Total Assets Ratio on Industry and Economy Average Ratios (3.2)

Year	Actual Ratio (x_{jt})	Estimated Ratio $(\hat{x}_{jt})$	Residuals $(u_{jt} = x_{jt} - \hat{x}_{jt})$
1952	.041	.046	−.006
1953	.059	.051	.008
1954	.080	.065	.015
1955	.058	.089	−.031
1956	.039	.072	−.033
1957	.039	.064	−.025
1958	.036	.032	.004
1959	.017	.041	−.024
1960	−.090	.023	−.114
1961	.049	.009	.041
1962	.062	.032	.031
1963	.079	.036	.044
1964	.082	.046	.036
1965	.082	.051	.031
1966	.081	.045	.036
1967	.062	.022	.039
1968	.047	.024	.023
1969	−.026	.010	−.036
1970	−.065	−.010	−.055
1971	.008	−.009	.017

specific aspect of operations. Accordingly, such early writers on financial analysis as Wall and Justin advanced extensive lists of ratios to be incorporated in any complete analysis of a firm.[21] It should be noted, however, that despite the use of several ratios in the analysis, the approach taken was still *univariate,* since each ratio was considered individually. The main shortcomings of such an approach are that (*a*) the interdependencies among the various ratios are ignored, and (*b*) ambiguous inferences resulting from conflicting signals (e.g., the firm's earnings-per-share are above the industry mean while the net income to total assets ratio is below the mean) are possible.

These shortcomings can be overcome by the use of a multivariate analysis in which several ratios are combined into a model or an index providing a unique signal. Accordingly, Wall and Dunning suggested the following index of credit strength. [22]

[21] A. Wall, "Study of Credit Barometers," *Federal Reserve Bulletin,* 5 (March 1919), 229–43; and W. H. Justin, "Operating Control through Scientific Analysis," *The Journal of Accountancy,* 38 (September 1924), 183–95.

[22] A. Wall and R. W. Dunning, *Ratio Analysis of Financial Statements* (New York: Harper Brothers, 1928), pp. 152–65. More recently, an index for financial solvency was suggested by M. Tamari, "Financial Ratios as a Means of Forecasting Bankruptcy," *Management International Review* (1966/4), pp. 15–21.

Ratio (R_i)	Relative Weight (w_i)
1. Current ratio	.25
2. Net worth to fixed assets	.15
3. Net worth to debt	.25
4. Sales to accounts receivable	.10
5. Sales to inventories	.10
6. Sales to fixed assets	.10
7. Sales to net worth	.05
Total	1.00

The index was thus calculated:

$$I = \sum_{i=1}^{7} w_i \left[1 + (1 - R_i/\bar{R}_i)\right] \tag{3.3}$$

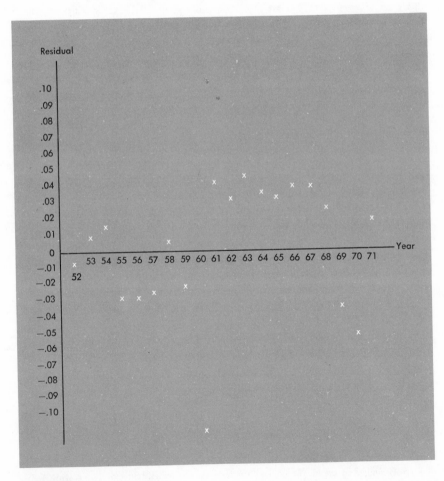

FIGURE 3.1

Regression residuals from Table 3.1

where

w_i = relative weight of ratio i,

R_i = the value of ratio i for the specific firm,

$\bar{R}_i$ = the standard or base ratio for the industry.

The main characteristic of the multivariate approach is thus the *simultaneous* consideration of several ratios in the analysis. However, the Wall and Dunning index and others proposed later suffer from a major deficiency—both the ratios and the relative weights used in the index are somewhat arbitrarily chosen.[23] The choice of ratios and relative weights was usually based on the writer's own experience, without any conceptual or empirical support. The resulting indexes were therefore of questionable generality.

It should be noted that the construction of a ratio index amounts to a formulation of a model designed to describe and/or predict some aspects of the firm's economic behavior. The specification problems involved in such model formulation are usually classified into three categories: (a) choosing the variables (e.g., the various financial ratios) to be included in the model, (b) deciding upon the mathematical relationship (e.g., linear) among the variables, and (c) assigning relative weights to the variables. Sometimes a well-defined theory (e.g., the portfolio selection theory presented in Chapter 12) can guide the analyst in the specification of variables, mathematical form, and relative weights. Often, however, well-defined theories are nonexistent, and the analyst must experiment with various alternative models and, on statistical grounds, choose the most appropriate one. This can be done, for example, by using the least-squares regression technique when appropriate. The variable to be explained or predicted (e.g., price-earnings ratios) is defined, and various combinations of independent variables (e.g., ratios) are examined for their explanatory power. The goodness-of-fit measures, such as the coefficient of multiple determination, R^2, the standard errors of the estimates, and the F-ratio will indicate the relative performance of the models examined. In addition, experimentation with various transformations of the variables (e.g., a logarithmic transformation) might suggest the optimal mathematical form of the model.[24]

The trend in modern financial analysis is clearly toward extensive use of multivariate models in the explanation and prediction of business phenomena. Such models usually incorporate accounting as well as nonaccounting data and are constructed by statistical means rather than based on well-developed theories. The discussion in Parts II and III of

[23] Wall and Dunning recognized the highly subjective nature of their index: "Each separate analyst must of necessity select for himself the importance which he will attach to any ratio." *Ibid.*, p. 154.

[24] The subject of model formulation for financial statement analysis is further discussed in Chapter 7.

the book is mainly concerned with the presentation and evaluation of these models.

RATIO ANALYSIS OF DIVERSIFIED COMPANIES

The unprecedented growth of corporate diversification that has taken place in recent years warrants some comments on the special problems involved in the financial statement analysis of diversified companies. A diversified company was defined as one that "experience(s) rates of profitability, degrees of risk, and opportunities for growth which vary within the company." [25] It is clear that when this variation is substantial, any financial analysis concentrating on the aggregate data of the company is meaningless. Accordingly, the need to disaggregate the financial results of diversified companies to homogeneous segments was recognized. Thus, the Securities and Exchange Commission in its July 14, 1969, release proposed the following criteria for the breakdown of sales and earnings of diversified companies:

> . . . State, for each of the registrant's last five fiscal years, or for each fiscal year ending after December 31, 1966, or for each fiscal year the registrant has been engaged in business, whichever period is less, the approximate amount or percentage of (i) total sales and revenues, and (ii) income (or loss) before income taxes and extraordinary items, attributable to each line of business which during either of the last two fiscal years accounted for:
>
> (a) 10 per cent or more of the total sales and revenues;
>
> (b) 10 per cent or more of income before income taxes and extraordinary items computed without deduction of loss resulting from operations of any line of business, or
>
> (c) a loss which equaled or exceeded 10 per cent of the amount of income specified in (b) above.[26]

Substantial efforts have also been made by accountants to provide, a conceptual framework for segmented reporting by diversified companies.[27] The general objective of these suggestions was to design the reports so as to facilitate the interpretation of financial results.

---

[25] R. K. Mautz, *Financial Reporting by Diversified Companies* (New York: Financial Executive Research Foundation, 1968), p. 7.

[26] "Adoption of Amendments to Forms S-1, S-7, and 10" (Washington, D.C.: Securities and Exchange Commission, Releases Nos. 4988 and 8650, July 14, 1969).

[27] For example, Mautz, *op. cit.;* A. Rappaport and E. M. Lerner, *A Framework for Financial Reporting by Diversified Companies,* NAA Research Studies in Management Reporting No. 2 (New York: National Association of Accountants, 1969). For a chronicle of the major events surrounding the segment reporting issue and an extensive bibliography of publications on the subject, see K. F. Skousen, "Chronicle of Events Surrounding the Segment Reporting Issue," *Journal of Accounting Research,* 8 (Autumn 1970), 293–99.

Segmentation of the financial results of diversified companies is desirable for both interfirm and intrafirm financial analyses. It was mentioned above that industry standards are used in the process of the analysis as a benchmark against which the specific ratios of the firm are evaluated. Industry data are sometimes also used for predicting future performance of the firm. Specifically, a forecast of the industry performance as a whole is performed, based, among other things, on the outlook of the specific demand and cost factors affecting the industry and on macroeconomic variables such as consumer spending and industrial production. Given the industry forecast, a prediction of the firm's performance is made based on an established relationship between the firm and the industry.[28] It is clear that the industry framework cannot be used for diversified firms which operate across industry boundaries, unless the company's financial results are adequately segmented to homogeneous operations.

Aggregate results of diversified companies also hinder any intrafirm analysis in which past patterns of the ratios are extrapolated to the future, since the results (e.g., earnings) of various segments may behave differently over time due to demand and cost-structure differences.[29] A segmental analysis of financial statements of diversified companies is therefore required for both interfirm and intrafirm ratio analyses.[30]

The main problem involved in the segmentation of financial statements of diversified companies concerns the allocation of common costs (e.g., interest, administrative expenses, etc.) to the various segments. It is well known that such allocations are to a large extent arbitrary and can even be manipulated by management to window-dress the performance of faltering segments. Generally, the more detailed (segmented) the report, the more serious the effects of common cost allocations. It would therefore seem preferable for the analyst to base the profitability analysis on the *contribution margin* of each segment (i.e., revenues less *traceable* costs) rather than on net income figures which involve common cost allocations.

---

[28] It was established (Ball and Brown, *op. cit.*) that the income of a specific firm is associated to a large extent with the income of other firms in the same industry (i.e., the industry-wide effect), and with income of all firms in the economy (economy-wide effect). Therefore, information concerning the extent of such association may be used for predicting the income of the specific firm, conditional upon the prediction of the industry- and economy-wide variables.

[29] Rappaport and Lerner, *op. cit.,* p. 17, comment: "Thus, when a corporation has two or more activities that are growing at sharply different rates, and each contributes materially to the performance of the total enterprise, the investor requires information about each segment to form a reasonable estimate of the security's future growth in earnings."

[30] An interesting segmentation procedure by growth rates rather than by industries or markets is suggested in Rappaport and Lerner, *ibid.*

SUMMARY

Three major issues concerning ratio analysis were discussed in this chapter: (*a*) Principles and postulates of financial analysis; it was concluded that available principles fail to provide the required conceptual basis for modern financial analysis. (*b*) Practical methods of ratio analysis; time-series and cross-sectional methods of ratio analysis were discussed, and a possible combination of the two—the residual method—suggested. In addition, a discussion of the shift from univariate to multivariate ratio analysis and the problems involved was presented. (*c*) Ratio analysis of diversified companies; financial analysis of such companies requires a disaggregation of the financial reports to homogeneous segments. Such segmentation usually follows product lines or markets to allow a meaningful analysis of the financial results.

CHAPTER FOUR

Decomposition Analysis of Financial Statements

Statistical decomposition analysis is generally designed for the study of allocation problems. In the analysis a total, such as total assets, total consumer's expenditures, or total portfolio investment, is regarded as given, and the changes over time in the *allocation* of this total to the various subunits is studied. Decomposition analysis has recently been applied to a wide range of administrative and social science areas—economics, sociology, psychology, and accounting.[1]

The application of decomposition measures to financial analysis seems natural, since firms' financial statements summarize the allocation of corporate inputs and outputs according to various classifications, such as assets, liabilities, revenues, and costs. Changes in such allocations are caused by environmental effects (e.g., a change in demand) and/or by management decisions (e.g., a drop of a product line). It is obviously of interest to the analyst to detect the occurrence and extent of such structural changes in the firm's resource allocation in order to evaluate their impact on its future performance.

The financial statement decomposition analysis presented in this chapter is designed to efficiently identify such allocation changes. It is

[1] For a comprehensive discussion of these applications, see H. Theil, *Statistical Decomposition Analysis* (Amsterdam: North-Holland Publishing Co., 1972).

especially suited for the analysis of mass data, such as large computer files of financial statements, or the study of detailed reports, such as those provided to regulatory agencies. In this case the decomposition measures are mainly used as a screening device to scan the data quickly and to detect unusual phenomena worthy of a detailed investigation. The application of decomposition analysis to various segments of the financial statements is discussed below along with a comparison between decomposition measures and financial ratios.

THE UNDERLYING CAUSES OF FINANCIAL STATEMENT DECOMPOSITION CHANGES

Consider the decomposition of Lockheed's total assets in 1969 and 1970, presented in Table 4.1

TABLE 4.1

Lockheed's Assets for the End of Years 1969 and 1970
(THOUSANDS OF DOLLARS)

	Absolute Values		Relative Shares	
	1969	1970	1969	1970
1. Cash	52,062	79,497	.041	.060
2. Receivables	244,775	179,087	.192	.135
3. Inventories	500,417	693,920	.394	.525
4. Prepaid expenses	129,643	19,407	.102	.015
5. Investment in affiliates	4,277	4,184	.003	.003
6. Property, plant, and equipment—Net	337,849	343,446	.266	.260
7. Other deferred charges	2,421	3,088	.002	.002
Total assets	1,271,444	1,322,629	1.000	1.000

The relative shares in Table 4.1 were obtained by dividing the balance of each asset item by the corresponding value of total assets. It is evident that during 1970 the relative shares of some items, such as cash, inventories, and prepaid expenses, changed to a larger extent than those of other items, such as property, plant, and equipment. In assessing the economic relevance of such structural changes in the firm's portfolio of assets, it is necessary to investigate the process underlying these changes. Specifically, what determines the relative shares of financial statement items, and how do changes in these shares occur?

A reference to the concept of homeostasis will be helpful at this stage. Homeostasis, which means an equilibrium maintained by a self-regulatory mechanism, is a major characteristic of all living organisms. When such an equilibrium—for example, a human body temperature of 98.6 degrees—is disturbed, forces are set in motion to restore it. It has been suggested by organization theorists and economists that the behavior of business organizations can also be characterized as homeostatic.[2] Optimal (equilibrium) relationships among the various inputs and outputs are determined by the organization, and efforts are made to maintain them in face of disturbances. Equilibrium relationships in business organizations are usually derived from economic optimality criteria designed to enhance operational efficiency. Thus, for any given level of activity there exist optimal relationships between labor and capital inputs, inventory and sales, cash and short-term securities, debt and equity capital, and so forth. The *actual* relationships among inputs and outputs, which might of course deviate from the optimal ones, are presented in the firm's financial statements.

The analogy between the homeostatic behavior of living organisms and that of business organizations is, however, incomplete, since the latter's equilibrium input and output relationships can and often do change over time. Such changes generally result from (a) *planned* actions by management, such as an increase in the ratio of short-term securities to cash induced by an increase in market interest rates, and/or (b) *unplanned* changes resulting from unexpected events, such as a change in the firm's capital structure caused by a general decrease in stock prices.[3] Variations over time in the relationships among financial statement items thus reflect significant business events, both planned and unplanned, and are therefore of interest to the analyst engaged in assessing the firm's future performance.

Indeed, the importance of changes in the relative shares of balance sheet and income statement items has been recognized in traditional financial analysis. The method often used to analyze such changes is the "common-size statements" in which financial statements are converted into fractions, and changes in these fractions are investigated. Such an analysis, however, is rather inefficient, since it requires an examination of all financial statement items for the various periods under study and does not provide summary measures. However, the decomposition analysis presented below offers an efficient and convenient device for identi-

[2] See D. Katz and R. Kahn, *The Social Psychology of Organizations* (New York: John Wiley & Sons, Inc., 1966), parts reprinted in *Readings in Organization Theory*, J. G. Maurer, ed. (New York: Random House, Inc., 1971). Also K. E. Boulding, *A Reconstruction of Economics* (New York: John Wiley & Sons, Inc., 1950).

[3] The existence of adjustment costs (e.g., those involved in stock flotation) will usually prevent the firm from an immediate and complete restoration of equilibrium after an unexpected change.

fying (*a*) whether a significant change in financial statement constructs has occurred, and (*b*) where most of the change is located.

THE ASSETS AND LIABILITIES DECOMPOSITION MEASURES

Denote the relative shares (fractions) of a financial statement decomposition by p_i, $i = 1, \ldots, n$ (in the order of appearance on the financial statement). In Lockheed's case for 1969 (Table 4.1), p_1 (cash) = .041, p_2 (receivables) = .192, etc., and $n = 7$. Denote by q_i the corresponding fractions of a later financial statement, say Lockheed's assets decomposition in 1970. Thus, $q_1 = .060$, $q_2 = .135$, etc. The *assets decomposition* measure, I_A, is defined as

$$I_A = \sum_{i=1}^{n} q_i \log \frac{q_i}{p_i}. \qquad (4.1)$$

This is a measure for the degree of change in the firm's assets decomposition during the period constrained by the two balance sheets. When there has been no change in the relative shares of the items (i.e., $p_i = q_i$ for all *i*), the measure will take its minimum value—zero.[4] As soon as some q_i's differ from the corresponding p_i's, I_A will be positive, and the larger the pairwise differences, the larger the measure.[5] The measure thus indicates the extent of change in the composition of the firm's assets portfolio. The base of the logarithm in (4.1) is left to the user's choice; when natural logarithms are used, as in this chapter, the unit of measurement is denoted as a *nit*.

Lockheed's assets decomposition measures for the period 1965 through 1970 and the aerospace industry averages are presented in Table 4.2. Lockheed's measures were larger than the industry averages in 1966/67, and especially in 1968/69 and 1969/70, indicating unusual changes in the composition of assets during these years. An examination of Lockheed's balance sheets reveals large changes in cash and inventory balances during 1967 and substantial changes in the relative shares of almost all asset items during 1969 and 1970. The instability of asset items (and especially of inventories) during 1969 and 1970 is, of course, a reflection

---

[4] Note that the relative shares may be unchanged while the absolute values of the items change. However, absolute values are of no concern in the decomposition analysis which focuses on *structural* changes.

[5] For elaboration on the mathematical properties of the assets decomposition measure and, especially, its nonnegativity, see B. Lev, *Accounting and Information Theory* (Evanston, Ill.: American Accounting Association, 1969), Chap. 3 and Appendix A.

TABLE 4.2

Assets Decomposition Measures
(In 10^{-4} Nits)

	1965/66	1966/67	1967/68	1968/69	1969/70	Average
Lockheed	197	571	82	906	921 a	535
Industry average	276	279	272	218	144	238

a Lockheed's measure for 1969/70 was calculated as follows:

$$I_A = .060 \ \log_e \frac{.060}{.041} + .135 \ \log_e \frac{.135}{.192} + .525 \ \log_e \frac{.525}{.394} + .015 \ \log_e \frac{.015}{.102}$$

$$+ .003 \ \log_e \frac{.003}{.003} + .260 \ \log_e \frac{.260}{.266} + .002 \ \log_e \frac{.002}{.002} = .09208 \ \text{nits.}$$

of the difficulties encountered by Lockheed mainly as a result of contract cancellation by the government.[6] The industry averages were stable during 1965–68 and decreased thereafter.

It should be noted that the example in Table 4.2 does not fully demonstrate the power of decomposition analysis. When a short period such as five years is examined, changes in assets composition can be observed by merely inspecting the financial statements. However, if the analyst is interested in a substantially longer time period and a more detailed assets breakdown (e.g., the breakdown in the 10-K reports), he can apply the decomposition analysis to select a few periods in which unusual events occurred and can concentrate his analysis accordingly. The efficiency and usefulness of decomposition analysis thus increases with the amount and complexity of the data.

A *liabilities decomposition* measure, I_L, can be computed in the same manner as the assets decomposition measure. The p_i's and q_i's in (4.1) will be the fractions of liabilities and stockholders' equity items at two points in time. In the case of Lockheed, three items were considered: short-term liabilities, long-term liabilities, and stockholders' equity. The liabilities decomposition measures for the period 1965 through 1970 are presented in Table 4.3. Lockheed's large measure for 1966/67 was caused by the substantial increase in long-term debt occurring in 1967. The large measures in 1968/69 and 1969/70 reflect the substantial changes that have occurred in all three liabilities and equity classes as a result of the deterioration in Lockheed's financial condition. The industry mean is very unstable throughout the period.

[6] In this context it is interesting to note that decomposition measures were found to be good predictors of financial failure; see Chapter 9.

TABLE 4.3

Liabilities Decomposition Measures
(In 10^{-4} Nits)

	1965/66	1966/67	1967/68	1968/69	1969/70	Average
Lockheed	8	1821	33	680	735 [a]	655
Industry average	429	1605	473	850	204	712

[a] Lockheed's decomposition measure for 1969/70 was calculated as follows:

$$I_L = .381 \log_e \frac{.381}{.483} + .442 \log_e \frac{.442}{.264} + .177 \log_e \frac{.177}{.253} = .07354 \text{ nits.}$$

Decomposition measures are not restricted to the balance sheet; measures similar to (4.1) can be defined for the income statement and funds statement designed for indicating the degree of change over time in the relative shares of the constituent items. For example, a decomposition measure for the income statement can be defined by breaking down total revenues (sales) to: direct materials, direct labor, overhead expenses, selling expenses, administrative expenses, fixed charges, and net income. This measure will reflect, among other things, structural changes in the firm's production and distribution methods (e.g., an increase in capital intensity reflected by a change in the relative shares of the direct and indirect production costs).

THE BALANCE SHEET DECOMPOSITION MEASURE

It is conventional to classify balance sheet items into four basic categories: current assets, current liabilities, long-term assets, and long-term liabilities (including equities). Dividing each of the four categories by *twice* the balance sheet total yields a set of four nonnegative fractions which sum to 1. These fractions will be denoted by p_{ij}. The index i takes the values 1 and 2 for current and long-term items, and j takes the values 1 and 2 for assets and liabilities, respectively. The balance sheet is thus arranged in the form of a two-way table as shown in Figure 4.1. The marginal total $p_{1.}$ and $p_{2.}$ refer to total current items and total long-term items, respectively, and both $p_{.1}$ and $p_{.2}$ equal $1/2$ due to the equality of assets and liabilities.

	Assets	Liabilities	Total
Current	p_{11}	p_{12}	$p_{1.}$
Long-term	p_{21}	p_{22}	$p_{2.}$
Total	$p_{.1} = \frac{1}{2}$	$p_{.2} = \frac{1}{2}$	1

FIGURE 4.1

A balance sheet decomposed

Suppose a firm's balance sheets are available for two consecutive years. Denote the four fractions of the earlier balance sheet by p_{ij} and those of the later balance sheet by q_{ij}. The *balance sheet decomposition measure* of the second year relative to the first is defined as

$$I_{BS} = \sum_{i=1}^{2} \sum_{j=1}^{2} q_{ij} \log \frac{q_{ij}}{p_{ij}}. \tag{4.2}$$

This is an index for the degree to which the decomposition (i.e., the set of four relative shares) of the later balance sheet differs from that of a former one. As with the preceding measures, when all four fractions remain unchanged (i.e., $p_{ij} = q_{ij}$ for all i and j), the balance sheet decomposition measure will equal zero. However, when the items do *not* change in proportion, there will be pairwise differences between the p_{ij} and q_{ij}, leading to positive values of the measure. The larger these differences, the larger the measure.

Consider the data for Lockheed presented in Table 4.4. The balance

TABLE 4.4

Balance Sheets of Lockheed Aircraft Corporation as of the End of Years 1969 and 1970, in Thousands of Dollars
(Relative Shares in Parentheses)

	Assets		Liabilities		Total	
	1969	*1970*	*1969*	*1970*	*1969*	*1970*
Current	926,897	971,911	614,153	503,495	1,541,050	1,475,406
	(.365)	(.367)	(.242)	(.190)	(.607)	(.557)
Long-term	344,547	350,718	657,291	819,134	1,001,838	1,169,852
	(.135)	(.133)	(.258)	(.310)	(.393)	(.443)
Total	1,271,444	1,322,629	1,271,444	1,322,629	2,542,888	2,645,258
	(.500)	(.500)	(.500)	(.500)	(1.000)	(1.000)

TABLE 4.5

*Balance Sheet Decomposition Measures for Lockheed
and the Aerospace Industry*
(In 10^{-4} Nits)

	1965/66	1966/67	1967/68	1968/69	1969/70	Average
Lockheed	20	104	39	12	107 [a]	56
Industry average	154	236	101	181	57	146

[a] Lockheed's measure for 1969/70 was calculated as follows (based on Table 4.4):

$$.367 \ \log_e \frac{.367}{.365} + .133 \ \log_e \frac{.133}{.135} + .190 \ \log_e \frac{.190}{.242} + .310 \ \log_e \frac{.310}{.258} = .01067 \ \text{nits.}$$

sheet decomposition measures (4.2) for Lockheed and the aerospace industry averages are presented in Table 4.5. In the case of Lockheed, the instability of balance sheet constituents as indicated by the decomposition measures is well below the industry average for the period 1965–69. In fact, only four of the nineteen firms in the industry had lower average decomposition measures. This relative stability probably reflects the large amount (about 85 percent) of Lockheed's sales made to the government on long-term contracts. However, that situation changed during 1970; heavy operating losses resulting from contract cancellations forced the firm to increase its long-term debt disproportionately in order to pay maturing obligations. This capital structure fluctuation and the disproportionate change in inventories, also a result of contract cancellations, are reflected in the large decomposition measure (.0107 nits) for 1969/70.

DISAGGREGATION OF THE BALANCE SHEET DECOMPOSITION MEASURE

The preceding discussion of the decomposition measures glossed over the question of uniqueness of mathematical form. Given that decomposition changes might be of interest to management and analysts, why should such changes be measured in the specific form of (4.1) and (4.2), that is, as a weighted logarithmic function of the items' ratios? The choice is based on the important mathematical property of *additivity*, which allows the user to disaggregate and compute weighted averages of decomposition measures. The usefulness of this property for financial analysis is most pronounced in the disaggregation possibilities. Specifically, measures such as those above can be broken down into component parts enabling the analyst to examine changes in finer classifications and subsets of the data and thus to identify more efficiently the disturbance causes.

Note that p_{11} and p_{21} in Figure 4.1 represent current and long-term assets, respectively, divided by twice the balance sheet's total. Therefore, $2p_{11}$ is the fraction of assets that are current, and $2p_{21}$ is the long-term fraction. Accordingly, we may define

$$\sum_{i=1}^{2} (2q_{i1}) \log \frac{2q_{i1}}{2p_{i1}} \tag{4.3}$$

as the assets decomposition measure based on two items—current and fixed.[7] Similarly, the liabilities decomposition measure for the general classes—short- and long-term items—would be defined as

$$\sum_{i=1}^{2} (2q_{i2}) \log \frac{2q_{i2}}{2p_{i2}}. \tag{4.4}$$

Consider now the following disaggregation of the balance sheet decomposition measure (4.2):

$$\sum_{i=1}^{2} \sum_{j=1}^{2} q_{ij} \log \frac{q_{ij}}{p_{ij}} = \sum_{j=1}^{2} q_{\cdot j} \sum_{i=1}^{2} \frac{q_{ij}}{q_{\cdot j}} \left[\log \frac{q_{ij}/q_{\cdot j}}{p_{ij}/p_{\cdot j}} + \log \frac{q_{\cdot j}}{p_{\cdot j}} \right] \tag{4.5}$$

$$= \sum_{j=1}^{2} q_{\cdot j} \sum_{i=1}^{2} \frac{q_{ij}}{q_{\cdot j}} \log \frac{q_{ij}/q_{\cdot j}}{p_{ij}/p_{\cdot j}} + \sum_{j=1}^{2} q_{\cdot j} \log \frac{q_{\cdot j}}{p_{\cdot j}}.$$

The last term of (4.5) vanishes, since $q_{\cdot j} = p_{\cdot j} = 1/2$, and the first term can be written as

$$\frac{1}{2} \sum_{i=1}^{2} (2q_{i1}) \log \frac{2q_{i1}}{2p_{i1}} + \frac{1}{2} \sum_{i=1}^{2} (2q_{i2}) \log \frac{2q_{i2}}{2p_{i2}}. \tag{4.6}$$

We therefore conclude that the balance sheet decomposition measure (4.2) is equal to the arithmetic average of the assets decomposition measure (4.3) and the liabilities decomposition measure (4.4).

Such an assets-liabilities disaggregation of the overall balance sheet measure provides the analyst with additional information concerning the source of disturbances. For example, a large liabilities decomposition measure relative to the assets measure would lead the analyst to con-

---

[7] Recall that Lockheed's assets decomposition measures were computed in Table 4.2 over seven asset items. The number of individual items over which the measure is computed should be determined according to the purpose of the analysis.

centrate his investigation of causes on the liabilities side of the balance sheet. Further useful disaggregations are also possible. The overall balance sheet decomposition measure could be broken down into current and long-term components, determining the individual contribution of each category to the total decomposition change. Thus, the mathematical form of decomposition measures allows the formation of various submeasures providing a more precise and sensitive search device.

INDUSTRY-WIDE DECOMPOSITION MEASURES

The indexes discussed thus far were restricted to the firm's own time series of financial data. It is possible to formulate a decomposition measure concerned with the extent to which the relative positions of the firm's financial statement items differ *at a point in time* from those of other companies in the same industry. This extension conforms to traditional financial analysis which emphasizes the relevance of the industry framework.

Consider an industry consisting of N firms, and denote by w_c the total assets of the firm c, measured as a fraction of the total assets of *all* firms in the industry on a given date. The fraction w_c is, of course, also the ratio of the firm's total liabilities to those of the industry. Denote by p_{ijc} ($i = 1$ for current and $i = 2$ for long-term items; $j = 1$ for assets and $j = 2$ for liability items) each of the four basic balance sheet constituents of firm c, measured as a fraction of the firm's total assets plus total liabilities. These four fractions are identical with the four fractions in Figure 4.1. By adding the corresponding items for all firms in the industry, an aggregate industry balance sheet can be derived. Denote by s_{ij} ($i = 1$ for current and $i = 2$ for long-term items; $j = 1$ for assets and $j = 2$ for liability items), the four balance sheet items of the industry, measured as a fraction of total assets plus total liabilities of the industry. By definition, we therefore have

$$s_{ij} = \sum_{c=1}^{N} w_c \, p_{ijc}, \quad \begin{matrix} i = 1, 2 \\ j = 1, 2 \end{matrix} \tag{4.7}$$

It is now possible to determine the degree to which the composition of firm c's balance sheet deviates from that of its industry contemporaries. This deviation, for each of the N firms in the industry, can be quantified by the following *industry-wide* balance sheet decomposition measure:

$$\sum_{i=1}^{2} \sum_{j=1}^{2} p_{ijc} \log \frac{p_{ijc}}{s_{ij}}, \quad c = 1, \ldots, N. \tag{4.8}$$

When firm c's balance sheet composition is identical with that of the industry (i.e., $p_{ijc} = s_{ij}$ for all i and j), the measure (4.8) will equal zero, which is also its minimum value. The measure will increase with the differences between the firm's composition and that of the industry and will thereby indicate the degree to which the firm's structure of assets and liabilities differs from its peer group.

Table 4.6 provides a five-year record of these industry-wide measures for three firms in the aerospace industry. It is evident from the small measures that Aerojet General's composition of assets and liabilities is very close to that of the industry, whereas the structure of Martin-Marietta's balance sheets differs substantially from the industry composition. Further investigation of the latter firm might reveal specific managerial policies, demand patterns, or factor input conditions as causing the observed differences. Indeed, it might logically be concluded that Martin-Marietta does not really belong to the aerospace industry and should therefore be analyzed with reference to a different milieu. In any case, the industry-wide decomposition analysis draws the analyst's attention to such systematic structural differences among firms within an industry.

PROPERTIES OF DECOMPOSITION MEASURES

The main objective of decomposition analysis is the study of changes over time in the allocation of the firm's inputs and outputs as reflected in its financial statements. Such allocation changes indicate the occurrence of important environmental and/or internal events worthy of detailed investigation. This objective obviously differs from that of conventional ratio analysis, in which two items from the same financial statement are related to yield a summary economic indicator. Decomposition and ratio analyses are therefore designed to answer different questions and should

TABLE 4.6

Industry-wide Balance Sheet Decomposition Measures for Three Firms in the Aerospace Industry
(IN 10^{-4} NITS)

Firm	1966	1967	1968	1969	1970	Average
Aerojet General	5	53	41	1	79	36
Lockheed Aircraft	332	83	101	252	180	190
Martin-Marietta	717	1,322	1,774	1,397	1,314	1,305

be regarded as complementary. Following are some important properties of decomposition measures which distinguish them from other statistical measures for use in financial statement analysis.

As indicated above, the additivity property of decomposition measures (resulting from the specific logarithmic function used) provides useful disaggregation of the measures. The general objective of such disaggregation is to allow the analyst to trace the overall variation to the individual contribution of each component in order to select candidates for further investigation. This is analogous to the objective of statistical analysis of variance in which the total variance of a variable is disaggregated according to various attributes.[8] However, for the study of financial statements, decomposition analysis seems to be better suited than variance analysis, since the latter presupposes that the underlying random variation is normal. As will be seen in the next chapter, this is a doubtful assumption in the case of financial statement data. Decomposition measures are inherently distribution-free and hence less restricted in application than the standard tools of variance analysis.

Decomposition measures belong to the family of statistical dispersion measures as do the variance and the standard deviations. Decomposition measures indicate deviation from proportional development of financial statement items, while the variance measures the extent of deviation from the mean. The main difference between the two is that decomposition measures can be applied to nominal variables, whereas the variance cannot. (Nominal variables are those that take qualitative rather than quantitative values, such as black and white or current and fixed assets.) This is so because decomposition measures depend exclusively on the fractions (relative shares), whereas the variance depends both on the probabilities (analogous to the fractions) and on the *numerical values* of the variable (e.g., the variance of a stock's return depends both on the possible values of the returns and on the set of probabilities). Decomposition measures therefore seem to suit the analysis of financial statements better than other statistical dispersion measures, since the variables dealt with (e.g., asset and liability items) are all nominal.

Unlike conventional dispersion measures, decomposition measures are scale-free. Changes in the *absolute* values of the variables alone do not affect the measures. However, decomposition measures indicate distance rather than direction. Thus, for example, the measures are unable to discriminate between a change in capital structure away or toward the optimal position. The measures focus on *something* that has been

---

[8] For the relationship between decomposition measures and analysis of variance, see W. Garner and W. McGill, "The Relation between Information and Variance Analysis," *Psychometrica*, 21 (September 1956), 219–28.

happening, rather than on *what* has been happening, and leave it to the analyst to pursue the matter further.

The contention that decomposition measures reflect the occurrence of important events worthy of investigation is supported by several recent studies which empirically established an association between certain key business events and decomposition measures. It was found, for example, that bankrupt firms had, for at least five years before bankruptcy, substantially larger balance sheet decomposition measures than those of comparable solvent firms.[9] In addition, the balance sheet decomposition measure outperformed a large set of financial ratios in predicting bankruptcy. In another study, a decomposition measure applied to the distribution of firms' export sales was found to be associated with the riskiness of these sales.[10] Decomposition measures were also found to be strongly associated with unexpected income changes, supporting the contention that the measures reflect the occurrence of unforeseen events.[11] It was also reported that small firms have, on average, larger decomposition measures than large firms and that the measures of durable-goods producers are larger than those of nondurable and service producers.[12] These results would appear to reflect the fact that the variance of growth rate is larger for small firms than for large ones.[13] The durable-nondurable contrasts can similarly be explained by the higher volatility of durable goods' demand over the usual business cycle.[14]

SUMMARY

Changes in the allocation of a firm's assets, liabilities, and costs may be caused by expected (planned) and/or unexpected events. In either situation, the occurrence of such events is of interest to the analyst. The decomposition measures presented above indicate the extent of such allocation changes and thereby draw the analyst's attention to the

---

[9] B. Lev, "Financial Failure and Informational Decomposition Measures," *Accounting in Perspective: Contribution to Accounting Thoughts by Other Disciplines*, R. R. Sterling and W. F. Bentz, eds. (Cincinnati: South-Western Publishing Co., 1971), pp. 102–11.

[10] S. Hirsch and B. Lev, "Sales Stabilization through Export Diversification," *The Review of Economics and Statistics*, 53 (August 1971), 270–77.

[11] R. Ball, B. Lev, and R. Watts, "Unexpected Income Changes and Balance Sheet Compositions," *Journal of Accounting Research*, 11 (Autumn 1973).

[12] Theil, *op cit.*, pp. 148–49.

[13] S. Hymer and P. Pashigian, "Firm Size and Rate of Growth," *Journal of Political Economy*, 70 (December 1962), 56.

[14] V. Zarnowitz, *An Appraisal of Short-Term Economic Forecasts*, National Bureau of Economic Research (New York: Columbia University Press, 1967); and V. Zarnowitz, *Cyclical Behavior of Orders, Production and Investment*, National Bureau of Economic Research (New York: Columbia University Press, 1970).

occurrence of the underlying events. As summary measures, the usefulness of the decomposition indexes increases with the number of financial statements analyzed and their degree of detail. As with other economic indicators, determination of the practical usefulness of decomposition measures is largely an empirical question. However, even at this early stage of development, the empirical results mentioned above indicate that decomposition measures do reflect basic firm characteristics and events which are of interest to analysts.

CHAPTER FIVE

Statistical Issues in Financial Statement Analysis

Most of the literature in financial statement analysis, textbooks in particular, is surprisingly naïve from a statistical point of view. A time-series and a cross-sectional analysis of ratios is generally advocated without due attention to the various statistical problems involved. It will be shown below that the conventional comparison of an investigated ratio with the industry mean is insufficient for meaningful inferences, that the correlation among ratios calls for parsimony in their use, and that the ratio form might sometimes cause statistical problems. All in all, the simplicity of ratio analysis is often deceiving, and great care should therefore be exercised in the use and interpretation of ratio analysis.

THE DISPERSION OF FINANCIAL RATIOS

Financial statement analysis is generally based on the comparison of an observed ratio with a standard, such as the industry mean. The inferences drawn from such a comparison depend both on the size and on the direction of deviation from the standard. For example, a well-known text on financial statement analysis provides, for each of the ratios discussed, a long list of industry medians, and an optimal "maxim" for the analyst based on these medians:

> From the figures in the preceding paragraph [the industry medians], it is obvious that a ratio of total liabilities to tangible net worth in excess of 100.0 per cent is unusual. Rarely, if ever, *should* total liabilities of a commercial or industrial concern exceed the tangible net worth, as in such cases creditors have more at stake in a business enterprise than the stockholders or the owners.[1]

Industry mean or median ratios are thus the major source of exogenous information conventionally used by financial analysts.[2]

However, the information contained in such measures of industry central tendency is incomplete; the significance (i.e., seriousness) of deviation of an observed ratio from the industry mean depends not only on the extent and direction of deviation but also on the *dispersion* and "shape" of the distribution of ratios from which the mean was calculated. Suppose, for example, that the distribution of the current ratio for a specific industry and time period is approximately normal, with a mean of 3.00. Suppose further that the current ratio of firm X, which belongs to this industry, is 2.50. The analyst has to evaluate the seriousness of the weaker short-run liquidity position of firm X relative to the industry. However, such an evaluation cannot be comprehensive unless the dispersion of the industry ratios is considered. If the standard deviation of the ratio distribution is .25, then, based on the normal distribution law, the analyst infers that about 98 percent of the firms in the industry have higher current ratios than that of firm X.[3] However, if the industry standard deviation is 1.00, then only 69 percent of the firms have a higher current ratio than that of firm X. The latter situation is ostensibly

---

[1] R. A. Foulke, *Practical Financial Statement Analysis,* 6th ed. (Princeton, N.J.: McGraw-Hill Book Company, 1968), p. 253, emphasis supplied.

[2] Such standard ratios are published periodically by Robert Morris Associates and by Dun and Bradstreet.

[3] The standard deviation σ (i.e., the square root of the variance σ^2) is a measure for the spread of the distribution around its mean (expected value). For a discrete distribution:

$$\sigma^2 = \sum_{i=1}^{m} p_i(x_i - \mu)^2 \quad , \tag{5.1}$$

where μ is the mean, i.e., $\mu = \sum_{i=1}^{m} p_i x_i$. The variance σ^2 is thus a weighted average of the squared deviations of each observation, x_i, from the mean, μ, the weights being the probabilities, p_i. (Corresponding definitions for continuous distributions entail integrations instead of summations.) In a normal distribution, roughly 95 percent of the observations will fall between the boundaries $\mu - 2\sigma$ and $\mu + 2\sigma$.

less serious for firm X than the former.[4] Thus, knowledge of the dispersion of the industry ratio distribution, in addition to its mean, is crucial for inferences based on ratio analysis.[5] Unfortunately, measures of dispersion are rarely provided to financial statement users, and hence only limited inferences regarding an observed deviation of a ratio from the standard can be made from currently available data.[6]

The previous example specified the distribution of the industry ratios as normal (Gaussian). This distribution belongs to a "two-parameter" family for which the mean and the standard deviation (or variance) completely specify the distribution.[7] Thus, in the example above, knowledge of the mean and the standard deviation enabled the analyst to determine the relative position of the current ratio of firm X within the industry. When the industry distribution departs substantially from normality, additional information should be available to determine the significance of deviation from the mean. In such situations, unless the distribution is well approximated by a symmetric, two-parameter, but nonnormal, distribution, either the complete frequency distribution should be available or at least various points on the distribution, such as the 10 deciles.

Ratio analysis will obviously be more complicated when the actual distributions of ratios deviate substantially from normality, since much of the standard statistical tools (e.g., analysis of variance) assume normality. Unfortunately, the available evidence indicates that nonnormality is common; the actual distributions of financial ratios tend to be asym-

[4] As is conventional in ratio analysis, "seriousness" is defined here in terms of deviation from the industry mean, relative to those of other firms. A complete evaluation of the implications of an observed deviation will, of course, incorporate additional factors, such as the cost of deviation.

[5] A similar situation is dealt with in quality control engineering. The seriousness of an observed deviation from a standard, such as the number of defective products in a sample, is based on both the mean and the standard deviation of the population. The standard deviation determines the area between the upper and lower limits of the "control chart" and consequently the decision whether to accept or reject the sampled batch. For a comprehensive discussion of the statistical issues involved in quality control engineering, some of which are also relevant to financial statement analysis, see A. J. Duncan, *Quality Control and Industrial Statistics*, 3d ed. (Homewood, Ill.: Richard D. Irwin, Inc., 1965).

[6] An exception is Dun and Bradstreet's list of "fourteen ratios" which provides some indication of the dispersion in the industry ratio distribution by reporting the values of the upper and lower quartiles.

[7] In other words, the density function of the normal distribution,

$$f(x) = \frac{1}{\sigma\sqrt{2\pi}} \exp\left\{-\frac{1}{2} \frac{(x - \mu)^2}{\sigma^2}\right\}, \quad (-\infty < x < \infty). \tag{5.2}$$

and, therefore, the cumulative distribution function, are completely defined given the mean, μ, and the variance, σ^2, of the distribution.

metric and are generally skewed to the right.[8] The main reason for the right-skewness is that most ratios have a lower limit of zero but an indefinite upper limit. Given this asymmetry, the standard deviation of the industry distribution may not always be an adequate dispersion measure for ratio analysis. To evaluate the significance of an observed deviation from the industry mean, the complete frequency distribution of the industry ratios should be available. For practical reporting purposes, such ratio distributions can be plotted or summarized by deciles. It should be noted, however, that asymmetry and departure from normality are relative concepts; the choice of the appropriate tools for ratio analysis therefore depends on the *extent* of departure from symmetry.[9] However, the available evidence on ratio distributions does not warrant firm conclusions regarding the extent of such departure.

CORRELATION AMONG FINANCIAL RATIOS

A high degree of correlation among financial ratios of a given firm can be expected, since (*a*) many ratios have common components (e.g., total sales in the various turnover ratios), and (*b*) some financial statement items tend to move in the same direction as other items (e.g., sales and distribution costs, or dividends and net income). This expectation was confirmed by the somewhat scanty evidence available. Short-term liquidity ratios, in a sample of petroleum and steel firms, were found to be highly correlated; [10] for example, the correlation coefficients between the current and the quick ratios for the twenty-four petroleum companies sampled were in the order of .85 to .90. This high correlation is obviously the result of common items. Short-term liquidity ratios were also found to be highly correlated with the working capital turnover ratio, again presumably the effect of common items; long-term solvency ratios were significantly associated with other types of ratios, and profitability ratios

---

[8] Empirical evidence on the asymmetry of financial ratios can be found in A. H. Winakor, *Standard Financial Ratios for the Public Utility Industry* (Bulletin No. 26, Bureau of Business Research, University of Illinois, 1929); J. O. Horrigan, "Some Empirical Bases of Financial Ratio Analysis," *The Accounting Review*, 40 (July 1965), 558–68; and Foulke, *op. cit.*, pp. 644–57. Foulke provides the interquartile ranges of fourteen ratios for seventy-two industries. In almost all cases, the difference between the lower quartile and the median is substantially smaller than the difference between the upper quartile and the median, suggesting a right-skewed distribution.

[9] The extent of departure from symmetry may sometimes be reduced by a transformation of the original variables. The logarithmic transformation is often used for this purpose.

[10] Horrigan, *op. cit.*

were only moderately correlated with ratios from other categories. Similar results were reported by Horrigan in a later study.[11]

The phenomenon of ratio correlations, if found to be general, would have important implications for financial statement analysis. Most important, a smaller number of ratios than expected would often convey the essential information contained in the financial statements. Generally, one, or at most two, ratios of a common type (category) would suffice for financial analysis.[12] The long lists of ratios usually provided to users (e.g., Dun and Bradstreet's fourteen ratios) or examined in empirical studies are therefore substantially redundant.

Ratio correlation may sometimes pose estimation problems, especially when financial ratios are used as independent (explanatory) variables in a multiple regression model. Specifically, when a high degree of correlation (multicollinearity) exists between two or more independent variables, it will be difficult to distinguish the *separate effects* of these variables on the dependent variable. A high degree of multicollinearity will result in large standard errors for the estimated coefficients and will therefore adversely affect the precision of the estimation. However, the effect of possible estimation difficulties resulting from multicollinearity should not be overstated; the important question for the analyst is whether a specific ratio actually contributes to the "explanation" of the dependent variable.[13] In the case of a positive contribution, it will usually be worthwhile to incorporate the variable in the model despite the resulting multicollinearity, since its addition will increase the model's predictive accuracy which generally is the main objective of the analyst.[14] The basic question is, of course, whether the analyst identified the appropriate structural relationships between the variables in constructing the model and whether these underlying relationships are reasonably sta-

[11] J. O. Horrigan, "The Determination of Long-Term Credit Standing with Financial Ratios," *Empirical Research in Accounting: Selected Studies, 1966,* Supplement to Vol. 4, *Journal of Accounting Research,* 44–62.

[12] Various statistical methods, such as factor analysis, can be used to screen a large number of ratios and choose the most appropriate candidates for further analysis. An example of a study using factor analysis for this purpose is provided in Chapter 10.

[13] The contribution of a specific variable can be measured by the increase in the squared multiple correlation coefficient resulting from the inclusion of the variable in the regression equation, given that the other K variables are used (i.e., the marginal contribution to the "explanation" of the dependent variable of the $K + 1$ independent variable equals $R^2 - R^2_k$).

[14] For a discussion of the statistical problems resulting from the existence of multicollinearity and means for increasing the precision of the estimated coefficients, see H. Theil, *Principles of Econometrics* (New York: John Wiley & Sons, Inc., 1971), pp. 147–54.

tionary (constant) over time. Failure to identify the underlying relationships and/or instability over time will obviously diminish the usefulness of the model.

The preceding discussion was concerned with the correlations among various ratios of a specific firm. Some evidence indicates a different form of ratio correlation; industry ratio distributions for individual ratios are correlated over time. Specifically, with respect to a given ratio (e.g., the current ratio), the relative positions of the various firms within an industry will tend to remain stable over a fairly long time period, resulting in a temporal correlation of ratio distributions. Empirical evidence on this phenomenon is, again, quite sparse; in a study of financial structures of firms it was reported that aggregate industry ratios for the years 1931 and 1937 were significantly correlated.[15] In another study, dealing with the quality of bank loans, it was found that the aggregate financial ratios of several industry-size groups maintained stable relative positions over the period 1953–57, despite changes in the absolute levels of the ratios.[16] Horrigan reported for his petroleum and steel sample:

> First, the short-term liquidity ratios showed the least correlations over time; but nevertheless, there were significant intertemporal correlations even in this group. . . . Second, the long-term solvency ratio distributions were very stable over time in both industries. These ratios were extremely highly correlated in adjacent years. . . . The profit margin ratio demonstrated essentially the same pattern as these long-term solvency ratios . . . the intertemporal correlations of turnover ratios involving long-term components were the most impressive.[17]

Ratio distributions tend to be correlated over time for various reasons: (a) It is believed that firms set and attempt to maintain optimal ratio levels *relative* to some industry target (e.g., the industry mean).[18] Consequently, ratio distributions will be correlated over time, since each firm maintains constant ratio levels relative to the industry target and

---

15 W. A. Chudson, *The Pattern of Corporate Financial Structure: A Cross-Section View of Manufacturing, Mining, Trade, and Construction, 1937* (New York: National Bureau of Economic Research, 1945).

16 A. M. Wojinlower, *The Quality of Bank Loans: A Study of Bank Examination Records*, Occasional Paper No. 82 (New York: National Bureau of Economic Research, 1962), pp. 3–4.

17 Horrigan, "Some Empirical Bases of Financial Ratio Analysis," *op. cit.*, p. 562.

18 For hypotheses regarding firms' attempts to maintain stable relative positions, see C. M. White, "Multiple Goals in the Theory of the Firm," in K. E. Boulding and W. A. Spiney, *Linear Programming and the Theory of the Firm* (New York: The Macmillan Company, 1960), pp. 189–91. For empirical evidence on the adjustment of ratios to the industry mean, see B. Lev, "Industry Averages as Targets for Financial Ratios," *Journal of Accounting Research*, 7 (Autumn 1969), 290–99.

therefore relative to other firms. (*b*) A certain degree of correlation among ratio distributions will result from industry- and economy-wide events which affect all firms within an industry. Specifically, empirical evidence indicates that about half the variability in the level of a firm's average earnings-per-share could be associated with economy-wide effects (e.g., changes of GNP).[19] It is reasonable to expect that in the presence of such a strong common effect operating on all firms within an industry, the relative positions of the firms' ratios will remain reasonably stable over time. (*c*) Inertia and persistence of firm operations will, of course, also contribute to temporal industry ratio correlation.

If, as the sparse evidence indicates, ratio distributions are substantially correlated over time, then past relationships can be used by the analyst to predict future values of ratios for a given firm. Specifically, knowledge of the past position of a firm's ratios within its industry, in addition to information regarding future changes in the industry, will enable the analyst to predict the future ratios of the specific firm.

LIMITATIONS IN THE CORRELATION AND REGRESSION OF RATIOS

It is common in both time-series and cross-sectional empirical studies to deflate (divide) the observations by a *size variable*. For example, in studies designed to estimate the relationship between cost and output in the railroad industry, the observations on these variables were usually divided by a size variable, such as miles of road.[20] One purpose of such a division is to reduce (i.e., transform) a three-variable relationship to a two-variable one. For example, to the extent that railroad cost is a function of output *and* size, this three-variable relationship can be reduced to a two-variable one by dividing the cost and output observations by a size variable (the transformed variables: cost/size and output/size). Deflation by size is also regarded as useful when the data are dominated by a few extremely large (or small) observations,[21] as in the

---

[19] R. Ball and P. Brown, "Some Preliminary Findings on the Association between the Earnings of a Firm, Its Industry and the Economy," *Empirical Research in Accounting: Selected Studies, 1967*, Supplement to Vol. 5, *Journal of Accounting Research*, 55–77.

[20] For a critical survey of these studies and a discussion of the statistical problems involved in size deflation, see Z. Griliches, "Cost Allocation in Railroad Regulation," *The Bell Journal of Economics and Management Science*, 3 (Spring 1972), 26–41.

[21] This result can also be achieved by other means, such as a logarithmic transformation of the data, i.e., substituting the logarithms of the observations for their absolute values.

railroad industry, since such extreme observations usually dominate the correlation coefficient.[22]

The preceding rationale for the deflation of observations by a size variable applies, of course, also to financial statement analysis. In fact, the main justification for the use of ratios in the analysis is to account for the size effect. For example, a comparison of the absolute profit levels of two different-sized firms will generally not be meaningful unless the size effect is accounted for (e.g., by a comparison of the earnings/total assets ratios of the two firms). Given the various advantages of size deflation, one would expect to find ratios with a common denominator extensively used in financial statement analysis. However, the correlation of such ratios may cause statistical problems:

> . . . correlating ratio variables and making inferences from these to the simple correlation between the series in the numerators is an *extremely hazardous business*. A possibly unexpected result is that in the context of spurious correlation the ratio correlation may just as well be spuriously low as spuriously high. Consequently, if primary interest centers on the simple correlation between the numerator series, it would usually be appropriate to proceed in a straightforward manner by relating these values to one another.[23]

Note that a distinction should be made between two different situations: (a) When the primary interest of the investigator is in the *ratio series* (rather than in the numerator series), then the possibility of spurious correlation does not arise at all. For example, when the hypothesis tested is concerned with the constant-dollar earnings of firms, then deflating reported earnings by a proper price-level index would obviously entail no difficulties. (b) The possibility of spurious correlation therefore exists only where the hypothesis (model) tested pertains to the undeflated variables, i.e., to the numerator series. For example, when the association between earnings and capital expenditures is investigated, it is possible to divide both variables by total assets and examine the association between the respective ratios. The analyst should be aware that in such cases, the ratio correlation might be a biased estimate of the correlation between the numerator series (e.g., earnings and capital expenditures). Here again, the real problem is that of model specifica-

---

[22] When the regression disturbance term is associated with size (e.g., when the conditional variance or standard deviation of the disturbance term is proportional to size), one would expect the homoscedasticity assumption of the linear regression model not to be met (i.e., the variance of the disturbance term will not be stable). In this case, deflation by size, under certain circumstances, may stabilize the disturbance variance and thus lead to a more efficient estimation, namely to estimators having lower dispersion.

[23] E. Kuh and J. R. Meyer, "Correlation and Regression Estimates When the Data Are Ratios," *Econometrica*, 23 (October 1955), 401, emphasis supplied.

tion; under certain conditions, the ratio estimate will still be optimal,[24] in other cases, a transformation of the original variables (e.g., by their logarithms) may reduce the size effect and thus fulfill the purpose of deflation. Thus, no strict rules or warnings can be given before carefully examining the behavior of the variables to be investigated.

Kuh and Meyer also show that in a multiple regression model consisting of ratios with common denominators, no serious adverse effects on estimation are usually to be expected. Under a wide range of circumstances, the regression coefficients of the deflated variables will not be greatly biased when application is made to cross-sectional data. However, bias may be encountered in time-series studies when the main purpose of deflation is to remove trend. Thus, it should be noted that "traditional textbook notions about 'spurious ratio correlation' have been inadequate or, in some cases, even misleading." [25]

The overriding question is, of course, whether the statistical model used is properly specified. If one is interested in the behavior of a certain variable (e.g., firms' earnings), then the specification question is twofold: What mathematical form will best describe the variable's behavior (e.g., a linear model), and which variables should be selected to "explain" the behavior? In a few situations, a well-defined economic theory can provide the appropriate specification of the model. However, in most situations, no such theory exists, and statistical testing procedures should guide the analyst as to the best specified model.[26] Models using ratios with a common denominator are therefore worth considering despite possible estimation problems. The ultimate choice among variables will rest on the relative predictive accuracy of the various models.

POSSIBLE PITFALLS IN USING RATIOS

Special care should be exercised in the analysis, interpretation, and presentation of ratios, since they can easily be misused, intentionally or unintentionally. Several examples of possible misuses of ratios are given below; each one is surprisingly straightforward, yet the frequency of misuse in practice warrants their brief mention here.

1. Ratios account for one variable only

It was stated in the preceding section that the major purpose for using ratios, or, in general, for deflating the original observations, is to

---

[24] For a comprehensive discussion of the use of ratio estimates, see W. G. Cochran, *Sampling Techniques* (New York: John Wiley & Sons, Inc., 1953), Chap. 6.

[25] Kuh and Meyer, *op. cit.*, p. 413.

[26] More on the problem of model specification in Chapter 7.

account for a variable which is correlated with the data studied.[27] Suppose, for example, that a time-series study reveals that a firm's earnings have been increasing over the last ten years. Since earnings are obviously associated with the level of investment, the ratios of earnings to total assets are formed to account for investment changes. However, even if the series of these ratios is still increasing it would be premature to draw any conclusions regarding the performance of the firm, since other important variables may have been unaccounted for. One such variable is the average increase in earnings of all firms in the economy and/or those within the industry. If such general increases are accounted for,[28] it might be found that the firm's earnings actually decreased over time relative to other firms.[29]

Since ratios can account for only one variable, they are insufficient for most practical uses in which the effect of several variables should be considered. In these cases, statistical techniques for dealing with more than two variables, such as the multiple regression analysis, should be used.

2. When is it appropriate to deflate?

The use of deflation to account for the size effect is appropriate only under special circumstances. Consider the railroad cost studies mentioned above in which the relationship between costs and output is to be determined. Size deflation will be appropriate only if the cost relationship is homogeneous in output and size, that is, when there are no costs that are independent of size. Specifically, such a homogeneous relationship is of the form:

$$C = \alpha S + \beta V, \qquad (5.3)$$

where C = cost, S = size, V = output.

Subsequent to a size deflation, this relationship becomes a two-variable one:

$$C/S = \alpha + \beta(V/S). \qquad (5.4)$$

However, if the true relationship is

$$C = \alpha S + \beta V + \gamma, \qquad (5.5)$$

[27] Namely, the reduction of a three-variable problem to a two-variable one.

[28] For a specific method of accounting for economy-wide effects, see R. Ball and P. Brown, "An Empirical Evaluation of Accounting Income Numbers," *Journal of Accounting Research*, 6 (Autumn 1968), 161–62. This study is further discussed in Chapter 15.

[29] Another relevant example is the ratio of airline fatalities to passenger miles flown, used as an indicator of airline safety. This ratio fails to account for important variables, such as the average number of takeoffs and landings, which may be associated with the number of fatalities.

deflation leads to

$$C/S = a + \beta(V/S) + \gamma/S, \qquad (5.6)$$

which is still a three-variable relationship. The correlation between the two ratios, C/S and V/S, obviously misrepresents the cost-output relationship.

3. Averaging ratios

Ratios, or percentages, can be averaged in various ways; consider the following hypothetical example and the two alternative averaging systems:

	Firm A	Firm B
Net income	100	200
Total assets	1,000	5,000
Return-on-assets ratio	.10	.04

One way of averaging the two return-on-assets ratios is to calculate the simple arithmetic mean (.10 + .04)/2 = .07. An alternative is to calculate a weighted average according to the different asset sizes of the firms:

$$1/6 \times .10 + 5/6 \times .04 = .05.$$

The latter average, .05, differs from the former, .07, since it reflects the different sizes of the firms. No general prescription can be given regarding the choice between averages; the use of a specific weighting system will be dictated by the objectives of the analysis. For example, suppose one is interested in the average rate of defective products in a production department. The relevant data for the three employees working in that department for a given week are as follows:

	Employees			
	1	2	3	Total
Defective products	10	15	20	45
Total production	100	100	400	600
Ratio of defective products	.10	.15	.05	.075

In this case, the simple average of the three ratios, .10, obviously does not represent the percentage of defective products produced during the week. The weighted average, .075, will be the appropriate indicator of the department's performance.

It should be noted that most of the published data on financial ratios is based on a simple averaging process of the individual firms' ratios (i.e., equal weights are assigned to each firm). Whether this or some other alternative is the most appropriate way of averaging ratios should be determined in relation to the specific objectives of the analysis.[30]

4. Interpretation of ratio changes

Many ratios, mainly from the profitability and turnover categories, are used as performance indicators. They are often required to be higher (or lower) than some standard or to reveal an increasing (decreasing) trend. Changes in such ratios should be interpreted with great care, as the following simple example demonstrates:

A retail store manager decides that his ratio between operating costs and sales, say 0.70, is too high and should be reduced. He reduces it to 0.65, yet finds that his operating profit to be applied against overhead costs is *less*, not more. Here are some hypothetical numbers that suggest how this could have happened:

	Before	*After*
Sales	10,000	8,500
Operating Costs	7,000	5,525
Operating Profit	3,000	2,975
Ratio, Costs to Sales	0.70	0.65

The reduction of costs (the numerator of the ratio of costs to sales) may itself have had an effect on sales (the denominator). For instance, the store manager might have reduced his sales staff and cut down his inventory, thereby losing sales because of inadequate service or failure to carry desired items in stock.[31]

Thus, a possible pitfall in interpreting ratio changes is to attribute the change solely to the numerator of the ratio or to the denominator. In many real cases, the variables in the numerator and the denominator are correlated, which complicates the economic interpretation of ratio changes.

5. Faulty use of percentages

Confusion regarding the base of comparison sometimes results in ridiculous statements:

[30] In some cases, such as when growth ratios in a time-series analysis are investigated, the use of the geometric mean would be most appropriate. For computation and applications of the geometric mean, see F. E. Croxton and D. J. Cowden, *Practical Business Statistics*, 3d ed. (Englewood Cliffs, N.J.: Prentice-Hall, Inc., 1960), pp. 232–35.

[31] W. A. Wallis and H. V. Roberts, *Statistics: A New Approach* (Glencoe, Ill.: The Free Press, 1964), p. 238.

Over the period of five years, the enrollment in a veterinary college in the United States declined from 3,160 to 641 students. The decrease was 2,519 students, or 79.7 per cent of the original enrollment; yet the dean of a midwestern veterinary college was quoted as having said that during the period in question, the enrollment had decreased 500 per cent! The dean may have actually said that the original registration figure was about 500 per cent of the later figure. A decrease of 500 per cent would mean a negative enrollment four times the size of the earlier registration.[32]

Percentages should not be calculated from very small numbers; or at least, the absolute numbers should also be provided:

A short time after Johns Hopkins University had opened certain courses in the University to women, it was reported that $33\frac{1}{3}$ percent of the women students had married into the faculty of the Institution. Of course, the important information was the number of women students. There were only three.[33]

Percentage comparisons are also awkward when one quantity is many times larger than the other. The population of the U.S. is about eighty times larger than that of Israel. It would be correct, though awkward, to state that the population of the U.S. is 7,900 percent larger than that of Israel.

Finally, it should be noted that percentage changes are not additive; changes that are equal in size but opposite in sign do not offset one another. As an example of such a mistake, consider the following statement which appeared in the July 2, 1932, issue of the *New York Times:*

The depression took a stiff wallop on the chin here today. Plumbers, plasterers, carpenters, painters and others affiliated with the Indianapolis Building Trades Unions were given a five per cent increase in wages. That gave back to the men one-fourth of the 20 percent cut they took last winter.

The 5 percent increase is, of course, not one-fourth but one-fifth of the 20 percent decrease. Also, the sum of two successive percentage changes is not equal to the total change. For example, an increase from 100 to 120, and later to 150, amounts to a total percentage increase of 50 percent, while the successive percentage changes are 20 and 25 percent, respectively.

[32] F. E. Croxton, D. J. Cowden, and S. Klein, *Applied General Statistics*, 3d ed. (Englewood Cliffs, N.J.: Prentice-Hall, Inc., 1967), p. 133.

[33] R. E. Chaddock, *Principles and Methods of Statistics* (Boston: Houghton Mifflin Company, 1925), pp. 13–14.

SUMMARY

Ratio analysis based solely on the comparison of observed measures for a specific firm with an industry measure of central tendency (e.g., the mean) is insufficient. Consideration of the dispersion of the industry ratio distribution is required for assessing the implications of an observed deviation. Preliminary evidence indicates that financial ratios are highly correlated both contemporaneously and over time. Such correlations may be a blessing as well as a curse for financial statement users. On the one hand, only a few ratios, carefully selected, will suffice for most purposes. On the other hand, ratio correlations may sometimes adversely affect estimation procedures, especially in multiple regression models. Statistical texts often warn users of the adverse effects of incorporating ratios with common denominators in correlation and regression analyses. Such general warnings are usually not helpful; the crucial question for the analyst is that of model specification, that is, choosing the most appropriate mathematical form and explanatory variables for the data investigated. The ultimate choice of ratios and/or deflators will be dictated by the predictive accuracy of the model. Finally, the simplicity of ratio analysis might in some cases be misleading. Therefore, special care should be exercised in the analysis, interpretation, and presentation of ratios.

CHAPTER SIX

Accounting Issues
in
Financial Statement Analysis

The dissatisfaction with currently reported financial data is widespread among both the users and the preparers of the information, as evidenced by the following sample remarks:

> . . . cross-section contemporaneous accounting data for different firms or plants give little if any information on so-called economies of scale.[1]

> Historical cost valuation of resources, which are most commonly available, are in principle irrelevant under changed conditions.[2]

> If accountants want to continue to enjoy a role in the investment management process, they should prepare to focus their energies on supplying whatever data a workable theory of security valuation requires, rather than defending the present ritual.[3]

---

[1] M. Friedman, "Comment," on C. Smith, "Survey of the Empirical Evidence on Economies of Scale," in *Business Concentration and Price Policy* (Princeton: Princeton University Press, 1955), p. 230.

[2] G. J. Stigler, *The Organization of Industry* (Homewood, Ill.: Richard D. Irwin, Inc., 1968), p. 72.

[3] J. L. Treynor, "The Trouble with Earnings," *Financial Analysts Journal,* 28 (September–October 1972), 43. Reprinted in *Modern Developments in Investment Management,* J. Lorie and R. Brealey, eds. (New York: Frederick A. Praeger, Inc., 1972), p. 667.

The accounting information that the SEC requires is, on the whole, not relevant for investors. In part, this is due to the basic inability of accounting data to measure economic events effectively.[4]

There appear to be two major reasons for the dissatisfaction: (*a*) the inconsistency between the economic and accounting concepts of income and asset valuation, and (*b*) the considerable leeway allowed by alternative accounting measurement techniques (e.g., the various generally accepted depreciation methods) in reporting financial results. Consequently, financial statement information is often alleged to be of little use because it does not reflect economic reality, and misleading because the data can be manipulated by the judicious use of alternative accounting methods.

This bleak view of financial data obviously contradicts empirical evidence which indicates that reported financial information has a substantial impact on investor decisions.[5] What then are the real sources of the widespread dissatisfaction with financial data and what can an analyst do to improve the usefulness of the reported information? These questions are dealt with in the current chapter: First, the process of modifying the hypothetical perfect certainty income concept to the real world of uncertainty is described, and the various conceptual sacrifices accountants make for the sake of reality and objectivity are examined. Having delineated the major problem areas concerning conventional income measurement and asset valuation, we turn to means open to the analyst to mitigate the adverse effects of these problems. Second, the allegedly harmful effects of alternative accounting methods are investigated and shown to be overly emphasized as well as clouding the real issue—that of adequate disclosure. Again, the implications for financial analysts are pointed out. Naturally, throughout the discussion the point of view taken is that of the analyst rather than that of management or the accountant.

ECONOMIC VERSUS ACCOUNTING INCOME AND ASSET VALUATION CONCEPTS

A firm's periodic income figure is by far the most closely watched and widely used financial statement item. The income figure is used, among other things, to evaluate the efficiency of management, to assist in predicting the future course of the firm, as a base for taxation, as a

---

[4] G. J. Benston, "The Effectiveness and Effect of the SEC's Accounting Disclosure Requirements," in *Economic Policy and the Regulation of Corporate Securities*, H. G. Manne, ed. (Washington, D.C.: George Washington University and American Enterprise Institute for Public Policy Research, 1968), p. 73.

[5] For elaboration, see Chapter 15.

means of regulating public utilities, as a focal point in labor negotiations, and as a performance measure for economic studies of the theory of the firm and industrial organization. This diversity in the use of the income figure contributes substantially to the dissatisfaction with the accountant's product. Specifically, since income is used for many purposes, often with conflicting motives (e.g., those of managers and regulators of public utilities), it is natural that a measure of income for one purpose will not be well suited to another. Thus, contrary to common belief, no unique or "true" concept of income exists; rather, many variant concepts can be conceived, each of which is especially suited for a particular purpose.[6]

The various concepts of income believed to be of practical use emanate from the fundamental view that periodic income is the amount of wealth that a person or a legal entity can dispose of (i.e., consume) over the course of the period and remain as well off at the end of the period as at the beginning:

> The purpose of income calculation in practical affairs is to give people an indication of the amount which they can consume without impoverishing themselves. Following out this idea, it would seem that we ought to define a man's income as the maximum value which he can consume during a week, and still expect to be as well off at the end of the week as he was at the beginning.[7]

Income is thus defined as the periodic increment to (or decrement from) the initial well-offness of a person, plus his consumption during the period. A step toward the practical application of the income concept is achieved by defining well-offness in terms of monetary values or *wealth,* that is, as the aggregate money value of the goods and service rights owned by a person. Periodic income is thereby defined as a person's consumption of wealth plus the change in wealth during the period, or the amount of wealth that can be consumed during the period without impairing the beginning-of-period wealth situation. Analogously, the income of a corporation can be defined as the amount of wealth that can be distributed to stockholders (i.e., dividends) while maintaining their wealth position in the firm (i.e., equity). Income determination thus depends on an appropriate measurement of wealth.

At first glance, the wealth measurement problem seems obvious; the

---

6 K. Arrow's well-known study, *Social Choice and Individual Values* (New Haven: Yale University Press, 1970), which showed that it is generally impossible to make interpersonal welfare comparisons, implies that no unique information source can be designed to satisfy different preferences.

7 J. R. Hicks, *Value and Capital,* 2d ed. (London: Oxford University Press, 1946), p. 172. Hicks's "week" refers to a specified time period not necessarily identical with a week.

value of the goods and services comprising wealth should be derived from their current market prices. However, even if dependable market prices were available for all the firm's assets, the aggregate value of these prices would not in general equal the firm's wealth, since the value of a firm as an income-generating unit is generally different from the net market value of its assets. This difference is usually known as goodwill and is recognized (i.e., recorded) in the case of corporate acquisition (merger) only. A corporation's wealth should therefore be measured in reference to its future net earnings stream rather than by the aggregate assets value.[8] Specifically, the firm's wealth should be determined by discounting the future stream of net earnings accruing to stockholders; periodic income will accordingly be measured as dividends plus the change during the period in the discounted value of future earnings.

The economic definition of income as the periodic change in the discounted value of future earnings would obviously be appropriate in a world of certainty, where future earnings and discount rates were perfectly known.[9] However, serious conceptual and practical difficulties are encountered when the certainty assumption is relaxed. In this case future earnings and discount rates would be random variables for which, at best, only their probability distributions are known.[10] Under these circumstances, the concept of a discounted value becomes rather vague; how does one discount future probability distributions of earnings? Obviously, as indicated by modern investment theory, the often suggested procedure of discounting the expected values (i.e., means) of these distributions is unsatisfactory, since the mean is not the only characteristic of the earnings distribution that interests investors; additional characteristics, such as the variance (indicating risk) and higher moments, will generally affect the investment decision. In fact, the process by which capital asset values are determined under conditions of uncertainty, and particularly the role of firms' income in this process, are not well understood.[11] Therefore, under real-world conditions the economic approach to income measurement is not even well defined, let alone operational.

---

[8] Conceptually, of course, it is possible to define goodwill as yet another asset owned by the firm, in which case the net value of assets will equal, by definition, the firm's wealth. This is, however, a semantic exercise, given the problems involved in obtaining market prices of goodwill.

[9] It should be noted that according to this income concept, a corporation that each year paid dividends equal to its economic income would always have the same level of income.

[10] A "random variable" is a nondeterministic value that is subject to a probability distribution; i.e., an observed value of the variable represents a drawing from some probability distribution.

[11] A promising and currently popular approach conceptualizing the process of capital value determination under uncertainty—the Sharpe-Lintner capital asset pricing model—is discussed in Chapter 12.

Before economic income can be measured, substantial progress must be made in (*a*) understanding the relationship between current asset values and future probability distributions of earnings and (*b*) the design of earnings prediction models.

Thus a modification of the economic income concept along the road to operationality is required. This brings us to the method currently employed by accountants—the determination of income from operations (rather than by discounting future earnings). Essentially, the costs of goods and services (inputs) consumed during the period are subtracted from the value of goods and services provided (outputs) to yield an income figure. Accounting income is thus obtained by a process of matching costs against revenues, applying a rather complex and controversial set of measurement procedures.

MAJOR DIFFERENCES BETWEEN ECONOMIC
AND ACCOUNTING INCOME

It is possible to define costs and revenues in such a way as to achieve congruity between the economic and the accounting income measurement. This will result when revenues are defined as any increase in the value of assets (both tangible and intangible) or a decrease in the value of liabilities, and costs are defined as any decrease in the value of assets and increase in the value of liabilities. The difference between revenues and costs will then equal the periodic change in the firm's equity, that is, economic income. However, accountants, in the process of matching costs against revenues, recognize only *realized* value changes, that is, those changes resulting from an exchange transaction.[12] Thus, a significant difference between the accounting and economic income concepts results from accountants' refusal to recognize changes in the value of assets *as they occur*.[13] Capital gains (e.g., an increase during the period in the market value of land) are ignored until they are actually realized by a sale. Accordingly, accounting and economic income would be equal only if

[12] The accounting *realization* principle means that revenues are recognized in the income measurement process only when an exchange or a severance has occurred. Specifically, goods or services must have been transferred to a customer, giving rise to the receipt of either cash or other assets. Thus, for example, revenues cannot be realized as a result of the production process alone. For elaboration, see E. H. Hendriksen, *Accounting Theory* (Homewood, Ill.: Richard D. Irwin, Inc., 1970), pp. 165–76.

[13] This is not strictly true, since under certain circumstances unrealized declines in the value of assets (e.g., when inventory market value is lower than its cost) are recognized as costs in the income measurement process. This biased treatment is justified by the accounting *conservatism* principle stating that accountants should report the lowest possible value for assets and revenues and the highest possible value for liabilities and expenses, see *ibid.*, pp. 118–20.

the original costs of all the firm's assets (including goodwill) not yet charged to operations equaled their market values (i.e., the present value of future receipts). Periodic changes in the values of specific assets will result in differences between accounting and economic income.

A second difference between accounting and economic income concerns changes in the general price level. The basic concept of income as the amount that can be distributed while keeping the beginning-of-period equity intact would require that equity values (or a person's wealth) be measured in *real* rather than in monetary terms. When the general price level is changing, equity values at two points in time should be expressed in terms of their command over purchasing power rather than in dollars. Thus, for example, if equity increased 20 percent during the period while the general price level increased 10 percent, distribution of 20 percent of the beginning equity value as dividends would result in the end-of-period equity having smaller command over purchasing power (i.e., smaller real value) than the beginning-of-period equity. Real economic income of a firm is therefore the real value of its equity at the end of the period minus the real value of its equity at the beginning of the period plus the real value of dividends paid during the period. However, accounting income is measured in monetary units,[14] thus ignoring the effects of general price-level changes on income and equity values.

A third difference between the accounting and economic definitions of income concerns the treatment of expected future business events that will affect the firm's earnings. Examples of such events are a future decrease in the demand for the firm's product because of an introduction of a substitute, a change in future employee productivity resulting from on-the-job training, or an expected sales increase because of a current advertising campaign. Future earnings in these cases are expected to change, and such changes will obviously be reflected in *current* economic income which is determined by the periodic change in the discounted value of future earnings. However, expected earnings changes will not be reflected in accounting income, since they do not affect current costs and revenues.

The highly defensive and often apologetic arguments advanced by accountants in support of their approach seem to suggest that measurement convenience is the only reason for deviating from the economic income concept. While economic income is generally considered to be the "true," most appropriate concept, it is argued that the highly subjective nature of the estimates underlying this concept precludes it from incorporation in financial statements. Thus, the accounting *objectivity,* or *verifiability,* principle is invoked to justify current accounting prac-

---

[14] This is known as the accounting *monetary unit* principle; see *ibid.*, pp. 117–18.

tices of income measurement and asset valuation.[15] Economic valuations, based on estimates of future events, obviously do not meet the objectivity criterion. Such a justification of the accounting approach naturally suggests that the real reason for accountants' reliance on historical values is to avoid any responsibility for judgmental errors. While there is probably some truth in this argument, it is an oversimplification.

As was seen above, the concepts of economic income and asset values are not well defined in a world of uncertainty. When probability distributions of future earnings are involved, it is by no means clear what is meant by the "discounted value of future earnings." Therefore, in the real world, the economic concepts of income and asset values cannot be accepted as the "true" variables to be reported in financial statements.[16] In fact,

> . . . in a dynamic economy, when values are changing both because of changes in prices and changes of expectations of future earning power, there is no unique well-defined ideal concept of income against which can be compared the actual practice of income measurement.[17]

The relevance of currently reported financial data should therefore be assessed not by reference to some "true" values but rather by their usefulness to potential users. Thus, the a priori case against financial statement data, based on their deviation from economic concepts, is to a large extent unsubstantiated.[18]

THE APPROPRIATE DATA FOR FINANCIAL ANALYSIS

An important question for financial analysts is, Which of the various variants of income and asset measurement is most appropriate for

15 The objectivity (verifiability) principle states that accounting measurement principles should be such as to allow ". . . qualified individuals working independently of one another to develop essentially similar measures or conclusions from an examination of the same evidence." Committee to Prepare a Statement of Basic Accounting Theory, *A Statement of Basic Accounting Theory* (Evanston, Ill.: AAA, 1966), p. 10. See also Hendriksen, *op cit.*, pp. 114–17.

16 It is interesting to note that when economists measure income, as in the national accounts, they use the accounting historical cost procedures, probably also for reasons of objectivity.

17 S. S. Alexander, "Income Measurement in a Dynamic Economy," in *Studies in Accounting Theory*, W. T. Baxter and S. Davidson, eds. (Homewood, Ill.: Richard D. Irwin, Inc., 1962), p. 127.

18 For example, "These [accounting definitions] are not *economic* definitions of earnings, but merely descriptions of the motions the accountant goes through to arrive at the earnings number. The analyst needs a definition that gives him an economic justification for using the earnings concept." Treynor, *op. cit.*, p. 663.

investment decisions? In answering this question, reference must obviously be made to how the income and asset values are used. However, a serious problem is encountered here, since the use or, more specifically, the valuation process of capital assets is not well defined. As was mentioned above, there is no well-specified and verified theory of the process that determines capital asset values under uncertainty.[19] Even the relatively advanced theories, like the Sharpe-Lintner "capital asset pricing model," do not specify the relationship between firm variables (e.g., income) and asset values determined in capital markets.[20] Therefore, given the imperfect knowledge regarding the optimal use of financial data, it is presently impossible to designate a specific measurement concept as "most useful." Moreover, it is also impossible to determine the seriousness of measurement errors involved in currently reported financial data.[21] Despite this imperfect state of knowledge regarding users' needs, it is still worthwhile to discuss briefly various suggestions for modifying currently reported financial data and the possible usefulness of such modifications for financial analysis.

A. Adjustment for specific asset price changes

It was pointed out earlier that an important difference between economic and accounting income results from accountants' refusal to recognize changes in the value of assets as they occur. In recent years, however, both accountants and nonaccountants have frequently proposed that accounting valuations rely primarily on measures of current prices of specific items.[22] The technical issues involved are quite complex and controversial; [23] for example, the current price of an asset can be determined as the price at which an identical asset can currently be purchased, the price at which equivalent service can currently be acquired, or the price at which the asset can currently be sold. Difficulties might also be encountered in obtaining market prices for specialized assets like work-in-process inventory. Despite such technical difficulties, adjustment of both

---

[19] It is sometimes suggested that the specific needs of financial analysts can be established by direct communication (i.e., questionnaire-type studies) rather than by the development of a theory. The frustrating results of such attempts can be largely ascribed to the fact that users of financial data are usually unaware of their needs. For example, without an established valuation theory, how can an analyst determine whether he prefers historical or price-level adjusted income?

[20] For elaboration on this point, see Chapters 14 and 15.

[21] A measurement error in this context is the difference between the reported value and the "true" value postulated by theory.

[22] For example, the AAA Committee on Concepts and Standards—Long-Lived Assets took a stand in favor of specific price adjustments in "Accounting for Land, Building and Equipment," The Accounting Review, 39 (July 1964), 693–99.

[23] For a comprehensive discussion of the technical issues involved in current price adjustments, see E. O. Edwards and P. W. Bell, The Theory and Measurement of Business Income (Berkeley: University of California Press, 1961).

balance sheet and income statement items to current values seems to have considerable advantages for financial analysis:

1. Interfirm comparability. Historical cost valuation hinders interfirm comparisons because financial data are dependent on the timing of asset acquisition. Consider, for example, two firms identical in all respects except the timing of asset acquisition; one firm purchased its assets during a period of low prices while the other purchased identical assets at a time of high prices. The various income statement and balance sheet ratios of these firms would differ because of the differences in the original asset costs and depreciation charges. Such differences, however, have little economic relevance.[24] When current values are used as the asset valuation base, differences due to timing of purchase (or, in fact, to changes in asset prices) will disappear, allowing a more meaningful interfirm comparison of financial results.

2. Income manipulation. The accounting realization principle opens the way to income manipulation by management. Thus, for example, if a firm holds securities whose market prices are higher than original cost, management can create a "profit" by selling these securities.[25] However, current value accounting will recognize capital gains (or losses) as they accrue, independent of the timing of sale, thereby stripping management of the power to create profits by mere asset sales.

3. Operating income and holding gains. Accounting income is determined by matching costs, which are partially based on historical prices (e.g., depreciation, cost of raw materials, etc.), with revenues, which are based on current prices. Income therefore contains two elements: (*a*) operating income, arising from the firm's production and exchange transactions, and (*b*) capital gains or losses, arising from the holding of assets prior to use (e.g., a speculative purchase of inventory in expectation of increasing prices). Since these two income elements might indicate different aspects of managerial performance, it might be desirable for the analyst to separate them.[26] Current value accounting provides such a

---

[24] Gas-producing utilities offer a clear example. Such companies are required by the Federal Power Commission to price their product according to the historical cost of the land and production facilities, which are substantially lower than current market values. As a result, gas utilities virtually ceased new explorations. For elaboration, see P. J. Garfield and W. F. Lovejoy, *Public Utility Economics* (Englewood Cliffs, N.J.: Prentice-Hall, Inc., 1964), pp. 303–11.

[25] Note that these securities can be sold on December 31 and repurchased on January 1, thereby creating a profit without changing the economic position of the firm (except for the transaction costs involved).

[26] For example, it has been suggested that such separation would improve the prediction of income; see Edwards and Bell, *op. cit.*, p. 99. For a critical view of this objective, see D. F. Drake and N. Dopuch, "On the Case for Dichotomizing Income," *Journal of Accounting Research*, 3 (Autumn 1965), 192–205.

separation; price changes of assets are recognized as they occur (rather than as they are realized) and are accordingly reported in the income statement as holding gains or losses, while the costs matched against revenues are measured in terms of current input prices resulting in a more appropriate indicator of operational performance. Current operating income thus indicates the net inflow of resources beyond those necessary to replace the expired assets at their prevailing prices.

4. A realistic statement of position. Adjustment for current prices results in the presentation of both assets and liabilities at their current values. Aggregations or measures (e.g., ratios) of these values will then be based on a common denominator—current prices—and will therefore be more economically meaningful than conventional balance sheet measures. In addition, the current prices of assets are of considerable importance for various purposes of financial analysis, such as short-term liquidity evaluation where debt coverage is examined. In some industries, notably in the real estate sector, appreciation in the value of assets is at least as important to lenders and investors as the creation of historical income.

The preceding discussion suggests that current value accounting is of considerable usefulness to financial analysts. It should be noted that the required adjustments (or, at least, a reasonable approximation) can be performed by the analyst even if the firm does not report its financial results on a current value basis. However, such adjustments would usually involve considerable effort and would require access to internal data (e.g., the timing of asset purchases).

B. Adjustment for general price-level changes

Accounting values are measured in monetary (money) units rather than in purchasing power (real) units. It has frequently been suggested that a conversion of monetary to real values by the use of general price-level indexes would enhance the usefulness of financial reports for the following reasons: (*a*) the changes in investor well-being reflected by income and equity figures will be measured in terms of command over purchasing power (rather than in money units), which seems to be conceptually consistent with the basic notion of maintaining well-offness positions,[27] (*b*) the firm's historical income figures will be comparable in terms of real purchasing power, thereby allowing investors to better evaluate the firm's past performance (e.g., an increasing monetary income series during an inflationary period is not necessarily a sign of favorable

---

[27] For example, when a person's wealth remains at the level of $100,000 while the general price level is increasing, it does not make much economic sense to argue that his well-being is kept intact.

performance), and (c) the profit or loss from price-level adjustment will provide analysts with an indicator regarding management's success in protecting the firm's wealth from erosion by price-level changes.[28]

As in the specific price changes discussed above, the mechanics of price-level adjustment is quite complex and controversial.[29] However, compared with specific price changes, the case for general price-level adjustment seems to have less merit for financial analysts. First, despite the intuitive appeal of the real income concept, there is no economic doctrine claiming that it is wrong to measure income (on both the macro and micro levels) in monetary values when price levels are changing. In fact, money values are used in economic measurements at least as frequently as real values.[30] Second, for various financial analysis purposes, there seems to be justification for ignoring general price-level changes. For example, credit analysis is concerned with the extent of debt protection in monetary rather than in real terms, since lenders' claims, and in fact almost all contractual relationships, are specified in money terms. Third, serious technical difficulties are encountered in the process of general price-level adjustment, particularly with the choice of an appropriate index. The problems involved in constructing price indexes, such as undependable data on prices, accounting for quality and consumer taste changes, and the continuous change in the relative weights of the sampled commodities, are extensively discussed in the economic literature and will not be elaborated here. However, these problems will obviously affect the quality of financial data when price-level adjustments are performed. Fourth, some of the objectives of price-level adjustments, particularly enhancing the cross-sectional comparability of financial data, can be achieved by the specific asset price adjustments discussed in the preceding section. Adjustment of financial data to changes in the general price level therefore appears to be less useful to financial analysts than specific asset price adjustments.

[28] In periods of serious inflation, management will usually attempt to hedge from inflationary losses by maintaining liabilities at least at the level of monetary assets (e.g., cash, government bonds, and receivables). Thus, losses in real purchasing power of the assets will be covered by gains from the decrease in the real value of liabilities.

[29] For a comprehensive discussion of the issues involved in price-level adjustments, see American Institute of Certified Public Accountants, "Reporting the Financial Effects of Price-Level Changes," *Accounting Research Study No. 6* (New York: AICPA, 1963). Also, American Institute of Certified Public Accountants, "Financial Statements Restated for General Price-Level Changes," *Statement of the Accounting Principles Board No. 3* (June 1969).

[30] Hakansson, for example, argued within the framework of a firm-behavior stochastic model that for a given set of utility functions, adjustment for general price-level changes is irrelevant to the firm's decision makers (i.e., the decisions that maximize the firm's objectives are independent of the price level). See "On the Relevance of Price-Level Accounting," *Journal of Accounting Research*, 7 (Spring 1969), 22–31.

C. Expected events affecting future earnings

The most problematic area of conflict between accounting and economic income and the one concerning analysts most is the treatment of foreseeable changes in the earnings power of the firm, usually known as goodwill changes. Given that investment decisions are based on the future prospects of the firm, it seems obvious that any event expected by management to affect future earnings (e.g., the development of a new product) should be reported in the financial statement. Accountants are naturally reluctant to report the effects on future earnings of expected events because of the highly subjective and unverifiable nature of the information. However, they should realize that any investment decision is based on estimation and valuation of future events. In a world of uncertainty, valuation cannot be both sound and objective. Therefore, the accounting objectivity criterion when in conflict with the relevance of information does not carry much weight, and the financial analyst must secure from the firm any relevant information concerning the effect of expected events on its future performance.

At present, analysts' needs for information on changes in future earnings power can be best served by providing operating statistics outside the conventional double-entry framework. Such statistics might be concerned with the products currently produced, the firm's market share for each product, and plans for the introduction of new products; plans for substantial capital expenditures; data on employee productivity, expenditures for employee development and training, statistics on absenteeism and turnover, and information on labor contracts and the process of labor negotiations; information on customers' attitudes, sales returns or cancellations, and order backlogs; data on research and development expenditures, advertising campaigns, and so forth, and the estimated effect of these expenditures on future earnings. To increase the reliability of such operating statistics, they should be verified as far as possible by the firm's independent auditors.

Of special importance are the suggestions for the disclosure of budgets and earnings forecasts in the financial reports.[31] Such data will provide investors with information actually used by management in formulating company policy. Naturally, objections to such disclosure are numerous; it is contended that forecasts are highly subjective and uncertain and might therefore mislead users, reporting future plans (e.g., the addition of a product line) might provide competitors with an advantage, and the publication of estimates might increase the legal liability

---

[31] For elaboration, see W. W. Cooper, N. Dopuch, and T. F. Keller, "Budgetary Disclosure and Other Suggestions for Improving Accounting Reports," *The Accounting Review*, 43 (October 1968), 640–48; and B. J. Belda, "Reporting on Forecasts of Future Developments," *The Journal of Accountancy*, 130 (December 1970), 54–58.

of management and auditors. While there is some merit in these objections, it should be realized that investors *must* use estimates in their investment decisions. At present, such estimates are not publicly announced or subjected to a third-party review. The suggested procedure can be expected to improve the quality of investor estimates. Forecast disclosure will also enable investors to compare the forecasts with subsequently realized results to evaluate the quality of management.

Summarizing, while it is impossible at this stage to specify the "true" or ideal income and asset value concepts, various modifications of, and additions to, currently reported data would considerably enhance the usefulness of financial reports to analysts. The major areas for such changes are current values for assets and income and information concerning future earnings changes. On balance, the advantages in relevance of such information would outweigh the disadvantages in lack of objectivity and secrecy. Until such information is regularly conveyed to the public, the analyst must attempt to secure it directly from the firm.

THE ALLEGED CONSEQUENCES OF ALTERNATIVE ACCOUNTING MEASUREMENT METHODS

Accountants are severely criticized for the lack of uniformity in accounting practices. As is well known, managements and accountants are free, within rather broad limits, to choose among alternative generally accepted accounting methods of measuring and reporting economic activities. The major areas in which such choices currently exist are [32] valuation of inventories, depreciation and depletion methods, income tax allocation, capitalization of research and development expenditures and of other intangibles (e.g., goodwill, advertising, employee training), the timing of income realization, income statement presentation of extraordinary and special items, the recording of business combinations (mergers and earnings of subsidiaries), and the treatment of complex security issues.[33]

The adverse effects of alternative measurement methods on investor decisions are usually demonstrated by means of hypothetical examples or real-life cases. An example of such a hypothetical case is provided in Table 6.1 where it is shown that by varying accounting measurement methods the earnings-per-share of a firm can be changed from $.80 to $1.79, given the same set of basic economic events. For those averse to hypothetical examples, an almost endless list of real-life examples of

---

[32] It should be noted that these areas change continuously; as more uniformity is achieved in some areas, larger diversity is usually observed in others.

[33] The various alternatives open in each area will not be discussed here, since they can be found in any accounting text.

TABLE 6.1

Accounting Magic
All "In Conformity with Generally Accepted Accounting Principles"

	Company A Col. 1	Use of FIFO in Pricing Inventory Col. 2	Use of Straight-Line Depreciation Col. 3	Deferring Research Costs Over 5 Years Col. 4	Funding Only the Pensions Vested Col. 5	Use of Stock Options for Incentive Col. 6	Including Capital Gain in Income Col. 7	Company B Col. 8
			Company B's Profits Are Higher Because of					
Sales in units	100,000 units $100 each							100,000 units $100 each
Sales in dollars	$10,000,000							$10,000,000
Costs and expenses:								
Cost of goods sold	$ 6,000,000							$ 6,000,000
Selling, general and administrative	1,500,000							1,500,000
LIFO inventory reserve		$(400,000)						–
Depreciation	400,000		$(100,000)					300,000
Research costs	100,000			$(80,000)				20,000
Pension costs	200,000				$(150,000)			50,000
Officers' compensation:								
Base salaries	200,000							200,000
Bonuses	200,000					$(200,000)		–
Total costs and expenses	$ 9,000,000	$(400,000)	$(100,000)	$(80,000)	$(150,000)	$(200,000)	$ –	$ 8,070,000
Profit before income taxes	$ 1,000,000	$ 400,000	$ 100,000	$ 80,000	$ 150,000	$ 200,000	$ –	$ 1,930,000
Income taxes	520,000	208,000	52,000	42,000	78,000	104,000	$ –	1,004,000
	$ 480,000	$ 192,000	$ 48,000	$ 38,000	$ 72,000	$ 96,000	$ –	$ 926,000

Gain on sale of property (net of income tax)	—	—	—	—	—	—	$ 150,000	
Net profit reported	$ 480,000	$ 192,000	$ 48,000	$ 38,000	$ 72,000	$ 96,000	$150,000	$ 1,076,000
Per share on 600,000 shares	$ .80	$ .32	$ .08	$ .06	$ .12	$ .16	$ .25	$ 1.79
Market value at:								
10 times earnings	$8.00	$3.20	$ .80	$ .63	$1.20	$1.60	$2.50	$17.93
12 times earnings	9.60	3.84	.96	.76	1.44	1.92	3.00	21.52
15 times earnings	12.00	4.80	1.20	.95	1.80	2.40	3.75	26.90

Source: L. Spacek, "Business Success Requires an Understanding of Unsolved Problems of Accounting and Financial Reporting," in J. Lorie and R. Brealey (eds.), *Modern Developments in Investment Management* (New York: Praeger, Inc., 1972), pp. 643–44.
( ) denotes deduction.

Column	Company A	Company B
2	Uses LIFO (last-in first-out) for pricing inventory	Uses FIFO (first-in first-out)
3	Uses accelerated depreciation for book and tax purposes	Uses straight-line
4	Charges research and development costs to expense currently (If R & D costs remain at same level, the difference disappears after five years. The difference of $80,000 in the chart is in the first year, where A expenses $100,000, and B capitalizes the $100,000 but amortizes 1/5.)	Capitalizes and amortizes over five-year period
5	Funds the **current** pension costs—i.e., current service plus amortization of past service (Difference in pension charges may also arise where, as in the case of U.S. Steel in 1958, management decides that current contributions can be reduced or omitted because of excess funding in prior years and/or increased earnings of the fund or the rise in market value of the investments.)	Funds only the present value of pensions vested
6	Pays incentive bonuses to officers in cash	Grants stock options instead of paying cash bonuses
7	Credits gains (net of tax thereon) directly to earned surplus (or treats them as special credits below net income)	Includes such gains (net of income tax thereon) in income

diverse methods can be provided.[34] Sun Oil elects to charge off its drilling costs for new wells right away, while competitor Continental Oil capitalizes the costs of successful wells and writes them off gradually; U.S. Steel takes the 7 percent investment tax credit on its capital expenditures into income over a period of several years, while Luken Steel among others recognizes all of its tax credits as current income; Delta Air Lines depreciates its planes over ten years, while United Air Lines writes off its 727 Boeing jets over as long as sixteen years; R. J. Reynolds values its leaf tobacco inventories by the last-in first-out method, while several other major tobacco companies use different inventory valuation methods (e.g., first-in first-out); in 1962 a profit of $80 million on the sale of Ethyl Corporation, jointly owned by General Motors and Standard Oil of New Jersey, was reported by the former in the income statement (thereby increasing net income), while the latter included it in the "Statement of Stockholders' Equity" (i.e., after net income); in 1964 Gulf and Western changed the method of accounting for exploration and development costs, thereby increasing by $1.6 million its earnings over the years 1965 and 1966. Given such cases of nonuniformity in the application of accounting methods and the substantial effect of changing methods on reported results, a cynical attitude toward financial data seems unavoidable: Ernest Henderson, chairman of Sheraton Corporation, was quoted by *Forbes* as saying, "My earnings, sir, are what you say they are." [35] And a recent book on finance concludes: "The intent of the [earnings] discussion is to emphasize the folly of attaching any great significance to reported earnings per share." [36]

A CLOSER LOOK AT THE EFFECTS
OF ALTERNATIVE ACCOUNTING METHODS

The heated arguments concerning the effects of alternative accounting methods seem somewhat paradoxical: How can expressions like "my earnings are what you say they are" or "the folly of attaching any great significance to reported EPS" be reconciled with the fact, indicated by both casual and empirical observations, that investors regard financial data as important? [37] A closer examination of the issue seems to suggest

[34] The following examples were taken from "What Are Earnings?: The Growing Credibility Gap," *Forbes Magazine*, May 15, 1967; reprinted in *Accounting: Socially Responsible and Socially Relevant*, R. G. J. Vangermeersch, ed. (New York: Harper & Row, Publishers, 1972), pp. 240–56.

[35] *Ibid.*, p. 246.

[36] J. H. Lorie and M. T. Hamilton, *The Stock Market: Theories and Evidence* (Homewood, Ill.: Richard D. Irwin, Inc., 1973), p. 154.

[37] See Chapter 15 for empirical evidence on the association between reported earnings and stock price changes.

the source of the paradox. Arguments concerning the adverse effects of alternative accounting methods must, at least partially, be based on the assumption that the investment community is extremely naïve in its financial statement interpretation. It is obviously necessary to assume such naïveté in order to argue that investors will be misled when a firm recognizes all its investment tax credit as current income rather than allocating it over the life of the assets; that stockholders will make different investment decisions when extraordinary items are reported before or after net income; or that investors will value a firm differently when it switches its inventory valuation method from LIFO to FIFO. A basic and systematic inefficiency must be assumed about a market setting in which a group of persons (accountants) can significantly affect the welfare of other persons (investors) by merely changing the *form* of reporting economic events. Recent evidence suggests that this is not the case.

The theory of efficient capital markets and the empirical evidence supporting it indicate that investors, on the average, are quite sophisticated in their interpretation of financial information.[38] While many "small investors" might be unfamiliar with the mechanics of accounting, a sufficient number of astute operators seem to be able to "see through the numbers" and recognize economic reality despite alternative reporting modes. Stock prices in efficient markets will reflect, on average, the firm's economic position in an unbiased manner, regardless of the *form* of financial reporting, since investors will adjust for differences in accounting techniques.[39]

Although the evidence on market efficiency is by no means conclusive, it suggests that the arguments concerning alternative accounting methods are somewhat exaggerated and misguided. In most cases, the real problem is not the existence of alternative reporting modes but the lack of adequate disclosure and/or the high costs involved in adjusting financial data. When essential facts, such as the firm's obligation under lease contracts, are omitted from the financial statement, the process of data adjustment by users will be curtailed. Sometimes even full dislcosure will not serve users' purposes, since the costs involved in the required adjustments would be excessively high. For example, even when a firm discloses the purchase dates and technical description of all its assets (as in utility reports to the regulatory agencies), it is still generally impractical for

---

[38] See Chapter 14 for elaboration.

[39] Note the use of the term *unbiased* rather than *correct*. Investor estimates might be erroneous, as is expected in a world of uncertainty, but such errors will not be systematically biased in an efficient market. A significant effect of alternative accounting methods should obviously be manifested by systematic biases (e.g., the market value of a firm using the FIFO inventory method is always larger than that of an identical firm using the LIFO method).

users to determine the current values of these assets. The firm's criteria in preparing financial reports should therefore be twofold: (*a*) Where adjustments from one method to another are relatively easy (e.g., investment tax credit), one method should be reported and sufficient information for adjustment supplied in footnotes.[40] (*b*) When the costs of obtaining the required information by users are high (e.g., the current value of assets), such information should be provided in the financial statements. Given the present situation, in which so little is known about users' informational needs, it makes little sense to enforce strict uniformity in accounting methods.[41]

In conclusion, it seems that financial analysts should not be overly concerned with the nonuniformity of financial reports. A cynical and disparaging approach toward financial information is clearly unwarranted. In most cases, the information required to achieve reasonable uniformity (i.e., to convert from one method to another) is available in the financial statement. In other cases, the analyst should attempt to secure the required information from the firm. The analyst's main concern should be full disclosure and minimization of information-processing costs rather than uniformity.

> In the end it is likely that the cries for abundant and relevant data will win out over the pleas for simplicity and uniformity, because analysts will become better trained and equipped to deal with such information.[42]

SUMMARY

The widespread dissatisfaction with currently reported financial data centers around two issues: (*a*) the inconsistency between accounting and economic concepts of income and asset values, and (*b*) the diversity of alternative accounting measurement methods. It has been argued above that the criticism of financial information is partially unfounded,

---

[40] The SEC's new disclosure rules are a step in the right direction. Firms will be allowed to continue choosing among generally accepted accounting principles, but in many cases they will be required to disclose in dollar amounts the impact on net income of the accounting alternative chosen. For example, firms will have to explain the differences between net income reported to stockholders and that reported to the Internal Revenue Service. In addition, firms will be required to fully explain the accounting principles used.

[41] It should also be noted that adaptation of accounting to a rapidly changing economy necessarily results in divergence of accounting practices. Enforcement of strict uniformity would place accounting in a straitjacket of rules and practices and would inhibit the desired progress.

[42] S. Davidson, "Accounting and Financial Reporting in the Seventies," *Arthur Young Journal* (Spring-Summer 1969); reprinted in *Accounting: Socially Responsible and Socially Relevant,* R. G. D. Vangermeersch, ed. (New York: Harper & Row, Publishers, 1972), p. 65.

since the economic concepts of income and asset values are ill-defined in the context of uncertainty, and in many cases analysts are able to recognize the effects of alternative accounting methods. However, it should be realized that the usefulness of financial data will be enhanced if they are supplemented by current asset values, relevant operating statistics, and forecasts of future events.

PART TWO

APPLICATIONS OF FINANCIAL STATEMENT ANALYSIS

CHAPTER SEVEN

Financial Statement Analysis as an Information System

The tools of financial statement analysis were developed in the preceding chapters. A large number of measures and indicators were presented and various related conceptual and practical problems discussed. The general objective in applying these tools is to provide information to decision makers, generally in the form of predictions of future business events. The remaining chapters of the book will mainly be concerned with such predictions. However, before we turn to an evaluation of the specific uses of financial statement analysis, a general discussion of the role of information systems in decision making is called for. Such a discussion will place the studies presented in the following chapters in the proper perspective and provide the background for the various suggestions and guidelines advanced for future research.

Financial statement analysis is an information-processing system designed to supply data on firm-related economic events. The number of possible information systems is obviously very large, given the numerous economic phenomena that can be described (e.g., profitability, size, liquidity, market share, etc.), each of which can be expressed in various ways (e.g., firm size can be measured by total assets, sales, number of employees, etc.). Accordingly, the basic concern of the financial analyst is to select the optimal information system(s) for a given purpose, that is, the system that will lead the decision maker to take the most preferred action. The choice of an information system therefore depends on the decision for which it is used; different decisions (and decision makers) will generally require different information systems. Accordingly, information systems should be developed within the framework of decision theory. The following section examines, in a general manner, the role of information systems in various decision situations. Discussion then focuses on financial statement information systems, particularly their objectives and optimal design.

INFORMATION AND DECISION MAKING

A decision is called for when a person faces a choice situation, that is, when he can choose among several alternative actions, such as various portfolios of securities.[1] When the consequences of these actions are not perfectly known at the time of decision, as in future portfolio returns, the person faces an uncertain choice situation. The major problem encountered in an uncertain choice situation is obviously the prediction of the various possible outcomes of each action (e.g., the various future rates of return on each portfolio considered). Information systems are generally designed to provide the data for such predictions.

A. Information in a perfectly specified decision process

A decision process is perfectly specified if the following four sets of data are available to the decision maker:

1. A set of mutually exclusive and exhaustive alternative *actions,* to be denoted by X. A specific action will be denoted by x, where $x \in X$.[2] One and only one action from X will be taken.

2. A set of mutually exclusive and exhaustive future *outcomes* associated with each possible action in X. The set of outcomes will be denoted by Y, and a specific outcome by y, where $y \in Y$. One and only one outcome will occur.[3]

3. A set of *probabilities*, $P(y)$, attached to the various future outcomes.

4. A set of *utilities* indicating the decision maker's subjective preferences with respect to the possible outcomes. The utilities are defined for each possible combination of action-outcome, and denoted by $U(x, y)$.

[1] This section draws on J. S. Demski, *Information Analysis* (Reading, Mass.: Addison-Wesley Publishing Co., 1972).

[2] The notation ϵ should be read as "belongs to" or "is a member of." Thus, $x \in X$ indicates that the action x is a member of the set X.

[3] The determinants of the various outcomes are usually known as *states*. The set of states often replaces the set of outcomes in decision theory.

The combined set of actions, outcomes, probabilities, and utilities, $\{X, Y, P, U\}$, thus constitutes a perfectly specified decision model. If the decision maker behaves according to the *expected utility theory*, he will choose the action $x \in X$ with the highest expected value of utility.[4] The expected utility from selecting a specific action x, to be denoted by $E\ (U|x)$, is

$$E(U|x) = \sum_{y \in Y} U(x, y)P(y). \tag{7.1}$$

The optimal action—the one that provides the maximum expected value of utility—is

$$E(U|x^*) = \max_{x \in X} E(U|x) = \max_{x \in X} \sum_{y \in Y} U(x, y)P(y). \tag{7.2}$$

For illustration, consider the following simplified decision problem facing a bank-lending officer evaluating a loan application. He can take one of two possible actions: x_1—grant the loan, or x_2—do not grant the loan. Each action is associated with two possible outcomes: y_1—loan will be repaid, or y_2—loan will be defaulted. The probabilities of these two outcomes are estimated as P(repayment) $= .95$, and P(default) $= .05$.

The utilities associated with each combination of action-outcome are specified in Table 7.1. If the loan is granted and repaid, the bank will realize the interest on the loan; the utility to the bank of this interest is estimated at 500 units. If the loan is granted and the borrower defaults, the bank will lose both interest and principal, and, in addition, its goodwill will be slightly impaired. The total loss is evaluated at $-9,000$ utility units. If the loan is not granted and the applicant remains solvent, the bank will lose the marginal interest that could have been charged and possibly even future business with the customer. This loss is evaluated in

TABLE 7.1

Utilities of Conditional Outcomes of a Lending Decision

Action	Outcome	
	Repayment	Default
Grant	500	−9,000
Do not grant	−300	200

[4] An axiomatic approach to the expected utility theory was first formulated by Von Neumann and Morgenstern in *Theory of Games and Economic Behavior* (Princeton, N.J.: Princeton University Press, 1947). The theory is usually discussed in decision theory and finance texts; see, for example, E. F. Fama and M. H. Miller, *The Theory of Finance* (New York: Holt, Rinehart & Winston, 1972), Chap. 5.

utility terms at −300 units. If the loan is not granted and the applicant subsequently goes bankrupt, the bank will realize a goodwill gain valued at 200 utility units (for example, the FDIC might decrease the insurance rate, given the favorable performance of the credit department).

The four components of the lending decision model—actions, outcomes, probabilities, and utilities—have been specified. Following (7.1), the expected utility values of the two actions are

$$\text{Grant} = 500 \times .95 + (-9,000) \times .05 = 25 \text{ units}$$
$$\text{Do not grant} = -300 \times .95 + 200 \times .05 = -275 \text{ units}$$

The loan will be granted, since the expected utility value of the "grant" action, 25 units, is higher than that of the "do not grant" action, −275 units.

When a decision model is perfectly specified, the purpose of an information system is to provide the decision maker with the set of probabilities associated with the various outcomes or to modify his existing probabilities. Other components of the decision model—actions, outcomes, and utilities—are, by definition, fully specified and hence unaffected by information systems. A bank financial analyst will thus be engaged in assessing the default probabilities of prospective borrowers for the use of loan officers.

B. Information in a simplified (imperfectly specified) decision process

In constructing a model, the decision maker must weigh the expected benefits against the expected cost of the model. For most practical purposes, the high cost involved in model construction (e.g., researchers' time, data collection and processing, etc.) will preclude the use of perfectly specified decision models. Instead, a *simplified* model will be used where some or all of the four data sets mentioned above are less than perfectly specified. For example, the decision maker will usually avoid the enumeration of all possible actions open to him and will consider instead a smaller subset of actions; he will also ignore many outcomes or states and focus on a few plausible outcomes; he will simplify the probability assignment to outcomes by applying a convenient function, such as the normal distribution; and he will similarly simplify the utility assignment to each action-outcome combination by using a general utility function, such as the quadratic or logarithmic functions, or even equate utilities with monetary values. A simplified decision model is thus based on a set of *assumptions* (e.g., that the probability distribution of outcomes is normal, or that the decision maker's preferences can be well approximated by a quadratic utility function). These assumptions are intended to abstract the common and crucial elements from the mass of complex and detailed circumstances surrounding the decision.

Practically all available decision models are highly simplified. In bank-lending decision models, it is customary to ignore the possible effects of rejecting a loan application on the future relationships with the customer because of estimation difficulties (i.e., high cost). In addition, the bank's utility function is usually assumed to be linear (i.e., the dollar values of the various outcomes are substituted for the utility values), thereby avoiding utility assessment. Capital budgeting models, which are extensively used for investment decisions by the firm, usually assume a single outcome (i.e., periodic cash flow) for each action and equate utilities with monetary values. Linear programming models, designed to determine the firm's optimal input and output mixes, are based on the assumption of linearity of technological relationships (e.g., between units of inputs and outputs). Sometimes the model's simplifying assumptions are extremely unrealistic. For example, the portfolio theory "capital asset pricing model," [5] designed to explain the formation of security prices in capital markets, is based on the following assumptions: all investors are (*a*) risk averse, (*b*) have identical predictions with respect to all security outcomes, and (*c*) can borrow or lend at the same riskless interest rate. These assumptions are obviously unrealistic; however, the fact that assumptions violate real-life conditions does not necessarily imply that the model's performance will be poor. Indeed, as was mentioned above, the main objective of simplifying a model by a set of assumptions is to abstract from real-life complexities. Assumptions, therefore, will usually be somewhat unrealistic, yet the decisions implied by the model might still lead to the desired outcomes.[6]

Recall that the function of information systems in a perfectly specified decision model is to provide data for the assessment and revision of the probabilities of outcomes. In a simplified decision model, the role of information is far more fundamental and far reaching. Given that the various components of a simplified model are at best approximations to the real choice situation, information can affect all the model's components (i.e., actions, outcomes, probabilities, and utilities), not just the set of probabilities. For example, in a bank-lending decision, a careful analysis might affect the set of outcomes by indicating that there are three rather than two possible outcomes: the loan can be fully repaid, partially repaid, or defaulted.

Generally, in simplified decision models, the role of information systems is threefold: (*a*) In the process of *constructing* the model, informa-

---

[5] See Chapter 12 for elaboration.

[6] M. Friedman, in "The Methodology of Positive Economics," *Essays in Positive Economics* (Chicago: The University of Chicago Press, 1953), pp. 3–43, took an extreme position by arguing that the realism of assumptions is largely irrelevant to the model's validity. This argument was challenged by many, e.g., E. Nagel, "Assumptions in Economic Theory," *American Economic Review*, 53 (May 1963), 211–19.

tion, usually from experience, will indicate the preliminary or a priori set of relationships (hypotheses) comprising the model. (*b*) In the process of *testing* (verifying) the model, information, usually from a sample, will indicate the adequacy of the model's assumptions and implications (predictions) and will suggest the required modifications. (*c*) In the process of *using* the model, information systems will be employed as a feedback control device to monitor the model and signal the required modifications in parameters and variables as the environmental conditions change.

THE ROLE OF FINANCIAL STATEMENT INFORMATION SYSTEMS

The development of investment theory, on both the firm and individual investor levels, is currently changing direction. The perfect certainty models of the 1940s and 1950s (e.g., capital budgeting) are gradually being replaced by new models allowing for explicit consideration of uncertainty in the decision process. However, these new models, which are mainly based on portfolio theory concepts, are still at a preliminary stage of development and suffer from serious implementation problems. The validity of basic relationships underlying the models (e.g., the relationship between expected rates of return and systematic risk in the capital asset pricing model), and the optimal estimation of required parameters (e.g., the estimation of portfolio risk), are far from settled issues. Consequently, for most financial decisions there are either no models available or only highly simplified ones. Given this situation, the potential usefulness of financial statement analysis is far reaching. In cases where decision models are unavailable, financial statement information systems should provide data for model construction and verification. In the few cases where reasonably well-specified models exist, financial information systems should provide, in the most efficient manner, the models' inputs and data for model control and modification.

A. Financial data for model construction

Most financial decisions are currently made in a heuristic and informal manner. Data are usually collected and evaluated, yet the final decision often seems to be made on intuitive grounds (sometimes referred to as judgment) rather than formally integrated with the data collection process. For example, the process of a bank-lending decision usually involves an extensive analysis of the applicant's financial data (e.g., the ratio "spread sheet"). However, both the evaluation of the data and the final decision are based mainly on the lending officer's experience and intuition. No formal models, not even simplified ones, are known to be used by banks in arriving at their lending decision. A similar situation exists in most other financial decision areas, such as the determination of underwriters' fees on prospective bond issues, the choice of an optimal capital structure (leverage) in a firm, the decision as to whether an asset should be leased or purchased, or whether and when to exercise call options or convert securities. Sometimes the intuitive nature of the decision process, i.e., the absence of a formal model, is even presented as an advantage. For example, bond rating institutions insist that the rating process [7] cannot be described in quantitative terms: "It [the bond rating] is a judgment of analysts. No computer can come up with the rating." [8]

Practically all investment decisions, both on the firm and on the investor level, are based on firm-related financial data. Therefore, it is natural for financial analysts to participate actively in the process of constructing decision models. In a situation where decision models are nonexistent or ill-specified, the distinction between model developers ("theoreticians") and information providers ("metricians") disappears:

> Whether it is the metricians who ought to become theoreticians or the theoreticians who ought to become metricians is not important. What is important is that theory construction and measurement development must be fused.[9]

Since so little is known about the process of actual financial decision making, it appears that the first stage of model development should be positive (descriptive). Research should be concerned with the question of *how* choices are made by decision makers. Normative (prescriptive) research, concerned with the question of how choices *ought* to be made, will naturally follow. Descriptive studies of financial decisions will generally be aimed at identifying the major determinants of the decisions (e.g., firm size and profitability in a bond-rating decision). Such an identification will then provide a system of generalization (i.e., a model) that could be used to make predictions (e.g., the rating on a forthcoming bond). The major test of a model will be the extent of conformity of its predictions with actual observations. However, the cost involved in model construction and data provision should also be considered in evaluating the model. Generally, the wider the scope of the model's predictions, the more precise the predictions; and the lower

[7] See Chapter 10 for elaboration on bond ratings.

[8] A quote from E. Vogelius, Moody's chief bond rater, in J. O. Horrigan, "The Determination of Long-Term Credit Standing with Financial Ratios," *Empirical Research in Accounting: Selected Studies 1966,* Supplement to Vol. 4, *Journal of Accounting Research,* 48.

[9] R. T. Sterling, "On Theory Construction and Verification," *The Accounting Review,* 45 (July 1970), 455.

the cost of operations, the better the model. Positive financial models, such as those designed to predict new bond ratings or banks' decisions regarding loan applications, are obviously of substantial importance. In addition, such models, by furthering our understanding of decision makers' behavior, will provide for the construction of normative models designed to improve upon current decisions:

> The conclusions of positive economics seem to be, and are, immediately relevant to important normative problems, to questions of what ought to be done and how any given goal can be attained. . . . Normative economics, and the art of economics, on the other hand, cannot be independent of positive economics.[10]

Consider again the example of bank-lending decisions, and suppose that the analyst's task is first to develop a model that describes these decisions and later to suggest improvements upon current practices. The first step would be to construct a set of hypotheses concerning the major determinants of the lending decision. These determinants will probably be classified into three groups: bank variables (e.g., size, deposits-to-loans ratio, etc.), applicant variables (e.g., various solvency and profitability ratios), and economic indicators (e.g., the prime interest rate, the Dow Jones index, etc.). Statistical techniques, such as regression and discriminant analyses, will then be applied to samples of real data from the bank loan files to answer the three basic questions of model specification: (a) Which of the various hypothesized variables actually affect the lending decision? (b) What are the relative weights of these variables? (c) What is the mathematical form of combining the variables? The final stage of the positive model construction will involve verification tests based on the accuracy of the model's predictions. Accordingly, a new sample of bank loan applications (both granted and rejected) will be collected, and the ability of the model to discriminate between the granted and rejected applications will be determined. Confidence in the model's descriptive power will increase as more and more tests confirm its ability to predict the actual decisions of loan officers. Once a satisfactory positive model has been developed, the analyst's attention will turn to the normative aspects of the lending problem. Specifically, the bank's objective (e.g., maximize profits for a certain level of loan-portfolio risk) should be determined, and various modifications of the model aimed at achieving this objective should be examined. For example, a substitution of the applicant's market-determined leverage for the accounting leverage might improve solvency evaluation and hence the lending decision. Here again, verification tests on various samples

[10] Friedman, *op. cit.*, p. 4.

will indicate whether the modified model consistently satisfies the bank's objective.

The studies presented and evaluated in Part II of the book (Chapters 7 through 11) provide numerous examples of the role of financial statement analysis in model construction. The models developed incorporate financial as well as nonfinancial variables and are designed to *(a)* predict economic phenomena, such as corporate earnings and growth rates, corporate failure (bankruptcy), and risk premiums on corporate bonds, *(b)* predict actual financial decisions, such as bond ratings and bank-lending decisions, and *(c)* examine normative questions, such as the improvement in earnings prediction resulting from interim report information.

B. Financial data for existing models

The preceding section dealt with the role of financial statement information systems in decision areas for which no satisfactory models are available. We now turn to cases where at least simplified models exist. Here the general role of financial statement analysis is to provide efficiently (i.e., at the lowest possible cost) some or all of the information inputs required by the models. Such information is usually provided in the form of predictions of future events.

Consider the portfolio selection model, which is probably the most advanced and well-defined investment decision model available.[11] The model, or more precisely its offspring, the "capital asset pricing model," stipulates that the systematic risk of a stock (Sharpe's β value) is the only firm-related characteristic that determines the expected rate of return (the other determinants are general market variables: the riskless rate of interest and the expected return on the "market portfolio"). The β value thus captures both the equilibrium return and the risk characteristics of the stock and is therefore a major determinant of the portfolio decision. Unfortunately, β values cannot be directly observed in the stock market; nor is their optimal estimation procedure specified by the portfolio model. Given that a security's systematic risk is determined by the firm's financial and operating characteristics (e.g., the firm's capital structure, operating leverage, etc.), it can be expected that financial statement data will assist in the optimal estimation of β values. Analysts involved in portfolio management should therefore attempt to design information systems for the optimal estimation of β values.

The design and selection of information systems obviously require a criterion to indicate the relative usefulness of the various possible systems, and to guide the analyst in choosing the optimal one. In prin-

[11] See Chapter 12 for a discussion of the portfolio model.

ciple this criterion is straightforward—the optimal information system is the one that when used by the decision maker maximizes his expected utility. The information value of a system thus depends on the specific model used by the decision maker. As an example, consider again the hypothetical lending decision described above (Table 7.1). Suppose that a clairvoyant offers to reveal the outcome of the loan, that is, whether it will be paid or defaulted. The value of such perfect information to the bank, or the maximum amount in utility units that the bank would be willing to pay for the clairvoyant's message, can be computed as follows: If the message states that the loan will be repaid, the bank will grant the loan and realize a gain of 500 utility units. However, if the message indicates that the applicant will default, the bank will decline to grant the loan and will realize a utility gain of 200 units. The *expected value* of the clairvoyant's perfect information is thus:

$$500 \times .95 + 200 \times .05 = 485 \text{ utility units.}$$

However, as was shown above, the expected utility value of the optimal action, that is, grant the loan, without the clairvoyant's information was 25 utility units. Hence, the expected improvement in the bank's situation brought about by the clairvoyant's message is $485 - 25 = 460$ utility units. Accordingly, the maximum value of information concerning the specific lending decision is 460 utility units. The bank would not be willing to pay more than this amount for any information.[12] Note, however, that the value of the clairvoyant's message will change when the decision situation is altered. Suppose, for example, that the utility of the combination grant-default changes from −9,000 to −5,000 units. The value of the clairvoyant's message would then be only 260 utility units.[13]

The preceding example shows that the value of an information system depends on the specific choice situation, and in particular, on the decision maker's set of utilities. Therefore, it is impossible for the financial analyst to select or design information systems without direct reference to the specific decision model used. This conclusion contra-

---

[12] The expected value of perfect information is computed by the following formula:

$$\sum_{y \epsilon Y} \left\{ \max_{x \epsilon X} U(y, x) \right\} P(y) - E(U|x^*). \tag{7.3}$$

For elaboration see Demski, *op. cit.*, pp. 13–17.

[13] The expected utility value of perfect information is still

$$500 \times .95 + 200 \times .05 = 485 \text{ units.}$$

However, the expected utility value of the "grant" decision (which is still the maximum expected utility action) is

$$500 \times .95 + (-5,000) \times .05 = 225 \text{ units.}$$

Therefore, the net expected value of the clairvoyant's message is

$$485 - 225 = 260 \text{ utility units.}$$

dicts a widespread belief that information systems can be selected solely on the basis of their ability to predict economic events:

> A prediction can be made without making a decision, but a decision cannot be made without, at least implicitly, making a prediction. In a world where little is known about the decision models, evaluating alternative accounting measures in terms of their predictive ability is an appealing idea, because it requires a lower level of specificity regarding the decision model.[14]

Thus, it is argued, the optimal information system is the one that consistently leads to the most precise predictions regardless of the decision model used. However, it can be shown that the information system having the lowest relative prediction error is not necessarily the one that will maximize the decision maker's expected utility.[15] Consequently, the design and selection of financial statement information systems cannot be made without direct reference to a decision model.

Consider again the example of a financial analyst designing a model for the estimation of β values. To evaluate the relative performance of several alternative models and choose the optimal one, the analyst must obtain the utility function of the decision maker. He will then use his various models for β estimation to select portfolios and will rank the models according to the values of the decision maker's utility. Such a test can be performed on actual (historical) security prices or on simulated data.[16]

Traditional financial statement information systems, such as ratio indexes, were usually developed without reference to specific decision models. At best, reference was made to some general and vague objective (e.g., that the information provided by the current ratio be useful for solvency evaluation). The preceding discussion indicates that there is no way to design financial statement tools and systems in a vacuum; the analyst must specify the decision model before performing the financial analysis.

SUMMARY

Financial statement analysis is an information-processing system designed to provide data for decision makers. The role of information

---

[14] W. H. Beaver, J. W. Kennelly, and W. H. Voss, "Predictive Ability as a Criterion for the Evaluation of Accounting Data," *The Accounting Review*, 43 (October 1968), 680.

[15] Demski, *op. cit.*, pp. 120–23, provides an example where a decision maker who is offered two prediction models will choose the one with the *larger* prediction error, because it maximizes his expected utility value.

[16] More on the role of financial statement analysis for portfolio decision in Chapter 13.

systems in decision making depends on the state of the model specification. In perfectly specified models, the role of information is limited to probability revisions. In simplified (imperfectly specified) models, information might change the entire structure of the model; the construction and verification of the model depend on the information obtained. Since in most financial decision areas no satisfactory models exist, financial analysts must actively participate in the process of model construction. Financial statement analysis can develop only as an integral part of financial decision making. In areas where reasonably well-specified models exist, notably the portfolio decision, the role of the financial analyst is to provide the model's input requirement in the most efficient (least cost) manner.

CHAPTER EIGHT

The Prediction
of Corporate Earnings
and Growth Rates

There appears to be a consensus among theoreticians as well as practitioners that a firm's future earnings constitute a major determinant of its current stock values. As will be shown below, both theoretical and practical stock valuation models generally incorporate anticipated earnings among the major explanatory variables. Given the importance of future corporate earnings in investment analysis, it seems warranted to examine the relationship between various aspects of the earnings prediction problem and financial statement analysis. The chapter opens with a background discussion concerning the role of anticipated earnings in capital assets valuation models. Next the relative predictability of various accounting income concepts is empirically examined, followed by an evaluation of the usefulness of interim (quarterly) reports for the prediction of annual earnings. The statistical characteristics of the process that generates earnings are then examined and inferences drawn for the optimal prediction of earnings.

BACKGROUND: EARNINGS AND CAPITAL VALUES

The strong relationship between anticipated earnings and capital values is among the few phenomena on which economists reached a consensus. As to the direction of this relationship, Irving Fisher stated, "Capital in the sense of capital value is simply future income discounted, in other words, capitalized. . . . The value of capital must be computed from the value of its estimated future net income, not vice versa." [1]

The precise relationship between capital values and anticipated earnings is most clearly seen in the context of the simple perfect certainty model, in which all real assets are assumed to yield uniform, known income streams in perpetuity, and in which the market interest rate, r, is given and remains constant over time. Under these conditions, it can easily be shown that the equilibrium current market value, V, of any capital asset is simply the present value of the perpetual earnings stream of x dollars per period:

$$V = \frac{1}{r} x. \tag{8.1}$$

Relaxation of the perfect certainty assumption obviously complicates the situation, yet the basic relationship between anticipated earnings and capital values still prevails:

> . . . if we retain the assumptions of perpetual streams, rational investor behavior, perfect markets, no taxes (and no "growth" in the sense to be more precisely defined later), then an analog of the certainty valuation formula does carry through to the case of uncertainty. In particular, if we restrict attention to what we have called a "risk equivalent class" of firms, then the equilibrium market valuation of any firm in such a class can be expressed as
>
> $$V = \frac{1}{\rho_k} \bar{x} \text{ for all firms in class } k$$
>
> where V is the the sum of the market values of all the firm's securities; $\bar{x}$ is the *expected* level of average annual earnings generated by the assets it currently holds; and where $1/\rho_k$ can be interpreted as the market's capitalization rate for the expected value of uncertain, pure equity earnings streams of the type characteristic of class k.[2]

Moving closer to reality by a further relaxation of assumptions complicates the relationship even more, as evidenced by the wide variety of stock valuation models advanced in the economics and finance literature. These models differ in their underlying assumptions, structure, and empirical validity, yet they share a common and basic feature—the

[1] I. Fisher, *The Theory of Interest* (New York: A. M. Kelley, Reprint of Economic Classics, 1965), pp. 12, 14.

[2] M. H. Miller and F. Modigliani, "Some Estimates of the Cost of Capital to the Electric Utility Industry, 1954–57," *American Economic Review*, 56 (June 1966), 337.

presence of an anticipated earnings surrogate among the explanatory variables. Following are several examples of stock valuation models which gained some recognition in the theory and practice of finance.

1. *The Value Line Ratings* constitute one of the early attempts to apply a scientific approach to practical stock valuation.[3] The objective is to predict the intrinsic ("true") value of a stock for the next twelve months. The usefulness of such a prediction rests, of course, on the assumption that actual market prices converge to intrinsic values, otherwise there is nothing to be gained from knowledge of the latter. The Value Line prediction is based on a time-series regression model including the following explanatory variables: the current year's average stock price, the estimated next year's dividends and earnings-per-share, and a "market sentiment" index based on the average annual yields of some fifty stocks.[4]

2. *The Whitbeck-Kisor Model*[5] predicts price-earnings ratios of common stocks by a cross-sectional linear regression model based on the following variables: the anticipated earnings-per-share growth rates, a measure of risk,[6] and the expected dividend payout ratio. The values of the anticipated variables are provided by security analysts based upon their appraisal of historical data and current firm and market conditions. Price-earnings ratios are based on "normalized" earnings, that is, "that level of net income which would currently prevail if the economy as a whole were experiencing mid-cyclical business conditions."[7] Predicted prices are then compared with actual prices to identify undervalued or overvalued stocks.[8]

---

[3] The first ratings appeared in 1937. The *Value Line Investment Survey* publishes three major ratings on some 1,100 stocks: the *quality grade*, which indicates the assurance with which the investor may expect dividend-paying ability to be maintained in the indefinite future; the *appreciation potentiality*, which indicates the relative appreciation that may be reasonably expected in the next three to five years; and the *probable market performance* (the Value Line Rating), which is the average price during a twelve-month period that is statistically determined to be normal or "right."

[4] For elaboration on the Value Line Ratings, see A. Bernhard, *The Evaluation of Common Stocks* (New York: Simon and Schuster, Inc., 1959). The Value Line predictions were found in a recent study to be quite successful; see F. Black, "Yes, Virginia, There Is Hope: Tests of the Value Line Ranking System," Paper presented at the Seminar on the Analysis of Security Prices, University of Chicago, May 1971.

[5] V. S. Whitbeck and M. Kisor, Jr., "A New Tool in Investment Decision-Making," *Financial Analysts Journal*, 19 (May–June 1963), 55–62.

[6] Risk is measured by the standard deviation of the firm's earnings.

[7] Whitbeck and Kisor, *op. cit.*, p. 56.

[8] For a somewhat similar valuation model, see D. M. Ahlers, "SEM: A Security Evaluation Model," in *Analytical Methods in Banking*, K. J. Cohen and F. S. Hammer, eds. (Homewood, Ill.: Richard D. Irwin, Inc., 1966), pp. 305–36.

3. *The Gordon Model*[9] predicts the value of a share on the basis of four variables: the current earnings, the firm's retention or investment rate, the rate of return on investments, and the rate of profit investors require on the share. The second and third variables (firm's investment rate and return on investment) reflect the firm's anticipated earnings.

4. *The Malkiel Model*[10] postulates that the price-earnings ratio is a function of the earnings growth rate and the dividend payout ratio. Both earnings and dividends are assumed to grow at a constant rate, and the discount rate is identical for all securities.

The preceding models dealt with uncertainty in a rather implicit and indirect manner, usually by discounting the expected value of returns by some risk-adjusted rate (e.g., Modigliani and Miller's ρ_k) or by incorporating a risk surrogate (e.g., past earnings variability). However, the situation in an uncertain environment is much more complicated; future earnings can, at best, be estimated in the form of probability distributions for which investors may have different preferences. Specifically, in making their portfolio decisions, investors will usually consider several characteristics of the probability distributions on earnings, such as the variance, and possibly even higher moments in addition to the mean (expected value). It is clear, therefore, that under these circumstances stock valuation cannot simply be described by a discounting process of the expected values of future earnings. The Sharpe-Lintner capital asset pricing model,[11] based on portfolio theory principles, is at present the most advanced attempt to deal explicitly with the uncertainty issue. Investors are assumed to act on the basis of predictions about the future performance of securities stated in terms of expected returns, standard deviations, and correlation coefficients of returns. Although the model's assumptions are highly restrictive, its major implications seem to be consistent with investor behavior.

Summarizing, a brief survey of valuation models revealed that anticipated earnings constitute a major explanatory variable of capital asset prices.[12] The various aspects of earnings prediction, to be discussed in this chapter, are therefore of major importance for investment decision making.

9 M. J. Gordon, *The Investment, Financing and Valuation of the Corporation* (Homewood, Ill.: Richard D. Irwin, Inc., 1962), Chap. 4.

10 B. G. Malkiel, "Equity Yields, Growth, and the Structure of Share Prices," *American Economic Review*, 53 (December 1963), 1004–31.

11 W. F. Sharpe, *Portfolio Theory and Capital Markets* (New York: McGraw-Hill Book Company, 1970), Chap. 5. This model is discussed below in Chapter 12.

12 Empirical evidence on the relationship between stock prices and earnings changes is quite convincing; for a summary, see R. A. Brealey, *An Introduction to Risk and Return from Common Stocks* (Cambridge, Mass.: M.I.T. Press, 1969), Chap. 7.

THE RELATIVE PREDICTABILITY OF VARIOUS
EARNINGS CONCEPTS

Accountants commonly regard the facilitation of earnings prediction as one of their major tasks:

> Almost all external users of financial information reported by profit-oriented firms are involved in efforts to predict the earnings of the firm for some future period. . . . The past earnings of the firm are considered to be the most important single item of information relevant to the prediction of future earnings. It follows from this that past earnings should be measured and disclosed in such a manner as to give the user as much aid as practicable in efforts to make this prediction with a minimum of uncertainty.[13]

Stated differently, given that corporate earnings can be measured in various ways by using alternative accounting techniques, the accountant should choose the specific measurement procedure that yields the most accurately predictable earnings series, thereby facilitating investment decision making. The question then is, Which measurement procedure yields such "optimal" earnings series?

Frank examined the question whether traditionally calculated accounting income or a measure incorporating current costs is more useful for predictive purposes.[14] The former income concept is based on historical costs while the latter is calculated by subtracting from revenues, which are already measured in current dollars, the replacement costs of goods and services used to provide those revenues.[15] The difference between the current and historical costs of goods and services is the amount of holding gains or losses realized during the period.[16] It has frequently been suggested (on a priori grounds) that current-cost operating income, excluding capital gains or losses, will be more accurately predictable than historical-cost income, since it abstracts from the nonrecurring consequences of holding assets.[17]

---

[13] *A Statement of Basic Accounting Theory* (Evanston, Ill.: American Accounting Association, 1966), pp. 23–24.

[14] W. Frank, "A Study of the Predictive Significance of Two Income Measures," *Journal of Accounting Research,* 7 (Spring 1969), 123–36.

[15] For elaboration and numerical examples of this procedure, see E. O. Edwards and P. W. Bell, *The Theory and Measurement of Business Income* (Berkeley: University of California Press, 1961), pp. 90–94.

[16] As discussed in Chapter 6, the profit-making activities of the firm can be divided into those that yield a profit by combining or transforming factors of production to final products, and those that yield a gain because the prices of assets rise or those of liabilities fall. The latter profit (loss) results from *holding* assets or liabilities and is accordingly termed a holding gain (loss).

[17] See, for example, Edwards and Bell, *op. cit.,* p. 99, and Committee on Concepts and Standards—Long-Lived Assets, "Accounting for Land, Building and Equipment," *The Accounting Review,* 39 (July 1964), 696.

Frank's sample was comprised of seventy-six firms operating in six industries. Each firm's cost of goods sold and depreciation expenses were restated in terms of current-year dollars (by using specific price indexes) to obtain an estimate of current-cost operating income. Two forecasting models were used to evaluate the relative predictability of the alternative income measures: a linear regression model and a moving average (smoothing) model. Of the nineteen years of data available for each firm, the first fourteen years were used to determine the parameters of the forecasting model and forecasts were made for the last five years. The two income series (historical and current-operating income) were used as inputs in the forecasting models, and the predictions were then compared with the actual income values to determine the prediction errors.

Surprisingly, results for both prediction models showed that the forecast errors of historical income were somewhat smaller than those of current income. This difference was statistically significant only for some of the sampled industries. Thus, contrary to common belief, no clear advantage in predictability seemed to exist for current-cost income.

Simmons and Gray examined a similar question by using the simulation technique.[18] They argued that in this case simulation of hypothetical data is preferable to using actual data, since

> insufficient information concerning asset acquisition dates, accounting methods used, and similar essential information tends to force arbitrary adjustments. In using actual data one is also limited to the events which actually occurred.[19]

The predictability of three income concepts based on historical cost, general price-level adjusted cost, and replacement cost was examined. A straight-line extrapolation was used to perform the forecasts. Several conditions, such as price levels, selling prices, inventory costs, and sales volume, were assumed to change during the period examined. Simulation results indicated that differences in predictability among the various income concepts were negligible. In some cases price-level adjusted income had a slight edge over historical- and replacement-cost income, while in other cases the ranking was reversed. No general superiority of one income concept was established.

Summarizing, results of both studies discussed above did not lend

---

[18] J. K. Simmons and J. Gray, "An Investigation of the Effect of Differing Accounting Frameworks on the Prediction of Net Income," *The Accounting Review*, 44 (October 1969), 757–76.

[19] *Ibid.*, p. 758. Note, however, that simulation studies are also quite restricted, since it is difficult to generalize results beyond the conditions assumed in the simulation process.

support to the frequent contention that current-cost income series can be predicted more accurately than income series based on historical costs. The predictability of the various income concepts examined was found to be quite similar. Note, however, that the above tests were aimed at determining which income concept best predicts *its own* future values. No attempt was made to tackle the broader question concerning the construction of prediction models incorporating, in addition to past earnings, other variables relevant to income prediction (e.g., current capital expenditures). The second important question left unanswered by the above studies is the *relevance* of the predicted series to potential users.[20] It was pointed out in the preceding chapter that predictability cannot serve as the sole criterion for preferring one information system over another. Reference must be made to the specific use (decision model) for which the information is required. Thus, the relevance, or usefulness, of the various income concepts to decision makers should be determined *before* predictability is examined. As a hypothetical example, suppose that a firm, by using various measurement procedures, reports a constant earnings series. Such a series will be perfectly predictable yet will bear no relevance to investors' needs.

THE PREDICTIVE POWER OF INTERIM REPORTS

The major purpose of interim (e.g., quarterly) reports is to provide more timely information than annual reports. The publication of interim reports has been required of most companies listed on the New York Stock Exchange since 1910 and of companies under the jurisdiction of the Securities and Exchange Commission since 1946. In 1962, the American Stock Exchange revised its listing agreements to include a requirement for the publication of quarterly reports. The Securities Act Amendment of 1964 has extended the interim-reporting requirement to over-the-counter companies with at least five hundred stockholders. However, most firms were quite reluctant to publish interim reports despite the persistent demand. The main arguments against publication concerned the additional costs involved and the computational difficulties inherent in short-term reporting. Specifically, the shorter the reporting period, the more severe the problems involved in matching the fixed costs (e.g., depreciation) with revenues, particularly when demand fluctuates sea-

---

[20] For elaboration, see J. G. Louderback, III, "Projectability as a Criterion for Income Determination Methods," *The Accounting Review*, 46 (April 1971), 298–305; and L. Revsine, "Predictive Ability, Market Prices, and Operating Flows," *The Accounting Review*, 46 (July 1971), 480–89.

sonally.[21] Despite this opposition, however, the publication of interim reports is at present a common procedure for publicly held corporations.

Given the current prevalence of interim reports and the argument concerning their merits, it seems warranted to determine their usefulness to decision makers. Green and Segall were probably the first to examine this question by testing the usefulness of 1964 first-quarter earnings-per-share (EPS) reports in predicting annual EPS.[22] The sample consisted of forty-six randomly selected companies listed on the New York Stock Exchange. Several naïve (i.e., based on the historical series) extrapolation models were employed to compare annual EPS forecasts that used the first-quarter reports with forecasts that did not use the interim report information. Results were rather surprising: forecasts using the interim report information were not found to be superior to those that did not incorporate this information. These results obviously run counter to intuition, since the former (i.e., forecasts using the interim report information) are predicting only the last nine months of the year, while the latter are predicting the full twelve months. The additional information (conveyed by the interim reports) can at worst be useless, but it is difficult to conceive how it can have an adverse effect on the prediction.[23]

These puzzling results led Green and Segall to replicate their study by adding the year 1965 to the original sample and increasing the sample size.[24] Results, however, were found to be consistent with the original study:

> We see no reason to modify the weasel-like conclusion of the original paper, "First-quarter reports as presently prepared are of little help in forecasting EPS." [25]

Green and Segall's findings prompted Brown and Niederhoffer to reinvestigate the usefulness of interim reports.[26] They used a sample of

[21] For a discussion of measurement problems involved in interim reporting, see D. Green, Jr., "Towards a Theory of Interim Reports," *Journal of Accounting Research*, 2 (Spring 1963), 35–49. Also R. G. Taylor, "An Examination of the Evaluation, Content, Utility and Problems of Published Interim Reports" (Ph.D. dissertation, Graduate School of Business, University of Chicago, 1963).

[22] D. Green, Jr., and J. Segall, "The Predictive Power of First-Quarter Earnings Reports," *Journal of Business,* 40 (January 1967), 44–55.

[23] Cohen and Zinbarg argue analogously, "But if data for the first two quarters already are available at the time of analysis, an estimate for the full year usually can be made quite readily." *Investment Analysis and Portfolio Management* (Homewood, Ill.: Richard D. Irwin, Inc., 1967), p. 250.

[24] D. Green, Jr., and J. Segall, "The Predictive Power of First-Quarter Earnings Reports: A Replication," *Empirical Research in Accounting: Selected Studies, 1966,* Supplement to Vol. 4, *Journal of Accounting Research,* 21–43.

[25] *Ibid.,* p. 36.

[26] P. Brown and V. Niederhoffer, "The Predictive Content of Quarterly Earnings," *Journal of Business,* 41 (October 1968), 488–97.

519 firms for the years 1962–65, drawn from Standard and Poor's Compustat tape. The tests employed were similar to those of Green and Segall: naïve predictions of annual earnings based on the information contained in both the interim and annual reports were compared with predictions that did not incorporate the interim report information. Prediction errors were then compared to determine the usefulness of interim reports. Test results revealed that

> on the basis of predictions made at the end of the first quarter the interim predictors as a group generally were superior to the annuals as a group. In addition, the best of the interim predictors was consistently better than the best of the annuals. Further improvements came with the release of each additional quarterly report.[27]

Brown and Niederhoffer, therefore, concluded that interim reports as currently published are useful in predicting annual earnings, and that predictability improved with each new report. In evaluating Brown and Niederhoffer's results it should be noted that they examined a substantially larger sample, longer time period, and more prediction models than Green and Segall.

Coates also tested the relative performance of various earnings prediction models with and without the interim report information.[28] The sample consisted of twenty-seven firms listed on the New York Stock Exchange and covered the period 1945–66. Results were consistent with those of Brown and Niederhoffer; regardless of the prediction model chosen, the effect of incorporating consecutive quarterly reports in the forecasts was to decrease the uncertainty (prediction errors) about the future outcome of annual reports.[29] Brown and Kennelly,[30] using the residual analysis method [31] aimed at examining the effect of public announcements on stock prices, found that quarterly earnings improved the prediction of annual earnings by at least 30 to 40 percent. Reilly *et al.* examined the predictability of various interim report items on a

---

[27] *Ibid.*, p. 496.

[28] R. Coates, "The Predictive Content of Interim Reports—A Time Series Analysis," *Empirical Research in Accounting: Selected Studies 1972,* Supplement to Vol. 10, *Journal of Accounting Research.*

[29] One feature in Coates's study differs from its predecessors and deserves special attention. For each sampled firm, he selected the *most appropriate* prediction model from a set of naïve models. Thus, for each firm, a particular, optimal model was chosen to accommodate the specific characteristics of the firm's earnings-generating process. Adjustments were also made for seasonality in earnings through modifications of the prediction models. This was a preliminary attempt to deal with the issue of the firm's earning-generating processes, which will be discussed in the next section.

[30] P. Brown and J. W. Kennelly, "The Informational Content of Quarterly Earnings: An Extension and Some Further Evidence," *Journal of Business,* 45 (July 1972), 403–15.

[31] This method was discussed in Chapter 3.

sample of forty firms randomly drawn from the Compustat tape.[32] They concluded that the prediction of annual earnings-per-share, net profit margin, and sales improved with the inclusion of the first quarter figures of these items. Incorporation of the second quarter figures resulted in further improvement of the predictions. Most pronounced was the improvement in the quality of sales predictions as a result of the quarterly report information. Additional evidence regarding the usefulness of interim financial data for investment decisions was provided by Latané et al.[33] and by Jones and Litzenberger.[34]

Summarizing, intuition as well as casual observation indicate that interim reports are useful to investors; summaries of such reports are regularly published in daily newspapers and are carried by the stock exchange wire services; the financial press publishes articles and projections based on interim results; and some security analysts reportedly incorporate interim report information in their forecasts of annual earnings. As was seen above, most empirical results are consistent with these observations; [35] it appears that the information contained in interim reports can be used to improve the prediction of annual financial data.[36] Note however that here, as in the preceding section, the scope of predictability tests was rather narrow; naïve prediction models using interim report information were compared with similar models excluding this information. Rather than restricting the models to past earnings data, the approach should have been to construct general earnings prediction models incorporating accounting as well as nonaccounting data and examine the improvement in the models' performance when the interim report information is incorporated. However, a necessary first step in the design of such comprehensive models involves the determination of the statistical nature of the process generating earnings to which we now turn.

[32] F. K. Reilly, D. L. Morgenson, and M. West, "The Predictive Ability of Alternative Parts of Interim Financial Statements," *Empirical Research in Accounting: Selected Studies 1972,* Supplement to Vol. 10, *Journal of Accounting Research.*

[33] H. A. Latané, D. L. Tuttle, and C. P. Jones, "E/P Ratios v. Changes in Earnings in Forecasting Future Price Changes," *Financial Analysts Journal,* 25 (January–February 1969), 117–23.

[34] C. P. Jones and R. H. Litzenberger, "Quarterly Earnings Reports and Intermediate Stock Price Trends," *Journal of Finance,* 25 (March 1970), 143–48.

[35] Note, however, that most studies used the Compustat tape data; hence, test results are to some extent replication rather than independent confirmation.

[36] For additional arguments regarding the interpretation of empirical results, see D. Green, Jr., and J. Segall, "Brickbats and Straw Men: A Reply to Brown and Niederhoffer," *Journal of Business,* 41 (October 1968), 498–502; V. Niederhoffer, "The Predictive Content of First Quarter Earnings Reports," *Journal of Business,* 43 (January 1970), 60–62; D. Green, Jr., and J. Segall, "Return of Strawman," *ibid.,* pp. 63–65; T. L. Holton and G. A. Welsch, discussions of D. Green, Jr., and J. Segall, "The Predictive Power of First-Quarter Earnings Reports: A Replication," *op. cit.,* pp. 37–39 and 40–43.

THE TIME-SERIES BEHAVIOR OF CORPORATE
EARNINGS AND GROWTH RATES

Determination of the statistical behavior of the process that generates corporate earnings is imperative to the construction of models designed to predict earnings. Since different forecasting models should be used for different processes, knowledge of the actual generating process will indicate the optimal forecasting model(s) to be used for predicting earnings series. The empirical studies on the usefulness of interim reports summarized above demonstrate the consequences of ignoring the behavior of earnings series; despite the large number of forecasting models used in each study, conclusions are at best tentative, since

> it is possible to continue creating imaginary situations in which other predictors could be expected to do best, but there is little advantage to be gained by doing so. *It clearly depends on the nature of the earnings process* (and the accountant's interpretation of it), a process that is yet to be studied rigorously.[37]

Thus, unless the specific earnings-generating process is identified, the researcher cannot determine the optimal forecasting model to be applied to the series, and hence no definite conclusions about the usefulness of data can be drawn from the relative performance of even a large number of models tested. Determination of the statistical behavior of the earnings-generating process is therefore imperative both to accountants concerned with the impact of alternative accounting techniques on investment decisions and to security analysts involved in the prediction of earnings for capital assets valuation.

A. Some possible earnings-generating processes

Since so little is known about the statistical properties of corporate earnings series, it seems appropriate to consider a broad range of well-known statistical processes as candidates for characterizing earnings behavior. Given the set of alternatives, the extent of fit of each process to actual earnings series can be empirically determined and the statistical behavior of corporate earnings thus characterized.

A possible earnings-generating process, which probably accords with the intuition of some accountants and financial analysts, is the *constant expectation,* or *mean-reverting,* process, implying that periodic earnings, Y_t, is a random variable whose expectation (i.e., mean value) remains constant over time. Specifically, suppose that the behavior of earnings is described by the following process:

$$\tilde{Y}_t = \mu + \tilde{u}_t, \tag{8.2}$$

[37] Brown and Niederhoffer, *op. cit.,* p. 490, emphasis supplied.

where μ is the expected value of earnings and $\tilde{u}_t$ is a random disturbance term (i.e., unexpected earnings) having a zero expected value,[38] $E(\tilde{u}_t) = 0$, constant variance, $\sigma^2(\tilde{u}_t) = \sigma^2$, and is serially independent, $\sigma(\tilde{u}_t, \tilde{u}_s) = 0$ for all t and $s \neq t$.[39]

Expression (8.2) implies that the expected value of earnings in period t, $E(Y_t)$ (the expectation made, of course, prior to t), is equal to the constant value μ. In other words, average periodic earnings are expected to be stable over the long run at the level of μ. When earnings expectation is constant over time, actual earnings will tend to *revert* to the mean; specifically, earnings that are in a given period higher than the mean will, on the average, be followed by lower earnings, and vice versa. The tendency of actual earnings to revert to the mean from either side results in a negative dependency in the time series of *earnings changes*.[40] Thus, for example, when earnings in a given period have increased to an extraordinarily high level relative to average earnings because of, say, some nonrecurring income items, one would expect a decline in the following period's earnings. Thus, positive earnings changes will, on average, be followed more frequently by negative changes than by positive ones, and vice versa. Figure 8.1 presents a hypothetical case of a firm whose earnings are generated by a constant expectation process. The firm's earnings-change in period t (relative to $t - 1$) is measured on the horizontal axis, while the earnings-change in the succeeding period, $t + 1$ (relative to t), is measured on the vertical axis. Each observation depicts the experience of two successive periods (e.g., changes in 1960/61 and 1961/62, etc.). Recall that in the constant expectation case positive changes (increases) in period t will tend to be followed by negative changes (decreases) in $t + 1$, and vice versa; hence the generally negative relationship presented in Figure 8.1.

A more general and probably more intuitively appealing version of the mean reverting process is one in which the expectation is a deterministic (known) function of time. The behavior of earnings will be described in this case by

$$\tilde{Y}_t = \mu_t + \tilde{u}_t, \tag{8.5}$$

---

[38] The tildes denote random variables.

[39] The process (8.2) is a special case of the mean-reverting process. There exist, for example, mean-reverting processes where the disturbance term, $\tilde{u}_t$, is serially correlated, i.e., $\sigma(\tilde{u}_t, \tilde{u}_s) \neq 0$.

[40] This means that the first order serial correlation coefficient, ρ, of the first differences (changes) in the series will be negative:

$$\rho[(Y_{t+1} - Y_t), (Y_t - Y_{t-1})] < 0. \tag{8.3}$$

The first order serial correlation of the original series will be zero:

$$\rho(Y_t, Y_s) = 0, \text{ for } s \neq t. \tag{8.4}$$

Higher order correlations for both the original series and the first differences will also be zero.

and the expected value of earnings, $E(\tilde{Y}_t)$, will be equal to the mean, μ_t.[41] The expectation function, μ_t, may take various mathematical forms, such as linear (e.g., $\mu_t = 5 + .2t$, indicating that the expected value of earnings-per-share is $5 plus an increase of $.20 in each period) and curvilinear (e.g., $\mu_t = 3 + .15t^2$, indicating that the periodic growth, $.15, is annually compounded). The conventional characterization of some firms as "growth" or "decline" companies probably refers to the situations where expected earnings are believed to be a function of time; increases in one period are likely to be followed by increases in the subsequent period, and vice versa. Thus, when the expectation of earnings is a known function of time, earnings-changes will tend to be followed by changes of the *same* sign, as shown in Figure 8.2. However, the first order serial correlation of earnings changes will be negative, since the *deviations* of earnings from the trend line (i.e., the changing mean) will behave as a mean-reverting process. In other words, a positive deviation from the trend line in period t will be followed more frequently by a negative deviation than by a positive one. Thus, while earnings changes will usually follow the same sign, deviations from the mean (depicted by the correlation coefficient) will usually follow the opposite sign.

Both processes, the constant expectation and the expectation that is a function of time, are thus characterized by negative first order serial correlation which, of course, reflects the mean-reverting nature of the processes. To distinguish between the two processes, the mean of the first differences (changes) of the earnings series should be examined; if the process is characterized by a constant expectation, the mean of the first differences will be zero, whereas in a process characterized by an expectation that is a deterministic function of time, the mean of the first difference in earnings will be nonzero.[42]

Both mean-reverting processes described above will generate a *dependent* (serially correlated) time series of earnings changes. There are, however, various processes known as *martingales,* which will generate *independent* series of earnings changes. The main characteristic of a martingale process is that the expectation changes randomly from

---

[41] The process described by (8.2) is, of course, a special case of (8.5) where $\mu_t = \mu$ for all t.

[42] In the constant expectation process (8.2), the first difference will be

$$\Delta\tilde{Y}_t = \tilde{Y}_t - \tilde{Y}_{t-1} = \tilde{u}_t - \tilde{u}_{t-1}. \tag{8.6}$$

The expectation (mean) of (8.6) is

$$E(\Delta\tilde{Y}_t) = E(\tilde{u}_t - \tilde{u}_{t-1}) = 0. \tag{8.7}$$

In an expectation that is a deterministic function of time (8.5), the first difference is

$$\Delta\tilde{Y}_t = \tilde{Y}_t - \tilde{Y}_{t-1} = \mu_t - \mu_{t-1} + \tilde{u}_t - \tilde{u}_{t-1}, \text{ and} \tag{8.8}$$

$$E(\Delta\tilde{Y}_t) = \mu_t - \mu_{t-1} \neq 0. \tag{8.9}$$

The mean of the first differences in earnings will thus equal the change in the means of the process which in general will not equal zero.

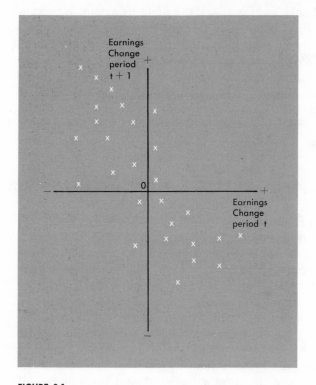

FIGURE 8.1

Hypothetical earnings changes generated by a constant expectation process

period to period.[43] For such a process, the expected value of next period's earnings is equal to the realized value of the recent period's earnings:

$$\tilde{Y}_t = \mu_t + \tilde{u}_t,$$

and

$$\mu_t = Y_{t-1}; \qquad (8.10)$$

therefore,

$$E(\tilde{Y}_t) = Y_{t-1}.$$

Earnings changes generated by a martingale process will be statistically independent over time, that is, behave as a series of random numbers.[44]

---

[43] Such processes, which seem to characterize stock price behavior, are usually referred to in the popular finance literature as *random walks*. A random walk is, in fact, a special case of the martingale process. For elaboration, see Chapter 14.

[44] The first order serial correlation coefficient of the first differences in the earnings series will be zero:

$$\rho[(Y_{t+1} - Y_t), (Y_t - Y_{t-1})] = 0.$$

The first order correlation of the original series (levels) of earnings will be positive.

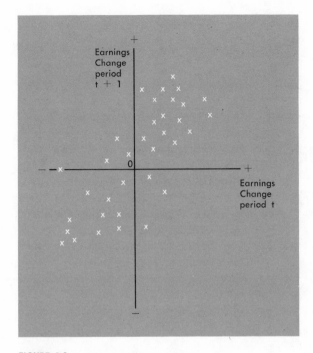

FIGURE 8.2

Hypothetical earnings changes generated by a process whose expectation is a deterministic function of time

Stated differently, no systematic patterns or trends will be revealed by the series of earnings changes. Figure 8.3 presents a hypothetical scatter diagram of earnings changes generated by a martingale process; the observations are scattered all over the space, indicating no systematic relationship between consecutive pairs of earnings changes.

It is possible for a martingale process to be combined with (superimposed on) a systematic trend, or drift. Such a process is known as a *submartingale* and might be caused by various factors, such as a general, economy-wide increase in corporate earnings or a constant decrease in the purchasing power of money (i.e., an increase in nominal earnings). When the systematic trend is positive, the expected value of next period's earnings will be larger than or equal to recent earnings:

$$E(\tilde{Y}_t) \geq Y_{t-1}, \text{ for all } t. \tag{8.11}$$

Note that despite the systematic trend factor, the first order serial correlation of the submartingale process will be zero. Thus, the two martingale processes (characterized by zero serial correlation) can be distinguished from the two mean-reverting processes (negative serial

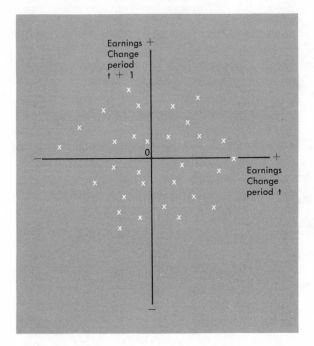

FIGURE 8.3

Hypothetical earnings changes generated by a martingale process

correlation). To distinguish between the martingale process and the sub-martingale process, the mean of the first differences (changes) of earnings must be examined; in the former process the mean will be zero while in the latter it will be nonzero, reflecting the trend (drift).

The distinction among the various processes discussed above may be clarified further by considering the implications for earnings prediction. If earnings were generated by a constant expectation process (8.2) or by a process whose expectation was a deterministic function of time (8.5), then past earnings data would be very useful for the prediction of future earnings. Specifically, the historical series of earnings can be used to estimate (e.g., by regression analysis) the constant expectation or the function of the expectation and thereby predict future earnings. However, if earnings were generated by a martingale process (8.10), the series of past observations would be *irrelevant* for the prediction of future earnings; the best estimate of next period's earnings would be the most recently realized earnings. The irrelevance of past earnings for prediction purposes is implied, of course, by the statistical independence of earnings changes, just as the historical record of tossing a fair coin is irrelevant for the prediction of a future toss. When earnings are generated by a submartingale process (8.11), past earnings will be useful for the prediction of the trend, or drift factor.[45] It is thus obvious that the identification of the statistical process actually generating corporate earnings is crucial for the construction of prediction models.

B. The evidence

The first study on the time-series behavior of corporate earnings was probably performed by Little [46] and pursued by Little and Rayner.[47] Results of correlating annual growth rates of earnings-per-share of 529 British firms indicated a substantial amount of randomness; most of the EPS correlation coefficients were very small, and negative correlations outnumbered the positive ones. These findings were alleged by the authors to challenge the fashionable doctrine that companies that had experienced above-average earnings growth in the past were likely to do so again in the future (i.e., "growth breeds growth"), since in a martingale process earnings growth can be expected to occur as frequently as a decline. However, as was shown above, a zero serial correlation of earnings changes is also consistent with a submartingale process where the random changes are superimposed on a positive growth trend (drift).[48] Consequently, the evidence on zero serial correlation of earnings changes does not preclude by itself the existence of growth companies.[49]

A study of earnings behavior in the U.S. yielded similar results to those of Little and Rayner. Lintner and Glauber examined the serial correlation of growth rates in sales, operating income, earnings before taxes, and earnings-per-share of 309 corporations listed on the Compustat tape, for the period 1946–65.[50] The degree of dependence between successive growth rates of the various series was found to be very small, yet the authors cautioned against any sweeping conclusions:

[45] For an empirical estimation of the drift term from past data, see R. Ball, B. Lev, and R. Watts, "Income Changes and Balance Sheet Compositions," *Journal of Accounting Research,* 11 (Autumn 1973).

[46] I. M. D. Little, "Higgledy Piggledy Growth," *Bulletin of the Oxford University Institute of Economics and Statistics,* 24, No. 4 (November 1962), 389–412.

[47] I. M. D. Little and A. C. Rayner, *Higgledy Piggledy Growth Again* (Oxford, U.K.: Basil Blackwell, 1966).

[48] As will be seen below, this is probably the process characterizing the earnings behavior of U.S. firms.

[49] Little and Rayner's conclusion (*op. cit.,* p. 64) that ". . . managements do not remain above or below average for very long" is even more questionable. Indeed, it can be argued that a firm's management is consistently "above average" if it succeeds in maintaining the *level* of earnings (as opposed to earnings changes) above the industry average.

[50] J. Lintner and R. Glauber, "Higgledy Piggledy Growth in America?" Paper presented at the Seminar on the Analysis of Security Prices, Graduate School of Business, University of Chicago, May 11–12, 1967.

". . . indeed any conclusion to the effect that nothing but a table of random numbers is relevant to growth in the real world would itself be premature and unwise." [51] Trent analyzed the growth rates of three ratios (earnings-per-share, return on common equity, and return on total capital) and two absolute measures (sales and common equity) for 459 U.S. firms during 1946–65.[52] The correlations between successive growth rates were again found to be very small and, in most cases, were statistically insignificant.

Brealey joined the "random walkers" by reporting that correlation coefficients of successive earnings changes of 700 U.S. firms for the period 1951–64 were very small.[53] However, a close examination of results revealed some systematic, though slight, deviations from randomness; in almost all the tests the correlation coefficients were found to be negative, as would be expected for a mean-reverting process. Runs tests [54] confirmed these results: ". . . a good year or succession of good years were more frequently followed by a poor year, and vice versa." [55] Beaver examined the time-series behavior of three rates of return measures: [56] the market rate of return,[57] earnings-per-share divided by the price-per-share at the beginning of the period (i.e., the reciprocal of the PE ratio), and earnings-per-share divided by net worth-per-share. Note that the first rate of return measure is a purely market-determined variable, the second incorporates accounting and market data, while the third is a purely accounting measure. In addition to the three rates of return, the time-series behavior of net income available to common stockholders was examined. The sample consisted of 57 firms randomly selected from those listed on the New York Stock Exchange. Serial correlation analysis and runs tests indicated a substantial negative dependence between successive return changes, suggesting that the three rates of return series behave as if generated by a mean-reverting process. The behavior of

---

[51] *Ibid.*, p. 18.

[52] R. H. Trent, "Corporate Growth Rates: An Analysis of Their Intertemporal Association," *Southern Journal of Business,* 4 (October 1969), 196–210.

[53] Brealey, *op cit.*, Chap. 8.

[54] A runs test, concentrating on the number and length of runs (e.g., a cluster of positive earnings changes), is a distribution-free test of serial independence; see J. V. Bradley, *Distribution-Free Statistical Tests* (Englewood Cliffs, N.J.: Prentice-Hall, Inc., 1968), Chap. 11.

[55] Brealey, *op. cit.*, pp. 94–95. Recall that negative correlation coefficients were also predominant in earlier studies.

[56] W. H. Beaver, "The Time Series Behavior of Earnings," *Empirical Research in Accounting: Selected Studies 1970,* Supplement to Vol. 8, *Journal of Accounting Research,* 62–99.

[57] Defined as $(d_t + p_t - p_{t-1})/p_{t-1}$, where d_t = cash dividends paid in period t, p_t and p_{t-1} = stock prices at end of period and beginning of period, respectively.

the net income series conformed quite closely to that generated by a martingale process.

Ball and Watts examined the twenty-year time-series behavior of net earnings, earnings-per-share, net earnings divided by total assets, and net sales series of about 450 Compustat firms.[58] They subjected the data to conventional runs tests and serial correlation analysis and, in addition, used "partial adjustment" models to determine the extent of dependence of income expectation upon past income.[59] Results of the various tests generally indicated that earnings and earnings-per-share series follow a submartingale process characterized by independence of successive earnings changes superimposed on an upward trend. The upward trend may have been the result of a sample selection bias; Compustat firms are, on average, large and successful enterprises for which a generally increasing earnings trend is expected.

C. Possible causes for the random behavior of earnings changes

The empirical evidence summarized above appears, with some exceptions, to be consistent with the hypothesis that corporate earnings behave roughly as if generated by a martingale process.[60] Earnings behavior thus appears to be similar to that of stock prices in efficient capital markets.[61] The analogy, however, appears to stop here; whereas the random behavior of stock prices is a natural implication of market efficiency, where no single group of investors exercises a monopoly power on information, the random behavior of corporate earnings seems to run counter to accountants' as well as analysts' intuition. It is a widely held view that corporate earnings tend to fluctuate around a stable expectation, sometimes termed "normal" or "permanent" earnings. The belief in such a stable expectation manifests itself most clearly in the "income smoothing" controversy. Specifically, it has often been suggested in the accounting literature that management uses discretionary accounting techniques (e.g., the alternative methods of interperiod tax allocation) to smooth reported income, that is, to moderate

---

[58] R. Ball and R. Watts, "Some Time Series Properties of Accounting Income," *The Journal of Finance,* 27 (June 1972), 663–81.

[59] Recall that when the expectation of earnings is constant or a deterministic function of time, it will be independent of past observations. On the other hand, in a martingale process, earnings expectation is equal to, and obviously dependent on, the recently observed earnings figure.

[60] The main exception is Beaver's study. It is difficult, however, to compare Beaver's results with others, since two of his three return measures incorporated stock market prices, while other studies concentrated on accounting numbers.

[61] For elaboration on the random behavior of stock price changes, see Chapter 14.

year-to-year fluctuations by shifting earnings from peak periods to less successful ones.[62] The underlying assumption of the smoothing hypothesis appears to be the existence of a stable, normal income value toward which reported earnings are smoothed in order to decrease their variability:

> These and other sources [the smoothing literature] imply that the expectation of income is a function of time or is constant. Smoothing implies a return to good times, on average, after bad times, during which income decreases are artificially reduced by smoothing practices. It implies that many increases in income are also temporary, and can therefore be smoothed in order to avoid the impression of permanence.[63]

Recall, however, that if earnings were generated by a martingale process, the expectation would change from period to period. Thus, good times are not necessarily followed, on average, by bad times, and hence attempts to smooth income under such circumstances are of questionable effectiveness. Indeed it can be shown that for certain random processes, attempts to smooth income can have exactly the opposite (increasing variability) effect.[64]

Given the apparent widespread belief of accountants and analysts in "normal" earnings (i.e., a mean-reverting process), it is interesting to investigate the reasons for the random walk behavior that appears to characterize the series of corporate earnings.[65] The major reason for the absence of persistent trends in earnings and growth rates is probably the *competition* prevailing in most inputs and outputs markets. The higher the degree of competition, the less likely it is that earnings changes of the same sign will persist over the long run. Competition may thus lessen the tendency of good (or bad) earnings records to persist and contributes to the random behavior of earnings changes. However, since the extent of competition varies considerably among industries, additional factors probably contribute to the random behavior of earnings changes. It is well known that the earnings figure is a *residual* of the income determination process and thus may be expected to reflect most,

---

[62] For a survey of the income smoothing literature and a rigorous definition of smoothing objectives and conditions under which smoothing will be optimal from management's standpoint, see N. J. Gonedes, "Income Smoothing Behavior under Selected Stochastic Processes," *Journal of Business,* 45 (October 1972), 570–84.

[63] Ball and Watts, *op. cit.,* p. 664.

[64] Beaver, *op. cit.*

[65] The belief in "normal" earnings is also prevalent among security analysts. "Discussion with the suppliers of data [security analysts] indicated that all firms were attempting to predict the same future figure, *the long-run average* ('normalized') earnings level, abstracting from cyclical or special circumstances." J. G. Cragg and B. G. Malkiel, "The Consensus and Accuracy of Some Predictions of the Growth of Corporate Earnings," *Journal of Finance,* 23 (March 1968), 68, emphasis supplied.

if not all, of the randomness of each of the components used in its determination (e.g., sales, cost of goods sold, etc.). Discretionary changes in accounting techniques, such as shifts from one method of reporting certain types of transactions to another method, or in the treatment of nonrecurring items, may exert an additional destabilizing effect on the pattern of reported earnings. With respect to earnings-per-share data, some randomness may be caused by the short-run impact of events such as the issuance of new shares, the irregular timing of conversions of outstanding hybrid securities, and mergers. It should be admitted, however, that the preceding causes for the observed behavior of corporate earnings are, at best, speculations. At this stage there seems to be no complete explanation for the rather consistent empirical findings regarding the random behavior of earnings changes.

EVALUATION OF EVIDENCE

The central question examined in this chapter concerned the extent to which financial data improve the prediction of future earnings, which is required for investment valuation models. This question involves two major issues: (a) Given the various alternative earnings concepts, what is the specific definition most relevant for financial decisions? and (b) What is the optimal model for earnings prediction? Concerning the former question, it has been shown in Chapter 6 that the various alternative definitions of income (e.g., historical-cost income, current-cost income, cash flow income, etc.) are all approximations to the "true" income required in principle for capital assets valuation models. Since this "true" income is as yet undefined in a world of uncertainty, it is impossible to directly estimate the extent of approximation, or relevance of the various practical income definitions. However, available evidence clearly indicates that investors react to currently reported earnings by rearranging their portfolios.[66] Such investor reaction implies, of course, that conventionally reported earnings are relevant for investment decisions and that the prediction of these earnings will probably improve financial decisions. In addition, several empirical studies concerned with the prediction of dividend changes [67] and the estimation of cost of capital [68] indicated that the explanatory power of conventionally reported (i.e., historical-cost) earnings was as good as that of alternative measures, such as cash flow earnings. It therefore seems that although the general question concerning the earnings measure most relevant to

[66] See Chapter 15.

[67] E. F. Fama and H. Babiak, "Dividend Policy: An Empirical Analysis," *Journal of the American Statistical Association*, 63 (December 1968), 1132–61.

[68] Miller and Modigliani, *op. cit.*

investors is still unanswered, the prediction of conventionally reported earnings is of substantial importance to analysts.

With respect to the second issue, concerning the optimal prediction model, the evidence on the statistical behavior of earnings series clearly indicates that simple extrapolation models exclusively based on past earnings will usually be ineffective.[69] Corporate earnings appear, on average, to behave as if generated by a martingale process in which successive earnings changes are largely independent over time. Past earnings, used in simple extrapolation models, are therefore of limited usefulness for prediction purposes.[70]

However, sweeping conclusions regarding the futility of earnings predictions are unwarranted; the evidence on the random behavior of earnings changes does not preclude the usefulness of financial statement data for the prediction of future earnings. Rather, it suggests that the role of financial data should be examined in the broader context of optimal prediction models incorporating both accounting and non-accounting data. Following are some general guidelines for the construction of such earnings prediction models based on the available evidence.

1. It should be noted that the evidence on the random behavior of earnings changes pertains to the means or medians of the sampled firms, that is, to the "typical" firm. There are some indications that earnings of atypical firms, mainly the most and the least successful, deviate systematically from randomness. Brealey, for example, found that when the firms with the least erratic earnings records were considered separately, some noticeable persistence (i.e., nonrandomness) in relative growth rate was apparent.[71] Watts, examining the earnings of thirty-two firms over the period 1927–64, found that earnings series of six firms revealed significant serial dependencies (i.e., nonrandomness).[72] It seems, therefore, that despite the evidence on the generally random behavior of earnings changes, an analyst concerned with a specific firm should still attempt to identify persistent patterns in its earnings record. Serial correlation tests, runs analyses, and

---

[69] Such extrapolation models are frequently used by researchers as well as practitioners. For example, Miller and Modigliani in their empirical study on the cost of capital, *ibid.*, p. 351, use highly sophisticated statistical tools (e.g., instrumental variables), yet predict earnings—a crucial variable in their model—by a simple extrapolation, exclusively based on past earnings. Cragg and Malkiel, *op cit.*, found that the five-year earnings growth rate predictions made by five investment firms were mainly based on historical figures. They conclude (p. 83) that ". . . the careful estimates of the security analysts participating in our survey, the bases of which are not limited to public information, perform little better than these past growth rates."

[70] If, as evidence suggests, earnings behave as though they are generated by a submartingale process (i.e., a martingale with a drift or trend), then past earnings are useful for estimating the drift factor.

[71] Brealey, *op. cit.*, pp. 98–100.

[72] R. Watts, Appendix A to "The Informational Content of Dividends," Paper, Graduate School of Business, University of Chicago, October 1970.

exponential smoothing models can be used to reveal such patterns to be subsequently used in the prediction model.

2. It has been empirically established that corporate earnings are to a large extent cross-sectionally correlated.[73] Such a dependency is, of course, expected, since the operating results of individual firms are substantially dependent upon the general situation of the economy (e.g., a recession) and that of the industry (e.g., a change in demand for the industry product). The extent of dependence upon industry- and economy-wide events differs among firms and industries, yet it can probably be used for prediction purposes. Specifically, given a statistically established relationship between a firm's earnings and those of the industry and the economy, a prediction of future earnings can be performed conditional upon expected industry and economy changes, such as devaluation, GNP changes, and imposition of import quotas. Thus, the outlook for the industry and the economy can be incorporated in an earnings prediction model.

3. In addition to data on industry- and economy-wide earnings changes, the prediction model should also incorporate any relevant information specific to the firm. The following items should be considered by the forecaster for possible inclusion in the model: new product plans, management's projections regarding capital expenditures and cash flows, changes in depreciation and inventory practices that might affect taxable income, expenditures on research and development, advertising and promotion programs, and special training and personnel policies. The effect on earnings of these factors is, of course, difficult to quantify, yet efforts should be made to incorporate them in the prediction process.[74]

4. The evidence on the usefulness of interim reports indicates the importance of timely and up-to-date information for prediction purposes. It therefore seems desirable to incorporate in the earnings prediction model information from such timely sources as recently released interim reports and management forecasts.

SUMMARY

There appears to be a consensus among academicians as well as practitioners that a firm's future earnings are a major determinant of its current stock values. Virtually all theoretical and practical stock valuation models incorporate anticipated earnings among the explana-

[73] Evidence is provided by R. Ball and P. Brown, "Some Preliminary Findings on the Association between the Earnings of a Firm, Its Industry and the Economy," *Empirical Research in Accounting: Selected Studies, 1967*, Supplement to Vol. 5, *Journal of Accounting Research*, 55–77; and by Brealey, *op cit.*, Chap. 9.

[74] For example, a recent study determined the effect of current advertising on future sales in various industries (Y. Peles, "Amortization of Advertising Expenditures in the Financial Statements," *Journal of Accounting Research*, 8 (Spring 1970), 128–37). Given such a relationship and current advertising expenditures, a conditional prediction of future sales and earnings can be made.

tory variables. The subject of earnings prediction is therefore of major importance to financial analysts.

The evidence presented above clearly indicates that earnings prediction is not a simple task; the findings concerning the random behavior of most earnings series cast serious doubts on the usefulness of simple extrapolation models based on past earnings. Improved earnings prediction can probably be achieved by the use of more involved models incorporating both accounting and nonaccounting data, and reflecting the firm's specific characteristics as well as industry- and economy-wide expected events.

CHAPTER NINE

The Prediction
of Corporate Failure

Financial statement analysis was developed at the end of the nineteenth century for the purpose of evaluating the solvency position (i.e., failure probability) of prospective borrowers. Shortly thereafter the first efforts were made to design models to predict corporate failure. The definition of failure is rather broad and somewhat ambiguous; to some it means a situation known as technical insolvency, where a firm is unable to meet its maturing obligations. Others restrict the term to the so-called real insolvency case where the total value of the firm's assets is smaller than its liabilities. Obviously, a firm may be temporarily insolvent yet keep operating for a while and even recover.[1] Sometimes business failure is interpreted in the strict legal sense of bankruptcy or liquidation where the firm ceases its operations (voluntarily or involuntarily).[2] The following discussion will not be restricted to a specific definition; rather, corporate failure will be broadly interpreted as severe financial and/or operational difficulties reflected in either insolvency or bankruptcy.

The ability to predict corporate failure is important from both

[1] Banks are not allowed to operate while insolvent (i.e., having negative capital).

[2] For a somewhat different set of definitions, see E. I. Altman, *Corporate Bankruptcy in America* (Lexington, Mass.: Heath Lexington Books, D. C. Heath and Company, 1971), pp. 2–4.

the private and social points of view, since failure is obviously an indication of resource misallocation. An early warning signal of probable failure will enable both management and investors to take preventive measures; operating policy changes, reorganization of financial structure, and even voluntary liquidation will usually shorten the length of time losses are incurred and thereby improve both private and social resource allocation.[3]

Model development for the prediction of corporate failure has generally followed one of two routes: failure prediction by *univariate* (single-variable) models, and prediction by *multivariate* models where several variables are used simultaneously in the prediction process. Prediction models of both types are presented and evaluated below.

BACKGROUND: THE CHARACTERISTICS OF CORPORATE FAILURE

Attempts to construct a theory of corporate failure, that is, to identify and generalize the major causes of failure, have been meager and generally unsatisfactory because of the complexity and diversity of business operations, the lack of a well-defined economic theory of the firm under uncertainty, and a surprising reluctance by many researchers to incorporate the failure phenomenon in their models.[4] Some progress has been made in identifying the major characteristics of failing firms, mainly by Dun and Bradstreet (D & B).[5] Such information will be use-

[3] Schumpeter, using the concept of "creative destruction," argued that the main advantage of corporate failures is the weeding out of inefficient and poorly managed firms, thereby increasing competition and innovation. L. Schumpeter, *Business Cycles,* Vols. 1 and 2 (New York: McGraw-Hill Book Company, 1939).

[4] It should be noted that modern finance theories, such as the Modigliani-Miller hypotheses on capital structure and dividend policy, portfolio theory, etc., explicitly ignore the possibility of corporate bankruptcy. Myron Gordon recently commented: "The academicians with first-hand knowledge of the subject [bankruptcy] have left the scene of action." "Towards a Theory of Financial Distress," *The Journal of Finance,* 26 (May 1971), 347. A recent attempt to investigate the relationship of bankruptcy to the Modigliani-Miller capital structure hypotheses was made in J. E. Stiglitz, "Some Aspects of the Pure Theory of Corporate Finance: Bankruptcies and Take-Overs," *The Bell Journal of Economics and Management Science,* 3 (Autumn 1972), 458–82.

[5] Business failure, as defined by D & B, includes businesses that ceased operations following assignment or bankruptcy; ceased with loss to creditors after such actions as execution, foreclosure, or attachment; withdrew voluntarily with unpaid obligations; were involved in court actions, receivership, reorganization, or arraignment; or voluntarily compromised with creditors. The Business Economics Department of Dun & Bradstreet, Inc., provides various statistical publications on financial failure, such as weekly publications on business failures with comment and analysis, monthly publication of numbers and liabilities of business failures in thirty-nine business lines, and quarterly analysis of failure.

ful in the construction of business failure theory. Following are selected findings from the D & B reports.

Table 9.1 presents the failure trend for the period 1950 through 1971. The failure rate peaked in 1961 (64 failures per 10,000 concerns in the Dun & Bradstreet *Reference Book*) and decreased thereafter, rising again in 1970. However, average liability per failure increased almost continuously. Table 9.2 presents data on the age of failing firms. It is evident that relatively new enterprises predominate in failure—over half the annual casualties are in the first five years of operations. Note, however, that the percentage of failed firms in business over ten years is higher in the 1960s (over 20 percent) than in the 1950s. Firm age, therefore, seems to be negatively associated with the probability of corporate failure.[6] Failed firms tend to be not only younger but also

TABLE 9.1

Business Failure Trends, 1950–1971

Year	Number of Failures	Total Failure Liability ($000)	Failure Rate Per 10,000 Listed Concerns	Average Liability Per Failure
1950	9,162	248,283	34	27,099
1951	8,058	259,547	31	32,210
1952	7,611	283,314	29	37,224
1953	8,862	394,153	33	44,477
1954	11,086	462,628	42	41,731
1955	10,969	449,380	42	40,968
1956	12,686	562,697	48	44,356
1957	13,739	615,293	52	44,784
1958	14,964	728,258	56	48,667
1959	14,053	692,808	52	49,300
1960	15,445	938,630	57	60,772
1961	17,075	1,090,123	64	63,843
1962	15,782	1,213,601	61	76,898
1963	14,374	1,352,593	56	94,100
1964	13,501	1,329,223	53	98,454
1965	13,514	1,321,666	53	97,800
1966	13,061	1,385,659	52	106,091
1967	12,364	1,265,227	49	102,332
1968	9,636	940,996	39	97,654
1969	9,154	1,142,113	37	124,767
1970	10,748	1,887,754	44	175,638
1971	10,326	1,916,929	42	185,641

Source: *The Failure Record through 1971* (New York: Dun & Bradstreet, Inc., 1972), p. 1.

[6] More on the association between failure rates and age in K. Lewis, "Business Failures—Another Example of the Analysis of Failure Data," *Journal of the American*

TABLE 9.2

Trend in Age of Business Failures, 1950–1971

Year	In Business 5 Years or Less (%)	In Business 6 to 10 Years (%)	In Business Over 10 Years (%)
1950	68.2	19.0	12.8
1951	63.2	23.5	13.3
1952	59.9	25.8	14.3
1953	58.5	26.7	14.8
1954	57.2	27.3	15.5
1955	56.6	26.0	17.4
1956	58.6	23.1	18.3
1957	58.9	21.8	19.3
1958	57.2	21.4	21.4
1959	57.1	22.3	20.6
1960	58.6	20.8	20.6
1961	56.2	22.4	21.4
1962	55.4	22.2	22.4
1963	55.4	21.7	22.9
1964	56.0	21.5	22.5
1965	56.9	21.4	21.7
1966	57.4	21.5	21.1
1967	55.3	22.5	22.2
1968	53.9	23.3	22.8
1969	53.2	24.4	22.4
1970	54.9	22.7	22.4
1971	54.2	22.2	23.6

Source: The Failure Record through 1971 (New York: Dun & Bradstreet, Inc., 1972), p. 10.

smaller, with liabilities seldom running over $1 million.[7] As evidenced by the data in Table 9.3, approximately 75 percent of the firms that failed during the 1950s and the 1960s had liabilities ranging from $5,000 to $100,000.[8] With respect to the industry classification of failed firms, in 1971 about 43 percent of total failures occurred in retailing, 15 per-

---

Statistical Association, 49 (December 1954), 847–52; and H. N. Broom and J. G. Longenecker, Small Business Management (Cincinnati: South-Western Publishing Co., 1971), Chap. 5.

[7] These findings are confirmed (and generalized) by Hymer and Pashigian, who found a systematic tendency for the growth rate variance to be larger for small firms than for large firms. "Firm Size and Rate of Growth," Journal of Political Economy, 70 (December 1962), 556.

[8] Note, however, that bankruptcy recently took a heavy toll of large corporations, such as Penn Central Transportation Company (total assets in 1969—$4,700 million), Boston & Main Railroad (total assets in 1969—$224.1 million), King Resources Company (total assets in 1969—$176.7 million), and Beck Industries (total assets in 1969—$156.9 million).

TABLE 9.3

Failure Distribution by Liability Size

Year	Under $5,000 No.	%	$5,000 to $25,000 No.	%	$25,000 to $100,000 No.	%	$100,000 to $1,000,000 No.	%	Over $1,000,000 No.	%
1950	2,065	22.5	4,706	51.4	1,975	21.6	407	4.4	9	0.1
1951	1,832	22.7	4,160	51.6	1,634	20.3	412	5.1	20	0.3
1952	1,428	18.8	3,884	51.0	1,769	23.3	512	6.7	18	0.2
1953	1,383	15.6	4,317	48.7	2,375	26.8	748	8.5	39	0.4
1954	1,640	14.8	5,640	50.9	2,946	26.5	829	7.5	31	0.3
1955	1,785	16.3	5,412	49.3	2,916	26.6	820	7.5	36	0.3
1956	2,032	16.0	6,152	48.4	3,431	27.1	1,022	8.1	49	0.4
1957	2,001	14.6	6,699	48.8	3,847	28.0	1,147	8.3	45	0.3
1958	2,028	13.5	7,015	46.9	4,456	29.8	1,408	9.4	57	0.4
1959	1,841	13.1	6,664	47.4	4,202	29.9	1,284	9.1	62	0.5
1960	1,688	10.9	6,884	44.6	5,078	32.9	1,703	11.0	92	0.6
1961	1,903	11.1	7,378	43.2	5,725	33.5	1,973	11.6	96	0.6
1962	1,647	10.4	6,700	42.5	5,425	34.4	1,876	11.9	134	0.8
1963	1,296	9.0	5,781	40.2	5,115	35.6	2,031	14.1	151	1.1
1964	1,093	8.1	5,202	38.5	5,051	37.4	2,003	14.9	152	1.1
1965	1,007	7.5	5,067	37.5	5,266	39.0	2,005	14.8	169	1.2
1966	932	7.1	4,569	35.0	5,332	40.8	2,042	15.7	186	1.4
1967	814	6.6	4,434	35.9	4,896	39.6	2,045	16.5	175	1.4
1968	481	5.0	3,332	34.6	4,016	41.7	1,686	17.5	121	1.2
1969	416	4.6	3,000	32.8	3,776	41.2	1,807	19.7	155	1.7
1970	430	4.0	3,197	29.7	4,392	40.9	2,450	22.8	279	2.6
1971	392	3.8	2,806	27.2	4,413	42.7	2,423	23.5	292	2.8

Source: The Failure Record through 1971 (New York: Dun & Bradstreet, Inc., 1972), p. 6.

cent in construction, 19 percent in manufacturing, 9 percent in wholesaling, and 14 percent in commercial services. Dun and Bradstreet also attempt to determine the causes of failure. Based on the opinion of informed creditors and D & B's own information, the major causes appear to be management incompetence and lack of experience (see Table 9.4).

Although it is definitely a step in the right direction, a classification of the characteristics of failed firms does not constitute a theory of corporate failure. Basic questions, such as *why* smaller firms fail more frequently than larger ones, *why* the rate of failure is changing over time, or *how* failure can be predicted and prevented, are still unanswered. Among the few attempts to answer such questions is Walter's critique of conventional technical solvency evaluation.[9] Technical insolvency refers to the inability of a firm to meet its currently maturing

[9] J. E. Walter, "Determination of Technical Solvency," *Journal of Business*, 31 (January 1957), 30–43.

TABLE 9.4

Causes for Failures in 1971

Underlying Causes	Manufacturers %	Wholesalers %	Retailers %	Construction %	Commercial Services %	All %
1. Neglect	1.3	2.6	1.9	1.7	1.6	1.7
2. Fraud	1.3	2.0	1.2	0.8	1.1	1.2
3. Lack of Experience in the Line	9.8	9.1	16.1	10.1	15.5	13.3
4. Lack of Managerial Experience	11.2	13.4	15.9	20.8	16.3	15.6
5. Unbalanced Experience *	18.6	14.1	19.3	19.5	17.1	18.4
6. Incompetence	54.6	55.0	41.3	43.0	44.3	45.7
7. Disaster	1.1	1.6	1.6	0.8	0.6	1.3
8. Reason Unknown	2.1	2.2	2.7	3.3	3.5	2.8
Total	100.0	100.0	100.0	100.0	100.0	100.0
Number of Failures	1,932	957	4,428	1,545	1,464	10,326
Average Liability per Failure	$368,846	$189,083	$100,290	$183,920	$243,800	$185,641

Source: *The Failure Record through 1971* (New York: Dun & Bradstreet, Inc., 1972), p. 11.

* Experience not well rounded in sales, finance, purchasing, and production on the part of the individual in case of a proprietorship, or of two or more partners or officers constituting a management unit.

obligations and is a special case of the general failure problem. The traditional, and probably prevailing, approach to the determination of technical solvency stresses the firm's working-capital position. The attitude taken is that liabilities that mature in the near future must be adequately covered by existing liquid assets (i.e., cash, short-term securities, receivables, and sometimes inventories). The popularity of the current and quick ratios is based on this approach. The major deficiency of the working-capital approach is its sole emphasis on *stocks* of assets and liabilities and the disregard of the *fund flows* aspect. Specifically, in the normal course of operations, current liabilities are discharged by the net cash flows emanating from sales rather than by the liquid assets at hand at the beginning of the period.[10] Accordingly, Walter's approach to the determination of technical solvency is based on cash flows indicators as well as the conventional stock measures.

Altman investigated the failure question from a macroeconomic aspect by examining the effect of aggregate economic factors on business failure experience.[11] His findings, based on linear regression analysis, indicate that the quarterly change in the failure rate is negatively correlated with the change in the GNP, the change in Standard and Poor's index of common stocks, and the change in the money supply. A firm's propensity to fail is thus increased during periods of reduced economic activity. It should be noted, however, that the explanatory power of Altman's model is rather modest—the three independent variables listed above account for somewhat less than 20 percent of the variability of failure rate during the period 1947–70. A few additional attempts have been made to develop a theory of corporate failure;[12] however, it seems safe to conclude that the way to a well-defined and accepted theory is still long and arduous.

UNIVARIATE CORPORATE FAILURE PREDICTION MODELS

The prediction of corporate failure has traditionally captured the imagination of financial analysts; the objective of empirical research was to compare the financial ratios of failed firms with those of nonfailed firms to detect systematic differences which might assist in predicting failure. Ramser and Foster analyzed eleven types of ratios for 173 firms

---

[10] Net cash flows are defined as the difference between dollar sales and costs, excluding noncash charges (e.g., depreciation).

[11] Altman, *op. cit.*, Chap. 2.

[12] For example, M. J. Gordon, "Towards a Theory of Financial Distress," *The Journal of Finance*, 26 (May 1971), 347–56.

whose securities were registered in the state of Illinois.[13] They found that the less successful and failing firms tended to have ratios that were lower than those of the more successful firms. FitzPatrick examined nineteen pairs of failed and nonfailed firms and found persistent differences in the ratios for at least three years prior to failure.[14] The net income to net worth and the net worth to debt ratios were found to be the best indicators of failure. Mervin, using a sample of over 900 firms, corroborated the ratio differences for as far back as six years before failure.[15] Winakor and Smith, using a sample of 183 bankrupt firms, reported a clear deterioration in the mean values of financial ratios of failed firms for ten years before failure; the rate of deterioration increased as the firm approached failure.[16] However, this study lacked a control group of solvent firms; thus, the observed deterioration in the ratios cannot be unambiguously attributed to the failure phenomenon. Saulnier *et al.* found evidence from RFC lending experience during 1934–51 that borrowing firms with poorer current ratios and net worth to debt ratios were more prone to loan default.[17] Seiden reported that certain financial ratios (e.g., net working capital to total assets) were inversely correlated with an index of trade credit difficulties,[18] and Moore and Atkinson found that the ability to obtain credit was correlated with several financial ratios.[19] Thus, despite the various statistical shortcomings of these early studies (e.g., small and biased samples, lack of control group, etc.), systematic differences between the ratios of failed and nonfailed firms were established. However, these studies were generally descriptive and did not face directly the normative problem of failure prediction.

Beaver was among the first to focus on the ability of ratios to pre-

[13] J. R. Ramser and L. O. Foster, *A Demonstration of Ratio Analysis*, Bulletin No. 40 (Urbana: University of Illinois, Bureau of Business Research, 1931).

[14] P. J. FitzPatrick, "A Comparison of Ratios of Successful Industrial Enterprises with Those of Failed Firms," *Certified Public Accountant*, 12 (October, November, and December 1932), 598–605, 656–62, and 727–31.

[15] C. L. Mervin, *Financing Small Corporations in Five Manufacturing Industries, 1926–36* (New York: National Bureau of Economic Research, 1942).

[16] C. H. Winakor and R. F. Smith, *Changes in Financial Structure of Unsuccessful Industrial Companies*, Bulletin No. 51 (Urbana: University of Illinois Press, Bureau of Economic Research, 1935).

[17] R. J. Saulnier, H. G. Halcrow, and N. H. Jacoby, *Federal Lending and Loan Insurance* (Princeton: Princeton University Press, 1958), pp. 456–81.

[18] M. H. Seiden, "Trade Credit: A Quantitative and Qualitative Analysis," *Tested Knowledge of Business Cycles*, 42nd Annual Report (National Bureau of Economic Research, 1962), pp. 86–88.

[19] G. H. Moore and T. R. Atkinson, "Risks and Returns in Small Business Financing," *Towards a Firmer Basis of Economic Policy*, 41st Annual Report (National Bureau of Economic Research, 1961), pp. 66–67.

dict corporate failure.[20] His study was restricted to financial ratios and thus excluded the consideration of nonaccounting data in failure prediction:

> The emphasis upon financial ratios does not imply that ratios are the only predictors of failure. The primary concern is not with predictors of failure per se but rather with financial ratios as predictors of important events— one of which is failure of the firm. . . .[21]

The sample consisted of 79 firms that failed and 79 nonfailed firms, selected by the *paired sample* technique.[22] Specifically, for each failed firm in the sample, a nonfailed mate from the same industry and similar asset size was selected. The objective of such a sample design was to control for systematic size and industry differences in financial ratios that might blur the relationship between the characteristics of failed and nonfailed firms. Generally, a paired sample analysis is designed to control for various factors that are believed to be unrelated to the phenomenon investigated.[23] However, as was indicated in the preceding section, size and industry factors are strongly related to the rate of corporate failure, and therefore sample stratification by these factors precludes the consideration of their contribution to failure prediction. Stated differently, the ability of the size and industry factors to improve failure prediction cannot be examined in a paired sample design where these factors are used as pairing criteria.[24]

Financial statement data for the failed firms were available for five years before failure. The data for each of the nonfailed mates corresponded to the same time periods of the failed firms. Thirty financial ratios from the various conventional ratio categories were computed for each firm in the sample. A comparison of the mean ratios for the failed and nonfailed firms (Figure 9.1) corroborated the findings of earlier studies:

[20] W. H. Beaver, "Financial Ratios as Predictors of Failure," *Empirical Research in Accounting: Selected Studies, 1966,* Supplement to Vol. 4, *Journal of Accounting Research,* 71–127. Also, W. H. Beaver, "Alternative Accounting Measures as Predictors of Failure," *The Accounting Review,* 43 (January 1968), 113–22.

[21] Beaver, "Financial Ratios," *ibid.,* p. 72.

[22] Beaver's definition of corporate failure is rather broad: Of the 79 failed cases, 59 were bankrupt, 16 were involved in nonpayment of preferred stock dividends, 3 were bond defaults, and 1 was an overdrawn bank account.

[23] For elaboration on the objectives and shortcomings of the paired sample technique, see B. Lev and G. Mandelker, "The Micro-Economic Consequences of Corporate Mergers," *Journal of Business,* 45 (January 1972), 85–89.

[24] By using multivariate analysis, it is possible to allow for cross-sectional systematic differences in firm characteristics (e.g., size) and at the same time to examine the predictive contribution of such characteristics. This can be done, for example, by incorporating size as an additional independent variable in a multiple regression model.

The difference in the mean values is in the predicted direction for each ratio in all five years before failure. Failed firms not only have lower cash flow than nonfailed firms, but also have a smaller reservoir of liquid assets. Although the failed firms have less capacity to meet obligations, they tend to incur more debt than do the nonfailed firms. The trend line of the nonfailed firms has a zero slope, and the deviations from the trend line are small. Yet the deterioration in the means of the failed firms is very pronounced over the five-year period. . . . The evidence overwhelmingly suggests that there is a difference in the ratios of failed and nonfailed firms.[25]

Differences in ratio means do not suggest directly the existence and extent of predictive power. To examine this possibility, Beaver employed various predictability tests, such as the *dichotomous classification* technique, which predicts a firm's failure status solely upon the knowledge of a given financial ratio, for example, the current ratio. Given that this ratio was found to be on average lower for failed firms than for nonfailed ones, the failed firm in each pair is predicted to be the one with the lower current ratio. Comparison of the actual status of the sampled firms with the predicted one yields a percentage error (i.e., the percentage of firms misclassified). The ratio with the smallest percentage error is considered the best predictor.[26] Results of this test indicated that the most successful predictor was the cash flow to total debt ratio (only 10 percent of the firms misclassified using the ratio of the first year before failure and 22 percent with the ratio of the fifth year before failure).[27] The net income to total assets ratio predicted second best (12 and 25 percent misclassified in the first and fifth year before failure, respectively). Surprisingly, the current ratio was among the worst predictors (20 and 31 percent of the sampled firms misclassified in the first and fifth year, respectively). Generally, the "mixed ratios" (i.e., those with income or cash flow in the numerator and assets or liabilities in the denominator) outperformed the short-term solvency ratios which were traditionally believed to be the best predictors of failure.[28]

[25] Beaver, "Financial Ratios," *op. cit.*, pp. 80–81.

[26] Beaver used additional versions of the dichotomous classification test and also applied a Bayesian analysis to prediction evaluation.

[27] Note that these error percentages were substantially smaller than would be expected from a random prediction model (i.e., a model with no predictive power), where the expected percentage error would be approximately 50 percent. The probability that a random prediction model would perform as well as this ratio is less than one in ten thousand.

[28] The importance of short-term solvency ratios in the traditional analysis is evidenced in the following statement: "The classification of current assets is undoubtedly the most important classification in a balance sheet, as current assets largely determine the going solvency of a business concern." R. A. Foulke, *Practical Financial Statement Analysis*, 6th ed. (McGraw-Hill Book Company, 1968), p. 71. Mervin, *op. cit.*, p. 99, reported that the net working capital to total assets ratio was the best indicator of firm discontinuance.

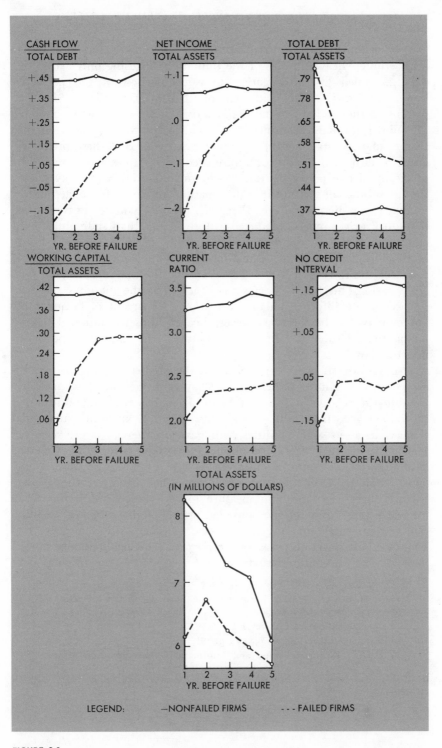

FIGURE 9.1

Means of selected ratios for failed and nonfailed firms

Source: Beaver, "Financial Ratios as Predictors of Failure," p. 82.

The univariate approach to failure prediction was pursued in other studies. Beaver, aware of the limitations in using only accounting data, extended his investigation to a comparison of the predictive power of financial ratios with that of stock market prices.[29] Since, according to the efficient capital markets hypothesis, stock prices impound all publicly available information (including, of course, that contained in the financial statements),[30] it can be expected that these prices will outperform financial ratios in failure prediction. However, a comparison of the predictive power of stock prices and financial ratios may suggest the usefulness of accounting information relative to nonaccounting sources in predicting failure. Using his original sample, Beaver found that stock prices indeed predicted failure sooner than individual financial ratios. However, the difference was rather small—the average length of time from the year of failure forecast to the failure date was 2.45 years for the stock prices and 2.31 years for the net income over total assets ratio. This finding seems to suggest that the marginal value of nonaccounting information in the market's assessment of failure probability may not be large. However, Beaver himself cautioned against taking these results at face value because of the limited scope of his investigation.[31]

Lev, using Beaver's sample, tested the predictive power of the decomposition measures presented in Chapter 4.[32] Since these measures indicate the relative stability of financial statement decompositions, it can be expected that failing firms, which usually experience substantial changes in assets and liabilities, will have on average larger measures than solvent ones. Results confirmed this expectation: The average decomposition measures of failing firms were found to be substantially larger than those of the nonfailing ones. For example, the average balance sheet decomposition measure for the failed group was .0423 nits versus .0075 nits for the nonfailed firms.[33] A dichotomous classification test indicated that the balance sheet decomposition measure had a lower misclassification percentage error (i.e., a higher predictive power) than all financial ratios tested except for the cash flow to total debt

---

[29] W. H. Beaver, "Market Prices, Financial Ratios, and the Prediction of Failure," *Journal of Accounting Research*, 6 (Autumn 1968), 179–92.

[30] For elaboration see Chapter 14.

[31] Beaver, "Market Prices," *op cit.*, p. 191.

[32] B. Lev, "Financial Failure and Informational Decomposition Measures," in *Accounting in Perspective: Contribution to Accounting Thoughts by Other Disciplines*, R. R. Sterling and W. F. Bentz, eds. (Cincinnati: South-Western Publishing Co., 1971), pp. 102–11.

[33] A *nit* is a unit of decomposition measures; see Chapter 4.

ratio which slightly outperformed the decomposition measure (a difference of only two firms misclassified).[34]

Wilcox derived a bankruptcy prediction measure from a firm behavior model based on a Markov chains process.[35] The measure performed well on a matched sample of failed and nonfailed firms. However, the novelty in Wilcox's approach was the attempt to base the failure prediction process on an explicit firm-behavior model. No such model underlies other failure prediction studies.

MULTIVARIATE CORPORATE FAILURE PREDICTION MODELS

The major feature of the multivariate approach to failure prediction is the *simultaneous* consideration of several indicators in the prediction process. Altman followed this approach by using the multiple discriminate analysis (MDA) technique which is designed to classify an observation into one of several a priori groupings, dependent upon the observation's individual characteristics.[36] This technique is primarily used for the classification or prediction of qualitative variables, such as sex, race, or solvency status. The first step in applying the MDA technique is to determine the a priori classification of the objects (failed and nonfailed in Altman's case). Data are then collected on various economic characteristics (e.g., liquidity, profitability, size, etc.) of the objects deemed relevant to failure prediction. The MDA technique derives a linear combination of all or some of these characteristics that best discriminates between the classes. The discriminant function is of the form:

$$Z = \beta_1 X_1 + \beta_2 X_2 + \ldots + \beta_n X_n \qquad (9.1)$$

[34] Note, however, that the balance sheet decomposition measure is restricted to balance sheet data, while the cash flow to total debt ratio incorporates both income statement and balance sheet information.

[35] J. W. Wilcox, "A Prediction of Business Failure Using Accounting Data," *Empirical Research in Accounting: Selected Studies, 1973*, Supplement to Vol. 11, *Journal of Accounting Research*.

[36] E. I. Altman, "Financial Ratios, Discriminant Analysis and the Prediction of Corporate Bankruptcy," *The Journal of Finance*, 23 (September 1968), 589–609. Of course, Altman was not the first to suggest the multivariate approach to financial analysis; the application of multivariate methods for discriminating between failing and solvent banks was suggested thirty years earlier by H. Secrist, *National Bank Failures and Non-Failures, An Autopsy and Diagnosis* (Bloomington, Ind.: Principa Press, 1938).

where

$\beta_1, \beta_2, \ldots, \beta_n$ = discriminant coefficients, and

$X_1, X_2, \ldots, X_n$ = independent variables (e.g., firm characteristics).

The discriminant function thus transforms the values of the individual variables into a single discriminant score, Z, which is then used to classify the firms into the failed or nonfailed groups.[37]

Altman used a paired sample consisting of thirty-three pairs of manufacturing firms, where industry and size were used as the pairing criteria.[38] Twenty-two accounting and nonaccounting variables were considered in various combinations as predictors of failure. The following combination (i.e., discriminant function) did the best overall job in discriminating the bankruptcy status of the sampled firms:

$$Z = .012X_1 + .014X_2 + .033X_3 + .006X_4 + .999X_5 \qquad (9.2)$$

where

X_1 = working capital/total assets (a liquidity measure)

X_2 = retained earnings/total assets (a measure for reinvested earnings)

X_3 = earnings before interest and taxes/total assets (a profitability measure)

X_4 = market value of equity/book value of total debt (a measure for the firm's financial structure or leverage)

X_5 = sales/total assets (a measure for the sales-generating ability of the firm's assets) [39]

To estimate the predictive power of the discriminant model, a classification test somewhat similar to Beaver's was used. The five-variable

---

[37] The statistical issues involved in the MDA technique are discussed in C. R. Rao, *Advanced Statistical Methods in Biometric Research* (New York: John Wiley & Sons, Inc., 1952). An example of an earlier study in financial analysis using this technique is J. E. Walter, "A Discriminant Function for Earnings Price Ratios of Large Industrial Corporations," *Review of Economics and Statistics*, 41 (February 1959), 44–52.

[38] Unlike Beaver, Altman restricted his sample to firms that were legally bankrupt and either placed in receivership or granted the right to reorganize under the provision of the National Bankruptcy Act.

[39] It is interesting to note that the five variables composing the most successful prediction equation were not the most statistically significant variables (among the twenty-two original ones) when measured *independently*. X_5, for example, was the least significant measure on an individual basis. This reflects a basic difference between the univariate and multivariate analyses; the most successful prediction equation which takes into account the *interactions* among variables is not necessarily composed of the most significant variables, measured individually. Hence, results of univariate studies cannot be directly applied to multivariate ones. For elaboration on this point, see W. W. Cooley and P. R. Lohnes, *Multivariate Procedures for the Behavioral Sciences* (New York: John Wiley & Sons, Inc., 1962), p. 121.

model using data of one year before bankruptcy correctly classified 95 percent of the total sample. The percentage of correct classification decreased to 72 when data of two years prior to bankruptcy were used for prediction. When earlier data were used, the predictive power of the model became unreliable. Altman further tested his model on a different sample and found the predictive power to be similar to that reported above—a 96 percent correct classification.[40]

Altman's model can be practically applied to the solvency evaluation of a given firm as follows. First compute the Z score of the firm based on the discriminant function (9.2).[41] Then relate this score to the cutoff point which discriminates between failed and nonfailed firms. For Altman's sample, the cutoff points were as follows: All firms that had a Z score greater than 2.99 fell into the nonbankrupt class, while all firms that had a Z score smaller than 1.81 were bankrupt. The group of firms having Z scores between 1.81 and 2.99 contained both bankrupt and nonbankrupt cases. Accordingly, a cutoff range (e.g., between 1.81 and 2.99) rather than a point is possible. Firms whose Z scores fall within the range obviously require further analysis to determine their solvency status. It should be noted that in a practical application, such as in bank-lending decisions, both the model's parameters and the sample cutoff points should be estimated from the user's data (e.g., the file of loan applicants). Given the small size of Altman's sample, it is doubtful whether his estimates will suit a specific application. Thus, when applying Altman's general approach, care should be exercised to adjust his estimates to the specific population and time period examined.

Meyer and Pifer developed a linear regression model for the prediction of bank failures.[42] The dependent variable was dichotomous (i.e., a dummy, taking the values of 0 for solvent banks and 1 for failed ones), while the independent variables were various financial statement measures. This special regression technique yields results similar to those of the discriminant analysis used by Altman.[43] A paired sample was again used according to the following criteria: The paired banks were in the same city, were of approximately equal size and age, and were subject to the same regulatory requirements. The sample consisted

---

[40] The desirability of testing models on "hold-out" samples (calibrated sample technique) is further discussed in the following section.

[41] Note that the ratios X_1 to X_4 should be expressed in absolute percents. Thus, for example, a working capital/total assets ratio of 20 percent should be expressed in the equation as 20.0. With respect to the fifth variable, X_5, a sales/total assets ratio of 200 percent should be expressed as 2.00.

[42] P. A. Meyer and H. W. Pifer, "Prediction of Bank Failures," *The Journal of Finance*, 25 (September 1970), 853–68.

[43] For a comparison of the two methods, see G. Ladd, "Linear Probability Functions and Discriminant Functions," *Econometrica*, 33 (October 1965), 873–85.

of thirty-nine pairs of banks and referred to the period 1948–65. Thirty-two financial measures were considered as independent variables in the various regression models tested.

An interesting feature of this study was the unconventional form of most measures used. An attempt was made to design the measures according to the a priori causes of bank failures. Following are some of the variables that entered the final regression equation.

1. *Errors in predicting cash and securities/total assets*—reflects the *unpredicted* liquidity change and supposedly measures managerial predictive power

2. *Coefficient of variation in the rate of interest on time deposits*—indicates the extent and frequency of change in management's objectives

3. *Growth of consumer loans/total assets*—serves as a proxy for the quality and aggressiveness of management

4. *Coefficient of variation of total loans*—is an additional indicator of management's quality, since well-managed banks adapt quickly to changing market conditions by altering their loan portfolio structure

5. *Growth of indebtedness of directors, officers, employees, and affiliates/total capital*—indicates questionable assets, or even potential embezzlement

A classification test was used by Meyer and Pifer to evaluate the predictive power of the regression model. With a lead time of one or two years before failure, approximately 80 percent of the sampled banks were correctly classified. For a lead time of three or more years, the model failed to discriminate between failed and solvent banks.

Westerfield investigated the market price movement of twenty bankrupt firms for ten years before bankruptcy declaration.[44] Using the residual analysis method,[45] he found that the market began bidding down the prices of bankrupt stocks as far back as five years before bankruptcy. Investors were thus aware of the firms' deteriorating condition for a relatively long time prior to failure, a finding consistent with the efficient market hypothesis to be discussed in Chapter 14.[46]

[44] R. Westerfield, "Pre-Bankruptcy Stock Price Performance," Working paper, University of Pennsylvania, Fall 1970.

[45] This method was discussed in Chapter 3.

[46] Additional studies related to failure prediction are N. Baxter, "Leverage, Risk of Ruin and Cost of Capital," *The Journal of Finance*, 22 (September 1967), 395–403; E. I. Altman, "Corporate Bankruptcy Potential, Stockholder Returns, and Share Valuation," *The Journal of Finance*, 24 (December 1969), 887–900; M. Blum, "The Failing Company Doctrine" (Ph.D. dissertation, Columbia University, 1969); R. O. Admister, "An Empirical Test of Financial Ratio Analysis for Small Business Failure Prediction," *Journal of Financial and Quantitative Analysis*, 7 (March 1972), 1477–93; E. I. Altman, "Railroad Bankruptcy Potential," *The Journal of Finance*, 26 (May 1971), 333–45; E. B. Deakin, "A Discriminant Analysis of Predictors of Business Failure," *Journal of Accounting Research*, 10 (Spring 1972), 167–79; and E. I. Altman, "Predicting Railroad Bankruptcies in America," *The Bell Journal of Economics and Management Science*, 4 (Spring 1973), 184–211.

EVALUATION OF EVIDENCE

The empirical evidence presented above was concerned with both the positive (descriptive) and normative (prescriptive) aspects of the corporate failure phenomenon. With respect to the positive aspect, the evidence clearly indicates that for a period of at least five years before failure, the economic indicators (e.g., ratios) of failed firms were significantly different from those of nonfailed firms. With respect to the normative aspect—the ability of financial measures to *predict* failure—the evidence is somewhat less conclusive. While the various models presented above appear to possess predictive power, it is difficult to generalize these empirical results because of the following shortcomings:

1. There is no well-defined theory of corporate failure to direct the design and performance of empirical studies. Lacking such a theory, researchers adopt a trial-and-error process of experimenting with a large number of measures (Beaver, for example, examined thirty financial ratios), various kinds of models (univariate and multivariate), and different statistical techniques (MDA, regression analysis, etc.). As expected, results of such unguided research efforts are often inconsistent,[47] and almost impossible to generalize.[48] It seems, therefore, that the main research effort should now be directed toward the construction of a testable theory of corporate failure.

2. Available research on corporate failure is plagued with serious statistical shortcomings. First, all studies were essentially *retrospective;* i.e., firms that have failed were compared with solvent ones. It is well known that retrospective (ex post) studies are susceptible to sample selection bias. For example, since in most studies firm age was not used as a pairing criterion, it is probable that the failed firms in the samples were, on average, younger than the nonfailed ones.[49] Consequently, the observed differences between the ratios of the two groups may be, at least partially, attributed to age differences rather than to solvency status. One way to overcome the selection bias inherent in retrospective studies is to use a *prospective* analysis. Specifically, select a random sample of solvent firms with different economic characteristics according to a priori knowledge about the determinants of failure. Then trace the performance of these firms over time to detect association between the economic characteristics and the rate of failure. For

47 For example, Beaver found liquidity measures (e.g., the current ratio) to be poor predictors of failure, yet a liquidity measure was included in Altman's most successful prediction model.

48 Due to differences in samples and statistical models it is impossible, for example, to compare directly the results of the univariate and multivariate studies.

49 Recall the association between failure rate and firm age presented in Table 9.2.

example, two random samples of solvent firms with very high and very low current ratios are selected, and the rate of failure during an interval of, say, ten years is determined for each sample. If the difference in the failure rates is statistically significant, it indicates that the current ratio may be used in failure prediction. This point is expressed in the following comment:

> Altman demonstrates that failed and nonfailed firms have dissimilar ratios, not that ratios have predictive power. But the crucial problem is to make an inference in the reverse direction, i.e., from ratios to failures. It must be demonstrated that stratified random samples of ratios' values can imply failure and nonfailure.[50]

Second, the requirement in all the failure studies that the control group be of the same size as the failed group is unwarranted. There seems to be no practical or statistical reason why the control group could not be much larger than the failed sample. The main advantage of a large control group will be the decrease in the sampling errors of the estimates of solvent firms' economic characteristics, and hence an improvement in the precision of measurements.

Third, several researchers (e.g., Meyer and Pifer) did not *calibrate* their samples. The advantages of calibration for failure studies were noted by Neter:

> . . . if you have a body of sample data, you can analyze these and come up with a criterion that is in some sense a good criterion according to the sample data. However, the indication of the predictive power of the criterion based on the sample data generally tends to be biased upward, because the criterion will usually work better for the data from which the criterion was developed than from another random sample from the population. Hence, it is desirable to use calibrating samples where, in effect, half of the data is used in order to develop the criterion and the other half is used to test the predictive power of the criterion.[51]

It thus appears that calibration is essential in any bankruptcy prediction study.

3. The performance of the above-mentioned bankruptcy prediction models, which were based mainly on financial data, should have been compared more systematically with that of other models incorporating nonaccounting data.[52] Beaver made a step in the right direction

---

[50] C. J. Johnson, "Ratio Analysis and the Prediction of Firm Failure," *The Journal of Finance*, 25 (December 1970), 1168. See also Altman's reply, pp. 1169–72.

[51] J. Neter, "Discussion of Financial Ratios as Predictors of Failure," *Empirical Research in Accounting: Selected Studies, 1966*, Supplement to Vol. 4, *Journal of Accounting Research*, 112.

[52] *Ibid.*, p. 115, suggests one such model.

by comparing the predictive power of ratios with that of stock prices,[53] but this approach was not pursued by others. Consequently, it is difficult to evaluate the usefulness of the models presented above. Ideally, financial statement data should be combined with nonaccounting data (e.g., stock prices, macroeconomic variables, etc.) to form optimal failure prediction models.

Despite the various methodological and statistical shortcomings of the available research, it appears that well-specified financial models (of the multivariate type and probably including nonaccounting as well as accounting variables) are capable of providing an early warning at least two to three years before bankruptcy. Such a warning system obviously has important uses: Lenders may use failure prediction models in the process of credit evaluation, investors may use such models for portfolio selection, management may use the models to evaluate the firm's solvency position and take corrective measures, regulatory agencies, such as the FDIC bank examiners, may use the models to determine the frequency and extent of examination of the regulated units.

SUMMARY

The ability of financial models to provide an early warning of failure was investigated in this chapter. Research on the subject, both of the univariate and of the multivariate type, suggests that models incorporating financial statement data are capable of discriminating (ex post) between failing and nonfailing firms for at least as far as five years before failure. The evidence regarding the predictive power of financial models is also favorable; yet, given the various methodological and statistical shortcomings of available studies, more and improved research is called for.

[53] Beaver, "Market Prices," *op. cit.*

CHAPTER TEN

The Prediction
of Bond Risk Premiums
and Ratings

The concept of risk was restricted in the preceding chapter to the possibility of corporate bankruptcy; additional aspects of risk associated with holding capital assets will now be presented.[1] Generally, a risky, or uncertain, situation exists when a realized (ex post) outcome *can* differ from an expected (ex ante) outcome.[2] Suppose, for example, that a particular stock has paid an uninterrupted annual dividend of five dollars per share for the past twenty years. Accordingly, a five-dollar payment is probably the best estimate for the next year's dividend. Nevertheless, some uncertainty with respect to this estimate prevails, since there is always the possibility that the firm will change its dividend policy because of earnings changes, fund requirement for investments,

---

[1] A comprehensive treatment of risk will be presented in Chapter 12 in the context of the portfolio selection theory.

[2] More precisely, *risk* is defined as the situation where each action of the decision maker leads to one of a set of possible specific outcomes, each occurring with a *known* probability. *Uncertainty* is defined as the situation where the probabilities of the various outcomes are completely *unknown*. For elaboration, see R. D. Luce and H. Raiffa, *Games and Decisions* (New York: John Wiley & Sons, Inc., 1957), p. 13. Modern finance and investment theories are mainly concerned with decision making under conditions of risk, i.e., the situation where the probabilities of future outcomes are known to the decision maker. The terms *risk* and *uncertainty* will be used synonymously hereafter.

and so forth. The possibility of future investment outcomes deviating from expectation thus constitutes the risk associated with holding these investments; the larger the possible deviation, the higher the risk.

The holding of capital assets usually involves various aspects of risk. One such aspect is known as *business risk* and is associated with the inability of investors to perfectly predict future revenues and costs of business enterprises. Actual corporate earnings can therefore differ from expectation, resulting in unanticipated changes in capital asset prices and hence in investors' wealth. Another risk aspect is the *market risk*, which emanates from the high degree of cross-sectional correlation among securities' prices and returns. Consequently, unexpected changes in general capital market conditions, such as those resulting from changes in the rate of money supply, will obviously affect the outcomes of all capital investments and portfolios.[3] The *financial risk* associated with holding the common stocks of high-levered corporations was discussed in Chapter 2. Additional risk aspects will be introduced below, yet in all cases risk is caused by the possibility of future investment outcomes deviating from expectation.[4]

The present chapter is concerned with risk aspects associated with the investment in corporate bonds. Although the management of a bond portfolio has always seemed dull compared with that of a stock portfolio, it should be realized that institutional investors buy far more bonds than stocks. Improved performance of such institutions therefore requires a careful analysis of bond characteristics such as the expected return and risk. The risk associated with bonds is reflected in two widely used indicators: the risk premium on bonds and bond ratings. Financial models designed to explain and predict these indicators are presented below, and their usefulness to financial analysts and bond portfolio managers is evaluated.

BACKGROUND: BOND RISK FACTORS

The risk involved in holding corporate bonds consists of the following factors:

1. *Default risk*, caused by the possibility that the firm's future resources will be insufficient to meet part or all of the bond interest and principal payments. Default, or bankruptcy, risk is, in fact, a special

---

[3] This aspect of risk is elaborated in Chapter 12.

[4] The dispersion of future probability distributions of investment outcomes, indicating the extent of possible deviation of actual from expected values, is therefore a natural measure of risk. Dispersion measures, such as the standard deviation of the probability distribution on outcomes, are extensively used in the finance literature as risk measures.

case of the firm's business risk where the unexpected negative change in earnings is large and persistent over time, forcing the firm to default on its bonds. Obviously, the extent of default risk associated with bonds depends not only on the firm's business risk but also on the specific provisions of the bond issue. Pledges on assets (mortgage bonds) and restrictions on the creation of additional debt or on excessive payments of dividends enhance bondholders' security by decreasing expected losses in the event of default.[5]

2. *Interest rate risk,* caused by unexpected changes in interest rates which will inversely affect the market value of bonds. Specifically, changes in prevailing interest rates, such as those induced by changes in monetary policy, will affect the opportunity costs of holding fixed interest bonds and hence their market prices. For example, when interest rates increase unexpectedly, the current bond yields are no longer sufficient to induce investors to hold them, and consequently a new equilibrium will be reached as bond prices decrease to the level where the higher yields equal the new interest rates.[6] The possible capital losses to current bondholders resulting from such unexpected price decreases constitute the interest rate risk associated with bondholding.[7] Note that this risk factor applies to all bonds: high grades as well as government bonds for which the default risk is negligible.

Interest rate risk is a function of the bond's term to maturity (i.e., its remaining duration); the longer the term to maturity, the larger the unexpected price changes and hence the higher the risk.[8] This association is caused by the coupon interest remaining fixed for the bond duration while market interest rates change. Hence, the longer the duration of the fixed coupon commitment, the stronger the effect of market interest changes on bond prices. Prices of long-term bonds are thus more vulnerable to unexpected interest rate changes than those of their short-term counterparts.

3. *Purchasing-power risk* refers to the loss in real terms sustained by bondholders during inflationary periods when the purchasing power of money decreases. The nature of the purchasing-power risk is clarified

---

[5] Bond provisions sometimes even restrict management's prerogatives (e.g., a veto power by bondholders' representatives on large capital expenditures) in order to exercise some control over the firm's business risk.

[6] Note that when the bond's coupon rate is fixed, any decrease in price amounts to an increase in yield, and vice versa.

[7] A bond can, of course, be held to maturity and its face value received regardless of market conditions. This possibility, however, does not eliminate the ex ante risk, since the bondholder may have to sell his investment before maturity because he either unexpectedly needs the money or wishes to maximize returns during rising interest periods.

[8] For elaboration, see R. A. Kessel, *The Cyclical Behavior of the Term Structure of Interest Rates,* Occasional Paper No. 91 (New York: National Bureau of Economic Research, 1965), pp. 9–10.

by the well-known distinction between *nominal* and *real* interest rates; the former refers to the interest stated in terms of money, while the latter refers to interest payments in terms of their command over commodities, that is, in terms of the purchasing power of money. Thus, when the general price-level increases (decreases), the real rate of interest will be lower (higher) than the nominal interest rate.[9] Changes in expectation of inflation rate will cause bond prices and yields to vary until investors obtain a nominal interest rate sufficiently high to insure the desired real rate of interest. Such unexpected changes in bond prices and consequently in bondholders' wealth thus constitute the purchasing-power risk factor.[10] As with interest rate risk, high grades and government bonds are also susceptible to purchasing-power risk.

4. *Marketability risk* refers to the ease in disposing of the bond. This risk is relatively low for large and dispersed issues traded in well-organized markets but is evidently higher for small issues and those traded over the counter. The marketability risk is associated with the possible loss sustained on sale, especially when the bondholder is pressed for time. The degree of marketability is a function of the individual properties of the bond (e.g., size of issue) as well as of the imperfections in the market in which it is traded (e.g., small number of traders, high transaction costs, etc.).

Considering the four risk factors discussed above, it can be concluded that no bond is risk-free. The lowest-risk security is probably a short-term (a week or two) government bond for which default and marketability risk are nonexistent, and because of the short term to maturity, the interest rate and purchasing-power risk are negligible.

It is generally observed that capital markets are dominated by risk averters, that is, by investors who demand a higher yield as a compensation for an increased risk.[11] This attitude toward risk underlies

---

[9] It can be shown that the real interest rate, i, is approximated by subtracting the expected price-level increase, g, from the nominal rate of interest, r, yielding: $i = r - g$. (See D. Patinkin, "Secular Price Movements and Economic Development: Some Theoretical Aspects," in *The Challenge of Development*, A. Bonné, ed. [Jerusalem: The Hebrew University, 1958], p. 28.) Thus, if a lender requires a 5 percent real interest rate per annum and, in addition, expects a 5 percent general price-level increase during the coming year, he will charge the borrower approximately a 10 percent per annum nominal interest rate. Consequently, *expected* price-level changes will be reflected in bond yields and prices.

[10] It is sometimes possible to hedge for the purchasing-power risk by linking bond interest and principal to a purchasing-power index (thus, for example, if the index increases by 10 percent, both interest and principal payments will increase accordingly). Such purchasing-power guarantees are quite common in countries suffering from serious inflation (e.g., Finland and Israel).

[11] For elaboration on risk aversion, see W. F. Sharpe, *Portfolio Theory and Capital Markets* (New York: McGraw-Hill Book Company, 1970), pp. 193–201. Sharpe defines a risk-averse investor as one who ". . . requires a higher expected return from a risky portfolio than from a riskless one. A risk-averse investor considers a risky

the concept of *risk premium,* which is the portion of the bond's yield compensating the investor for the risk bearing:

> The risk premium on a bond has been defined as the difference between its market yield to maturity and the corresponding pure rate of interest. Market yield is defined as the rate of interest at which the principal and interest payments specified in the bond contract must be discounted if their present value is to equal the current market price of the bond. The corresponding pure rate of interest is defined as market yield on a risk-less bond maturing on the same day as the bond under consideration.[12]

It was concluded earlier that no bond is riskless; the pure rate of interest mentioned by Fisher thus refers only to investments free of default and marketability risk (i.e., government bonds). The risk premium on a bond therefore reflects the default and marketability risk factors. Stated differently, the risk premium reflects the specific characteristics of the bond and those of the issuing firm, and abstracts from the risk elements pertaining to general economic conditions.[13]

THE DETERMINANTS OF BOND RISK PREMIUM: FISHER'S MODEL

The determinants of risk premium on corporate bonds were investigated by Fisher, who hypothesized that the default risk can be estimated by the following three variables:

> There are three sorts of variables that it is plausible to use together in estimating risk of default: measures of the variability of the firm's earnings; measures showing how reliable the firm has been in meeting its obligations; and measures depending on the firm's capital structure.[14]

Variability of past earnings as a surrogate for the probability of default was suggested as early as 1904.[15] The implicit assumption in using this measure is that the time series of a firm's earnings may be treated as a

---

portfolio less desirable than a riskless portfolio with the same expected wealth" (pp. 194–95). The evidence pertaining to the risk aversion of most investors is abundant: High-grade bonds usually yield less than the riskier low-grade bonds; over long periods stocks yield more than bonds, etc.

[12] L. Fisher, "Determinants of Risk Premium on Corporate Bonds," *The Journal of Political Economy,* 67 (June 1959), 221.

[13] Changes in economic conditions, such as an increase in interest rates, will probably affect the absolute values of bond risk premiums.

[14] Fisher, *op. cit.,* p. 222.

[15] J. P. Norton, "The Theory of Loan Credit in Relation to Corporation Economics," *Publications of the American Economic Association,* 3d series, 5 (1904), 298.

random sample from a normally distributed population of potential future earnings. The variation of the historical series is thus an estimate of the variation in the underlying population. Therefore, other things equal, a firm with a low variation of earnings is less likely to default than a firm experiencing a high variation.[16] Fisher measured earnings variability by the coefficient of variation of the firm's net income after taxes over nine years and denoted this variable by X_1.[17]

Since the coefficient of earnings variation is obviously only a surrogate for default risk, Fisher considered additional explanatory variables. One such variable was the firm's reliability in meeting obligations; other things equal, the longer a firm does not require its creditors to take a loss, the less likely it is that the estimated earnings variation, X_1, will be substantially less than the true one. Reliability in meeting obligations, X_2, was measured as the length of time since the latest of the following events occurred: the firm was founded, the firm emerged from bankruptcy, or a compromise was made in which creditors settled for less than 100 percent of their claims. Another element of default risk is inherent in the firm's capital structure (leverage). Capital structure indicates how much the firm's assets can decline in value before they become smaller than the liabilities, in which case the firm becomes insolvent. The equity/debt ratio, X_3, was chosen to measure this aspect of default risk.[18]

In addition to the surrogate variables for default risk, a measure for marketability risk was required. The variable chosen to reflect this risk element, X_4, was the total market value of the firm's bonds. The use of this variable was justified by the assumption that the smaller the amount of bonds outstanding, the less frequently they would be traded, and hence "thinner" and less perfect is their market.[19]

Fisher examined the explanatory power of the four-variable model with respect to risk premiums on a sample of U.S. industrial corporate bonds. Various least-squares regressions were run cross-sectionally on the 366 observations available, applying a logarithmic transformation to all the variables. Following are the estimated coefficients of the basic equation:

$$X_0 = .987 + .307X_1 - .253X_2 - .537X_3 - .275X_4; \quad (R^2 = .75)$$
$$ (.032) \quad\quad (.036) \quad\quad (.031) \quad\quad (.021)$$

[16] This approach to the measurement of ex ante variability is consistent with most practical applications of portfolio theory where past volatility is used to predict volatility in the future. More on the adequacy of past volatility estimates in Chapter 13.

[17] The *coefficient of variation* is the ratio of the standard deviation of the sample (adjusted for degrees of freedom) to its arithmetic mean.

[18] Note that equity is defined as the total *market value* of all shares of stock outstanding, rather than the accounting figure of equity.

[19] Volume of trading is an alternative and more intuitively appealing measure of marketability risk. However, Fisher found that the total amount of bonds outstanding is a better predictor of risk premium than volume of trading.

where X_0 is the logarithm of the average bond risk premium, and X_1 through X_4 are the logarithms of the four risk surrogates defined above. The numbers in parentheses are the estimated standard errors of the coefficients, and R^2 is the coefficient of multiple determination. Thus, the logarithms of the four risk surrogates accounted for 75 percent of the variance in the logarithm of risk premium, indicating a reasonably good explanatory power of the model. All the coefficients had the expected signs, they were all statistically significant at the 1 percent level or lower, and they were found to be relatively stable over time. It can be concluded, therefore, that the four variables—earnings variability, reliability in meeting financial obligations, capital structure, and bond marketability—adequately reflect the major determinants of risk premium on corporate bonds.

A model for the prediction of risk premium on corporate bonds may be of significant importance to the firm's financial managers as well as to investors. With respect to a prospective bond issue, the model provides a prediction of risk premium which, when added to the riskless interest rate, gives an estimate of the bond yield required by the market and hence of the effective cost of debt to the firm. Knowledge of this cost element is essential to management for such financial decisions as whether to finance investments by borrowed capital, equity capital, retained earnings, or a combination of these sources.[20]

A risk premium prediction model may also be used by investors and bond portfolio managers to assess the riskiness of bonds, by bank credit managers to evaluate the credit worthiness of prospective borrowers, and by underwriters to examine the potential of a prospective bond issue.

It should be noted, however, that the predictive power of Fisher's model was *indirectly* inferred from the relative stability over time of the estimated coefficients. No direct tests of the model's predictive power (e.g., by using the calibrating sample technique discussed in the preceding chapter) were reported by Fisher. Therefore, the normative usefulness of the model is yet to be verified.

BOND RATINGS

Bond ratings assigned to issues by rating agencies, such as Moody's and Standard and Poor's, are well known, respected, and extensively used

---

[20] It should be noted that when the effects of income taxes are considered, financial decisions are no longer independent of investment decisions (as is the case under perfect capital markets—the well-known Modigliani and Miller separation principle). Therefore, knowledge of the cost of debt is also important for investment decisions.

indicators of bond quality.[21] These agencies provide investors with a relatively up-to-date record of their opinions on the quality of most large, publicly held corporate, municipal, and governmental bond issues.[22] The quality of bond ratings is highly regarded by the investment community and by official regulatory commissions; the latter often utilize the ratings in evaluating the safety of securities held by banks and insurance companies.

Bond ratings are designed essentially to rank issues in order of their default probability.[23] In Standard and Poor's twelve-ratings system,[24] AAA bonds are regarded as having a negligible default risk; AA bonds are still high-grade obligations yet not quite so free of default risk as the preceding class; A and BBB bonds are regarded as upper-medium and medium-grade quality, respectively, where the obligation is adequately protected yet some default risk is evidently present; [25] BB and B bonds are regarded as speculative, while CCC and CC bonds are considered extremely speculative from the default risk point of view; C, DDD, DD, and D bonds are issues with interest not regularly paid (C ratings), or bonds in default. It was estimated that only about 5 percent of all industrial bonds get an AAA rating from Standard and Poor's, and about 40 percent of the bonds get a BB rating or lower.[26] The agencies are engaged in a continuous process of reviewing and reconsidering their ratings, and they change the ratings when circumstances warrant.

The high regard of the business community and regulatory agencies for bond ratings seems to be justified by experience; bond ratings have been found to be highly correlated with default rates.[27] Harold, in his study of corporate bond experience during 1929–35, reports an inverse relationship between bond ratings and default rates.[28] Burrell found an

---

21 In addition to these principal rating agencies, two other organizations publish bond ratings—Fitch and Dun & Bradstreet; the latter specializes in municipal bond ratings.

22 The value of rated bonds is substantial: At the end of 1964, Moody's ratings covered about $57 billion of outstanding bonds—about half the value of all publicly and privately held bonds.

23 Some weight is also given to marketability risk.

24 The interpretation of Moody's nine-ratings system (from AAA through C) is quite similar.

25 BBB bonds are the lowest grade qualifying for bank investment under present commercial bank regulations.

26 See H. C. Sherwood, "How They'll Rate Your Company's Bonds," *Business Management*, 29 (March 1966), 78.

27 It should be noted, however, that the adequacy of bond ratings, especially with respect to municipal bonds, has sometimes been questioned. See, for example, S. B. Packer, "Municipal Bond Ratings," *Financial Analysts Journal*, 24 (July–August 1968), 93–97.

28 G. Harold, *Bond Ratings as an Investment Guide* (New York: The Ronald Press, 1938), pp. 93–106, 141–46.

inverse relationship between bond ratings and the proportion of corporate bonds whose income was interrupted and whose market values suffered relatively great declines.[29] Hickman, in a comprehensive study of corporate bond experience, confirmed these findings.[30] He reported that issues rated as high grades at offering had, with great regularity, lower default rates than those rated at low grades; capital losses were consistently smaller for the high grades that went into default than for the low grades; and the highest returns were obtained, on average, on low-grade offerings reflecting their higher riskiness. In general, he found agency ratings able to predict default occurrences as well as default losses.

THE PREDICTION OF BOND RATINGS

Ratings agency officials frequently claim that their ratings cannot be statistically determined from published data, arguing that subtstantial weight is given in the rating system to judgmental, nonquantifiable factors. For example, Albert C. Esokait, senior vice-president of Moody's, says that bond rating ". . . is not a number game. You couldn't rate bonds on a computer. It would blow a gasket. Bond-rating is a comprehensive analysis of the position of a company in whatever industry it is in." [31] While judgment is undoubtedly exercised in the determination of bond ratings, it is obvious that various quantifiable financial and operating factors relating to the rated bond and the issuing company play an important role in the rating process. Louis Brand, who presided for twenty-six years over Standard and Poor's bond department, disclosed that rating committee members mainly focus on four factors: the company's future earnings power, the company's financial resources (mainly its liquidity position), the extent of property protection (i.e., how heavily the property is encumbered by other debt), and the bond's indenture position (i.e., the restrictions under which the company must operate after the bond issue.) [32] Since most of these factors are quantifiable, it would seem possible to develop financial models that simulate the rating process. If successful, such models could then be used by management and analysts to predict new ratings and rating changes.

Horrigan was probably the first to develop a model for the pre-

[29] O. K. Burrell, *A Study in Investment Mortality* (University of Oregon, Bureau of Business Research, School of Business Administration, 1947), pp. 10–11.

[30] W. B. Hickman, *Corporate Bond Quality and Investor Experience* (Princeton, N.J.: Princeton University Press, for the Naitonal Bureau of Economic Research, 1958), Chap. 3.

[31] "The Men Who Make Treasures Tremble," *Forbes*, September 1, 1970, p. 19.

[32] Sherwood, *op. cit.*

diction of bond ratings.[33] His initial sample was comprised of firms whose bond ratings did not change during 1959–64. This sample included 201 firms rated by Moody's and 151 firms rated by Standard and Poor's (137 of the firms were rated by both agencies). Results (i.e., estimated regression coefficients) obtained from the initial sample were then used to predict the ratings of two subsequent samples: (a) 130 firms obtaining new ratings during the period 1961–64 and (b) 85 firms whose previously assigned ratings were changed during 1961–64.

The analysis was performed by running multiple linear regressions on the initial sample of bond ratings with various combinations of financial ratios as the independent variables.[34] The model with the highest explanatory power included the following variables: total assets, working capital to sales, net worth to total debt, sales to net worth, and net operating profit to sales. Note that the ratios in this model represent the four conventional ratio categories discussed in Chapter 2.[35] Size of firm (total assets) was found to be the most important variable in terms of explanatory power, and net worth to total debt (a capital structure measure) was the most important ratio.[36] These regression results confirm the well-known and documented phenomenon discussed in the preceding chapter that default risk (reflected in the bond rating) is highly correlated with firm size and degree of leverage, the latter variable indicating the firm's financial risk. The coefficient of multiple determination, R^2, for the various samples was slightly below .50, indicating that about 50 percent of the cross-sectional variation in bond ratings was "explained" by the five variables listed above.

The regression coefficients derived from the initial sample were then used to develop indexes for predicting *new* sets of ratings as well as *changes* in the ratings. The predictions were made on the basis of the firm's financial data for one and two years prior to the new rating or

33 J. O. Horrigan, "The Determination of Long-Term Credit Standing with Financial Ratios," *Empirical Research in Accounting: Selected Studies, 1966*, Supplement to Vol. 4, *Journal of Accounting Research*, 44–62.

34 The ratios used in the regressions were adjusted by dividing them by the industry average ratio. This adjustment was intended to serve as a "correction" for cyclical and seasonal conditions as well as for industry classification.

35 Horrigan notes (*op. cit.*, p. 56), "Given the presence of intercorrelation among the various ratios, this model, or some variation of it, probably represents the maximum amount of information which can be squeezed out of financial ratios."

36 For example, the following estimated coefficients (and their standard errors in parentheses) were obtained from running the regression on Standard and Poor's 1960 ratings (*ibid.*, p. 57):

$$X_0 = .035X_1 + .289X_2 - .506X_3 + 4.570X_4 - .223X_5; \quad R^2 = .48$$
$$\quad\;\; (.006) \qquad (.071) \qquad (.124) \qquad (1.469) \qquad (.162)$$

The independent variables (in order of X_1 through X_5) are total assets, net worth to total debt, working capital to sales, operating profit to sales, and sales to net worth.

the change in rating and were then compared with the actual rating. Approximately 58 and 52 percent of Moody's and Standard and Poor's new ratings, respectively, were correctly predicted, and most of the remaining predictions were within one rating of the actual ones. With respect to rating changes, approximately 54 percent of Moody's and 57 percent of Standard and Poor's were correctly predicted. Based on these results, Horrigan concluded that ". . . financial ratios and accounting data can be useful in long-term credit administration." [37] The main use of the model for analysts, financial officers, and underwriters obviously lies in its ability to predict the value of a new rating. With respect to bond-rating changes, the usefulness of the model is less straightforward:

> The prediction results in regard to the bond-rating changes should be viewed mainly as a test of the model with a new set of data, rather than as a test of the model's power to predict the *timing* of changes. To establish that power, the results would have to be much better and a control group would be necessary.[38]

The main shortcoming of Horrigan's model lies in the restriction of the explanatory variables to conventional financial ratios. The restrictiveness of this approach was confirmed by Horrigan when a non-accounting dummy variable, representing the subordination status of the bonds, was added to the model:

> The addition of the subordination dummy variable improved the results considerably. . . . These results tended to "swamp" the role of accounting data, and the financial ratios in particular.[39]

The argument concerning the restrictiveness of accounting data was pursued by Richard West, commenting on Horrigan's study:

> In closing, I would like to echo several remarks made earlier by other discussants. I am referring to comments that accounting data should be viewed rather broadly and that empirical research using accounting data need not be limited to using only accounting data. It just might be that

[37] *Ibid.*, p. 62.

[38] *Ibid.*, p. 61.

[39] *Ibid.*, p. 58. Following are the regression results for Standard and Poor's 1960 sample, including the subordination dummy variable:

$$X_0 = 1.197SUB + .034X_1 + .272X_2 - .501X_3 + 4.519X_4 - .203X_5; R^2 = .63.$$
$$(.159) \quad (.007) \quad (.073) \quad (.124) \quad (1.462) \quad (.161)$$

The first variable (SUB) represents the bond's subordination status; the remaining variables are as defined in footnote 36. Note the high statistical significance of the subordination variable (t value $= 7.54$), and the improvement in R^2 resulting from the addition of this variable to the model (from .48 to .63).

the real usefulness of accounting data can only be appreciated, and measured, when it is looked at in this broader context.[40]

To prove his point, West later examined the predictive power of Fisher's model (discussed earlier in this chapter) with respect to bond ratings:

> The basic rationale behind the use of Fisher's model to predict corporate bond ratings is extremely simple. The model does an excellent job of estimating risk premiums and these are highly correlated with ratings. Therefore, the model should also perform well as a predictor of ratings.[41]

Using Fisher's data, West found that the four-variable model (earnings variability, reliability in meeting financial obligations, capital structure, and bond marketability) accounted for more than 70 percent of the variability in the logarithms of the ratings and predicted the ratings correctly in about 60 percent of the cases. Thus, while Fisher's model accounts for a larger percentage of the ratings variability than Horrigan's, the improvement in predictive power is rather modest.

Additional models, based mainly on financial data, were recently developed for the description and prediction of bond ratings.[42] The performance of these models was basically similar to those of Horrigan and West. Of special interest is a recent study by Pinches and Mingo in which the "factor analysis" method was used to screen the data in order to choose the most appropriate explanatory variables.[43] The principal objective of factor analysis is to attain a parsimonious description of the observed data, thereby expediting the statistical analysis. The savings are substantial when the number of original variables is large but the number of factors or distinct dimensions (patterns) of the data is small.[44] In the Pinches and Mingo study, thirty-five financial variables (financial ratios, coefficients of variation, etc.) were considered, yet only seven factor patterns or basically different dimensions were identified by the factor analysis method: size, leverage, long-term capital intensiveness, return

[40] R. R. West, discussion of J. O. Horrigan, *op. cit.*, p. 70.

[41] R. R. West, "An Alternative Approach to Predicting Corporate Bond Ratings," *Journal of Accounting Research*, 8 (Spring 1970), 121. See also Horrigan's comment, *ibid.*, pp. 126–27.

[42] See T. F. Pogue and R. M. Soldofsky, "What's in a Bond Rating?" *Journal of Financial and Quantitative Analysis*, 4 (June 1969), 201–18; W. T. Carleton and E. M. Lerner, "Statistical Credit Scoring of Municipal Bonds," *Journal of Money, Credit and Banking*, 1 (November 1969), 750–64; and J. J. Horton, Jr., "Statistical Classification of Municipal Bonds," *Journal of Bank Research*, 1 (Autumn 1970), 29–40.

[43] G. E. Pinches and K. A. Mingo, "A Multivariate Analysis of Industrial Bond Ratings," *The Journal of Finance*, 28 (March 1973), 1–18.

[44] For elaboration on the factor analysis method, see R. J. Rummel, *Applied Factor Analysis* (Evanston, Ill.: Northwestern University Press, 1970).

on investment, short-term capital intensiveness, earnings stability, and debt coverage. The use of factor analysis thus reduced the thirty-five variables to seven rather homogeneous groups, each representing a different characteristic of the firm. One variable was then chosen from each group (factor dimension) to be included in the bond-rating prediction model.

Using a sample of 180 Moody's rated bonds (B rating or above), Pinches and Mingo found that their multiple discriminant analysis model (incorporating the variables chosen by the factor analysis method) correctly predicted the ratings of 64.6 percent of the bonds. The prediction in all cases was within one rating of the actual. The bond subordination status was found to be the most important independent variable. Note that these results are quite similar to those reported by Horrigan.

EVALUATION OF EVIDENCE

Whether bond risk premiums and ratings can be predicted from financial data is obviously of great importance to management,[45] investors, and regulatory agencies. The evidence, however, is somewhat sparse to warrant conclusive answers. The determinants of bond risk premiums were thoroughly investigated only once (Fisher's study), emphasizing the positive (descriptive) aspects of the problem and leaving the normative (predictive) aspects to be indirectly inferred from the stability of the regression coefficients. The bond-rating prediction problem fared better; various studies demonstrated that agency ratings can be simulated reasonably well by financial models, and new bond ratings predicted rather accurately within one-rating bounds. The inclusion of nonaccounting data (e.g., the bonds' subordination status) and the transformation of some accounting data (e.g., earnings variability) proved warranted in most cases. The evidence thus suggests that despite the arguments of rating agency officials to the contrary, well-constructed financial models might be helpful in indicating a reasonable range of rating for a prospective bond issue and the possibility of a change in the ratings of outstanding issues.

It should be noted that the inability of financial models to predict the ratings more accurately may be a reflection on the quality of the rating process as well as on the performance of the models. Although the ratings were generally found to be reliable, exceptions were noted from

---

[45] It was estimated that in 1966 an AAA-rated bond had to pay about 4.95 percent interest annually while a BBB bond had to pay about 5.40 percent. If the firm is seeking $50 million repayable in thirty years, this difference in interest amounts to $6.65 million in additional interest expenses to the firm. Sherwood, *op. cit.*, pp. 39–40.

time to time.[46] In addition, the change of ratings by agencies, as opposed to risk premium changes, is not a continuous process. There is probably a substantial lag between the change in the firm's financial and operating characteristics affecting the quality of its bonds and the actual change in the rating. It has also been alleged that bond issuers or underwriters might sometimes affect the ratings by exerting pressure on the rating agencies.[47] Accordingly, the following two avenues of research are suggested: (a) constructing financial models aimed at *improving* the rating system rather than simulating it, and (b) directing more research toward the prediction of risk premiums which are based on the capital market's assessment of bond quality and might therefore be more updated and reliable risk indicators than bond ratings.

SUMMARY

The risk associated with bond holding was examined in this chapter, particularly the default and marketability risk factors which are reflected in bond risk premiums and ratings. The major determinants of bond risk premiums were found to be the earnings variability, the firm's reliability in meeting its financial obligations, the degree of financial leverage, and the bond's marketability measured by the size of issue. Financial models aimed at predicting new bond ratings and changes in the ratings were also examined. Results suggest that well-constructed models are useful for indicating a reasonably accurate range of ratings for a prospective bond issue and the possibility of changes in the ratings of outstanding issues.

[46] For example, Harold, *op. cit.*, p. 144, reports that during 1929–35, the actual default rate for BBB bonds was lower than that of the higher quality ABB bonds (14 percent vs. 18 percent, respectively).

[47] See, for example, "New York State Asks 2 Services to Upgrade School Bond Ratings," *Wall Street Journal*, August 13, 1971, p. 15. It is well known that extensive negotiations between corporate executives and rating agency officials are sometimes undertaken prior to the rating determination.

CHAPTER ELEVEN

Credit Evaluation
by Banks

The optimal allocation of credit is probably the most important problem facing a bank. The bank loan analyst must provide loan officers with an evaluation of the extent of an applicant's credit risk and assess the trade-offs among the terms of a loan, such as interest rate, maturity, and face value. Since the loan analyst's time is a scarce resource, it should be allocated in an efficient manner; a formal screening process that would segregate loans into several categories requiring different amounts of analysis would obviously improve such resource allocation. Additional objectives of formalizing the currently heuristic and subjective loan evaluation process are (a) to gain better understanding of the process and thereby improve its consequences, and (b) to assist in the training of bank loan officers and analysts.

The majority of existing credit evaluation models have been designed for consumer credit.[1] The development of commercial credit models seems to be more difficult for the following reasons:

First, commercial borrowers do not belong to large homogeneous populations as do customers for consumer credit. This lack of standardization

---

[1] See J. H. Myers and E. W. Forgy, "The Development of Numerical Credit Evaluation Systems," *Journal of the American Statistical Association*, 58 (September 1963), 799–806.

presents a problem in obtaining data for a statistically significant study. Second, there are substantial variations among commercial loans with respect to their size, terms, collateral types, and payment procedure, all of which are relatively uniform in the case of consumer loans. Finally, there is a lack of reliable up-to-date financial data on small commercial borrowers and particularly on those who defaulted in their loans.[2]

However, since our main interest lies in the usefulness of financial statement data for credit evaluation, we will focus on commercial borrowers for which such data are usually available. The models presented and evaluated below deal with the following aspects of bank credit operations: the determinants of lending terms, the evaluation of loan applications, and the prediction of loan examiner ratings.

THE DETERMINANTS OF BANK LENDING TERMS

Hester conducted an econometric investigation of commercial banks' lending behavior.[3] His study is unique among bank credit models in that he attempted to construct a theory of a general loan offer (supply) function. His model specified the efficient set of terms at which a bank with particular characteristics will be willing to lend to a borrower with "a known profit level, balance sheet, credit history, and prospects for the future." [4] Four kinds of lending terms were considered: the loan rate of interest, the maturity of the loan, the amount of the loan, and the requirement of security.

Based upon an efficiency definition in the Pareto optimality sense, Hester hypothesized that a bank with certain characteristics and information about the prospective borrower will not grant a more liberal loan from the standpoint of one lending term (e.g., interest rate) without worsening other terms (e.g., maturity). Therefore, the final loan terms will depend not only upon the economic characteristics of the loan applicant and those of the bank but also upon the trade-offs among the four terms of lending.

Having conceptualized the loan offer function, Hester formally defined the two models to be empirically tested:

$$\log F_1(R,M,A,S) = \log G_1(W_1, W_2, \ldots, W_I) \qquad (11.1)$$

$$\log F_2(R,M,A,S) = \log G_2(Z_1, Z_2, \ldots, Z_J) \qquad (11.2)$$

[2] Y. E. Orgler, "A Credit Scoring Model for Commercial Loans," *Journal of Money, Credit and Banking*, 2 (November 1970), 436.

[3] D. D. Hester, "An Empirical Examination of a Commercial Bank Loan Offer Function," *Yale Economic Essays*, 2 (Spring 1962), 3–57.

[4] *Ibid.*, p. 3.

where

R = the loan rate of interest (percent)
M = the maturity of the loan (months)
A = the amount of the loan (dollars)
S = "1" if the loan is secured, and "0" otherwise
W_i = the ith relevant characteristic of loan applicants, $(i = 1, \ldots, I)$
Zj = the jth relevant characteristic of lending banks, $(j = 1, \ldots, J)$.

The independent (explanatory) variables in (11.1) were classified into two categories: financial ratios as well as other measures of the firm's past performance and present financial position, and quantitative measures reflecting the firm's previous relationship with the bank, such as its average deposit balance. The independent variables in (11.2) were various bank characteristics, such as the level of deposits and asset size. In each case, Hester selected variables that were expected to cause the rate of interest on the loan to increase, and/or the amount of the loan to decrease, and/or the maturity of the loan to decrease, and/or the likelihood of demanding security to increase, holding all other variables constant.

Data for model (11.1) were obtained from three large commercial banks. The data included information about the lending terms, the borrowers' financial position, and previous relationships between the borrowers and the banks. This sample included only term-loans (i.e., loans with maturity exceeding one year) granted during the period January 1955 through October 1957. Regression results indicated that four financial ratios derived from borrowers' statements contributed significantly to the explanation of lending terms—average profits,[5] current ratio, average deposit balance, and the ratio of profits to total assets. However, four other borrower variables—total assets, changes in average profits, working capital, and changes in working capital—were found to be statistically insignificant.[6]

Inspection of the regression results (11.1) for each of the four terms of lending indicates that the three regressions (one for each bank) determining the rate of interest provided the best overall statistical explanation (R^2's ranging from .80 to .74). The model's performance with respect to the other three lending terms was not as high; the R^2's for the amount of the loan, loan maturity, and likelihood of requiring security were on average, .49, .35, and .24, respectively.

In testing model (11.2), Hester's data were collected from surveys of

---

[5] These averages were calculated for a three- to five-year period, depending upon data availability.

[6] The insignificance of the total assets variable for loan terms is somewhat surprising in light of its importance in predicting bankruptcy and bond ratings, discussed in Chapters 9 and 10.

business loans taken by the Board of Governors of the Federal Reserve System from 1955 through 1957. This sample included information obtained from a large number of banks on loans of varying amounts and maturities, as opposed to the large, long maturity loans from three banks considered in model (11.1). To test the relevance of bank characteristics as determinants of loan terms, four independent variables were used in estimating the loan offer functions. Three of these variables relate to bank characteristics (i.e., level of deposits, ratio of commercial and industrial loans to total assets, and a location dummy variable), while one, total assets, relates to the borrower.

Regression results for model (11.2) suggest that the bank's level of deposits is the most significant factor in determining the loan terms; large banks charge higher interest rates and are more likely to require security than small banks, given an equivalent borrower. The bank location variable and the ratio of commercial and industrial loans to total assets were statistically insignificant in more than one of the regressions. The most interesting result was that borrowers' total assets dominated, in explanatory power, the regression equations. Generally, the explanatory power of the (11.2) models was inferior to that of (11.1) models. These results suggest that bank characteristics play a minor role relative to borrower characteristics in the determination of lending terms.

Hester's model suggests some important extensions. In particular, if bank loan offer functions can be formulated, it will be possible to evaluate loan officer decisions in light of the stated policy of the bank. This would provide management wtih a powerful control device, and external analysts would be able to compare and evaluate the policies of different banks. However, a major shortcoming in Hester's model should be noted. The separation of borrower and bank characteristics into two functions ignores the interaction that may actually take place when loans are made. Thus, although borrower characteristics seem to dominate the bank characteristics in the regression equations, we do not know on the basis of Hester's analysis their *combined* effect on the determination of lending terms. This problem can be overcome by developing a lending terms model which incorporates both borrower and bank variables.

A SIMULATION MODEL FOR THE EVALUATION OF LOAN APPLICATIONS

Cohen, Gilmore, and Singer have attempted to model the heuristic process followed by bank loan officers in evaluating commercial loan applications.[7] The model was intended to reflect both the type of analysis

---

[7] K. J. Cohen, C. Gilmore, and F. A. Singer, "Bank Procedures for Analyzing Business Loan Applications," in *Analytical Methods in Banking*, K. J. Cohen and F. S. Hammer, eds. (Homewood, Ill.: Richard D. Irwin, Inc., 1966), pp. 218–50.

followed and the specific factors considered so as to allow a computer simulation program "to make the same decisions on particular business loan applicants that commercial bankers actually make." [8] While the authors state that their model draws heavily on the particular evaluation procedures followed by two large banks, they do not feel that this fact will hinder the general applicability of the model to at least major money market banks and hopefully also to medium-sized and small banks.

It is important to note that since the model is intended to simulate the loan officer's decision process, the model incorporates the strengths and weaknesses of the human decision maker. That is, the model is not intended to provide "better" (in the sense of screening out loans that are likely to result in losses) decisions than are currently obtained by loan officers. The authors recognize this fact but state that once a computer program can simulate loan officer decisions

> it is probable that variations in the [computer] program would result in loan decisions which are even better, i.e., which will lead to increased net earnings for the bank.[9]

Although the model's eight phases cover the entire application evaluation procedure, only one of these phases—the credit evaluation—utilizes financial statement information. The other seven phases deal with evaluation of such matters as the requested loan's conformity with legal and bank policy requirements, the purpose and proposed repayment method of the loan, and the applicant's value to the bank as a future customer.

The credit evaluation phase of the model was designed to answer the following questions:

1. Is the bank's share of risk clearly unreasonable?
2. Does the applicant have enough current assets?
3. Are the applicant's current assets sufficiently liquid?
4. Is the applicant sufficiently profitable?
5. What is the final credit rating of the applicant?

The model inputs consist of historical and *pro forma* financial statements data of the applicant as well as industry standards.

In answering the first of the five questions, the model compares the applicant's ratio of tangible net worth to total debt with various industry percentile values of this ratio. If the firm's ratio does not exceed some

---

[8] *Ibid.*, p. 219.
[9] *Ibid.*, p. 221.

specified percentile value, the amount of the loan requested is reducd accordingly. The model next (question 2) deals with funds from operations, defined as net income plus nonoperating income and expense plus depreciation, depletion, and amortization. Various historical and projected amounts are tested to determine whether they will cover the total funds required to service both present and proposed debts for the next year. Liquidity (question 3) is evaluated by comparing the following ratios for the firm with various percentile rankings for the industry: cash to current liabilities, cash plus receivables to current liabilities, and inventories to current assets. In addition, the model compares the firm's present level of inventories with a three-year average of the firm's inventories. The authors present various decision tables to be used in the computer program to make comparisons and arrive at a solvency rating. Profitability (question 4) is evaluated by means of thirteen factors. In this stage, the minimum desired ratio of pretax profits to total tangible assets is estimated by the current prime interest rate or some multiple of this rate. *Pro forma* values for such measures as net profits and pretax profits to tangible assets are compared with industry standards to arrive at a profitability rating. Finally, in answering question 5, two decision tables, one for seasonal and one for term loans, combine the solvency and profitability ratings into an overall credit rating for the firm. This credit rating then serves as an input to the comprehensive loan evaluation model.

Regarding the usefulness of such a model, the authors state that it can be used to train loan analysts and that variations in the computer program will probably result in improved loan decisions. The problem, however, is that the model is based on current loan officer practices, and it is difficult to see how it can *improve* upon these practices without the explicit consideration of an optimization model designed to indicate what ought to be done rather than what is done. Nevertheless, a formalization of heuristic loan evaluation procedures may serve as an initial step in the construction of such a normative optimization model.

THE PREDICTION OF LOAN EXAMINER RATINGS

Orgler has constructed a multiple regression model to predict which commercial loans will be "criticized," that is, classified as doubtful, substandard, or loss, by bank examiners.[10] This dependent variable (i.e., criticized or uncriticized loans) was investigated earlier by Wojnilower [11]

10 Orgler, *op. cit.*
11 A. W. Wojnilower, *The Quality of Bank Loans,* Occasional Paper 82 (New York: National Bureau of Economic Research, 1962).

and Wu.[12] Wojnilower, using the examination files of three Federal Reserve Banks, reported that

> the annual changes in the criticism rate were quite consistent with the changes in industry and size composition of loans and in financial ratios, as well as with those in other indicators of loan quality, such as credit ratings and business failures and discontinuances.[13]

Wu tested directly the relationship between examiner criticisms and subsequent loan defaults, concluding that examiners were reasonably accurate in their criticisms. Examiners' predictability was more accurate for small banks and for large borrowers. Loan examiner ratings were thus found to be associated with the quality of loans, and it may therefore be of interest to construct a model for the prediction of such ratings. In addition, such a model ". . . can be considered a tool for allocating the time of bank officers and bank examiners in the review and evaluation of existing commercial loans." [14]

Orgler's sample consisted of three hundred loans; each of the seventy-five criticized loans in the sample was matched with three uncriticized loans from the same industry. A multiple regression analysis was used where the dependent variable took the value of one for a criticized loan and zero for an uncriticized loan. Of the six independent variables included in the final model on the basis of their statistical significance, five were dummy variables reflecting whether the loan was secured or unsecured, current or past-due, whether the borrower's financial statements were audited, whether his income was positive or negative, and whether the loan was criticized during the last examination. The sixth independent variable was the borrower's working capital to current assets ratio. The overall performance of the model was rather modest, as evidenced by the R^2 of .364. Tested on a validation (hold-out) sample of forty criticized loans and eighty uncriticized loans, the model correctly classified 75 percent of the criticized loans while classifying as marginal and uncriticized 22.5 percent and 2.5 percent, respectively. Of the uncriticized loans, 35 percent were correctly classified, 47.5 percent were classified as marginal, and 17.5 percent were classified as criticized.

In evaluating the usefulness of Orgler's model, it should be noted that the variable to be predicted (i.e., loan examiner ratings) is in itself a surrogate of somewhat questionable value for the quality of loans. Thus

If examiner judgment is less than completely accurate, a model based on

---

[12] H. K. Wu, "Bank Examiner Criticism, Bank Loan Defaults, and Bank Loan Quality," *Journal of Finance*, 24 (September 1969), 697–705.

[13] Wojnilower, *op. cit.*, p. 3.

[14] Orgler, *op. cit.*, p. 445.

their studied opinions will be less satisfactory in distinguishing between actual good and bad loans than [a] more objectively defined model.[15]

Therefore, the normative value of the model for predicting loan default is still unsubstantiated. Given the uncertainty regarding the value of examiner ratings, doubts are also raised with respect to Orgler's main objective in constructing the model, which was:

> . . . [to release] loan officers and bank examiners from routine evaluations of all loans and allocating their time to a small proportion of riskier borrowers.[16]

Obviously more has to be known about the ability of examiner ratings to predict loan failures before such ratings can serve as a useful economic indicator.

EVALUATION OF EVIDENCE

Given that banks are probably the major users of financial statement information, it is striking that so few models have been developed for bank credit operations. Difficulties in obtaining reliable data from banks may provide a partial explanation for the meager research in the area. However, the main problem here, as elsewhere in financial analysis, is clearly the lack of an adequate conceptual framework for credit-granting operations. Such basic questions as the optimal trade-offs among the terms of lending, the efficient risk-return combination for a bank loan portfolio, and the relationship between borrower economic characteristics and the risk of default are largely unanswered.

The models summarized in this chapter, despite their methodological shortcomings, represent a step in the right direction. They provide some descriptive information on the relationship between the characteristics of banks and borrowers and the terms of lending, and on the factors that probably guide loan officers and bank examiners in their decisions. Obviously much more has to be known on how credit decisions *are* made, but, more important, models must be designed to indicate what *ought* to be done. Normative models must be developed for the improvement of current credit operations. Probably the most promising approach at this stage would be the application of portfolio theory principles designed to indicate the optimal structure of an investment portfolio.[17]

---

15 J. A. Haslem and W. A. Longbrake, "A Credit Scoring Model for Commercial Loans," *Journal of Money, Credit and Banking*, 4 (August 1972), 734.

16 Orgler, *op. cit.*, p. 443.

17 For elaboration, see Chapter 12.

Such basic portfolio theory concepts as risk diversification and the effect of correlation among investment returns on the portfolio's risk are clearly applicable to bank credit operations. The shift in research should therefore be from descriptive to normative studies, taking advantage of existing optimization models and developing others when necessary.

SUMMARY

Banks are among the major users of financial statement data for investment decision making. A few models using such data have been developed to describe the decision process involved in lending operations. The main shortcoming of these models lies in their descriptive nature. Although they provide insight into the lending process, they fail to indicate the optimal decisions that ought to be made by bank officers.

PART THREE

RELATIONSHIP WITH MODERN FINANCE THEORIES

CHAPTER TWELVE

Principles
of
Portfolio Theory

The portfolio selection model has recently had a considerable impact on both the theory and the practice of finance. The model provides researchers with a wide range of empirically testable implications and offers practitioners various useful analytical tools, such as a framework for the evaluation of mutual funds' performance. The role of the financial analyst in the portfolio decision process is to assist in the optimal estimation of the model's parameters, particularly the systematic risk of securities. Specifically, given that conventional estimation of securities' systematic risk is rather unsatisfactory, the objective of the financial analyst is to design an information system that will improve upon current risk estimation.

The present chapter presents various basic principles and implications of the portfolio model relevant to financial statement analysis.[1] The next chapter (Chapter 13) discusses the role of financial statement analysis in the portfolio selection process.

[1] It should be noted that this discussion is not a comprehensive presentation of the portfolio model. The model's aspects that are unrelated to financial statement analysis, such as the expected utility theory, are not discussed below. Various texts provide a comprehensive presentation of the portfolio model; for example, W. F. Sharpe, *Portfolio Theory and Capital Markets* (New York: McGraw-Hill Book Company, 1970).

THE INADEQUACY OF CLASSICAL APPROACHES
TO THE INVESTMENT DECISION

The main body of the microeconomic theory of investment was developed within the context of perfect certainty. It was generally assumed that future outcomes of investment projects, their replacement costs and interest rates, were perfectly known in advance. Given such information on future outcomes, an optimal investment strategy could be determined: Capital stock should be adjusted by investment or disinvestment until the marginal rate of return on further investments is equal to the interest rate (i.e., the cost of capital).[2] Computational techniques such as the net present value method were developed to implement this optimal investment criterion.

The perfect certainty investment model violates real-life conditions not only in its assumptions (i.e., future investment outcomes are perfectly predictable) but also in its implications. The major implication, or prediction, of the model is that each decision maker will choose the project that offers the highest rate of return (or net present value), because investors are only interested in rates of return. Accordingly, the perfect certainty investment model implies that investors will usually hold a *one-asset portfolio*—a prediction that is obviously inconsistent with the observed behavior of portfolio diversification. Stated differently, the perfect certainty model does not explain the prevalent phenomenon of investment diversification. The failure of classic investment theory to cope with positive as well as normative real-life phenomena paved the way for new approaches to the investment decision.

Given that the development of a comprehensive investment theory under conditions of uncertainty is a major endeavor, some researchers attempted to devise partial solutions to the investment decision problem. One such solution involved the substitution of the expected values of future investment outcomes for the "known" outcomes in the certainty model. Specifically, it was argued that in an uncertain environment, the investment's future outcomes (e.g., the periodic net cash flows) are random variables subject to a known probability distribution. Therefore, the adjustment required is to replace the deterministic values of the certainty model by the expected values (i.e., means) of the probability distributions. Note, however, that such an investment model implies that investors base their decisions solely on the expected value of future outcomes and will therefore also predict a single-asset portfolio; each in-

---

[2] In a world of certainty and perfect markets, there will be a unique (i.e., single) interest rate in each period. This rate will also be the cost of capital for all investors in the economy.

vestor will hold only that asset offering the highest expected return.[3] The major shortcoming of the expected value approach is its failure to recognize that in making decisions investors will usually consider, in addition to the expected value, other characteristics (e.g., the standard deviation) of the probability distribution on future outcomes. Therefore, an investment model under uncertainty cannot be fully described by a simple discounting mechanism of the expected values of future investment outcomes.

Another attempt at a partial solution to the uncertainty problem employs the concept of risk-equivalent class developed by Modigliani and Miller.[4] Since investments belonging to a certain risk class have, by definition, the same degree of business risk, any analysis of behavior confined to a given risk class can abstract from the risk element.[5] Risk is thus accounted for, but only at the cost of restricting consideration to investments within a given risk class. Such a restriction did not adversely affect Modigliani and Miller's objective, that is, the proof that in perfect capital markets the firm's capital structure (leverage) is independent of its market value. However, the risk class notion cannot be used in an investment decision model where the main issue of interest is the relative riskiness of investments belonging to different risk classes.

The unsatisfactory solutions offered by the above models to the investment decision problem under uncertainty initiated the development of the portfolio model. Unlike earlier approaches, this model deals with decisions involving uncertain outcomes by considering *explicitly* the risk element involved. A discussion of various basic principles and implications of the portfolio model follows.

PRINCIPLES OF PORTFOLIO SELECTION THEORY

Portfolio theory is concerned with decisions involving outcomes that cannot be predicted with complete certainty, such as investment in common stocks, acquisition of real estate, choice of employment, and purchase of an insurance policy. It thus extends the classical microeconomic

---

[3] Investors basing their decisions solely on the expected (monetary) values of future outcomes are defined as risk-indifferent. For such investors, there will indeed be no incentive to diversify in order to reduce risk. For elaboration on investors' attitudes toward risk, see Sharpe, *op. cit.*, Chap. 9.

[4] F. Modigliani and M. H. Miller, "The Cost of Capital, Corporation Finance, and the Theory of Investment," *American Economic Review*, 47 (June 1958), 261–97. Investments (or firms) belonging to a risk-equivalent class are defined as those fulfilling the following two conditions: (*a*) the probability distributions of expected returns differ at most by a scale factor and (*b*) the returns are perfectly positively correlated.

[5] Risk and uncertainty will be used in this chapter synonymously. The difference between the two concepts was discussed in Chapter 10, footnote 2.

theory of investment under certainty to the real world of uncertainty. The origins of portfolio theory can be traced back to 1730 when Bernoulli published his celebrated "Exposition of a New Theory on the Measurement of Risk," laying the ground for the expected utility theory. However, Bernoulli's work had little impact on investment theory until the early 1950s when Markowitz's portfolio model was published.[6] Markowitz's contribution initiated an unprecedented amount of research in finance aimed at extending the theory and testing its empirical implications.[7]

A. The two-dimensional risk-return investment decision

In a broad sense, the portfolio selection process encompasses all the uncertain choices an individual must make, such as accepting a job, taking a trip abroad, and purchasing an insurance policy. However, for practical reasons, the portfolio model is usually restricted to investments in capital markets, that is, to the choice of securities to be included in a portfolio. Essentially, the portfolio selection problem is the following: Given a set of estimates regarding the future outcomes (i.e., rates of return) of each security, what is the optimal portfolio an investor should select? The estimates regarding future outcomes may be the investor's own based on his experience and outlook on the future, or they may be obtained from an analyst. The crucial point is that predictions in the form of "point estimates" only (e.g., an IBM stock will yield 15 percent next year) are insufficient for optimal investment decisions. The reason is that predictions in the real world are very rarely perfectly accurate; it is therefore imperative to account in the investment decision for the extent to which the subsequently realized outcomes may differ from those predicted. The larger the possible difference between predicted and realized outcomes, the larger, on average, the uncertainty of the estimate and hence the risk involved in the portfolio decision. The following example clearly demonstrates that this uncertainty element should be considered in the process of portfolio selection. Suppose an analyst predicts next year's return on a specific security to be 10 percent. However, he perceives a chance of one out of ten that the actual return will be

---

[6] H. Markowitz, "Portfolio Selection," *Journal of Finance*, 7 (March 1952), 77–91; and *Portfolio Selection: Efficient Diversification of Investments* (New York: John Wiley & Sons, Inc., 1959). An important contribution to portfolio theory was also made by J. Tobin, "Liquidity Preference as Behavior toward Risk," *Review of Economic Studies*, 25 (February 1958), 65–86.

[7] For a comprehensive bibliography, see Sharpe, *op. cit.*, pp. 303–12. For a survey article, see M. C. Jensen, "Capital Markets: Theory and Evidence," *The Bell Journal of Economics and Management Science*, 3 (Autumn 1972), 357–98.

9 percent and an equal chance for the actual return to be 11 percent (the chance of 10 percent return is obviously eight out of ten). Suppose further that for a second security the analyst's point estimate is still a return of 10 percent, yet he perceives the following possible outcomes:

Rate of Return	Chance
1%	1 of 10
7	2 of 10
10	5 of 10
15	1 of 10
20	1 of 10

It is obvious that the analyst's uncertainty regarding next year's return is larger for the second security than for the first, since the actual outcome of the second security might deviate from the predicted one (10 percent) to a larger extent than in the case of the first security (e.g., the lowest return perceived for the first security is 9 percent, while that for the second is 1 percent). Thus, despite the identical expected or average return for both securities (i.e., 10 percent), it is clear that most investors would not be indifferent between them, because of the different degree of uncertainty involved. Some investors, for example, would be reluctant to hold the second security given the possibility of 1 percent return. The uncertainty element involved in the prediction should therefore be taken into account in the portfolio decision.

The preceding example, despite being oversimplified, highlights a major principle of portfolio theory. Whereas in a world of certainty investment decisions should be exclusively based on the value of future returns, in an uncertain situation the decision maker must consider two factors simultaneously: the security's expected rate of return and the uncertainty involved in this expectation, the latter element being measured by the extent to which the actual return may deviate from the predicted one. The explicit consideration of an uncertainty factor in the decision process is a significant extension of classical investment theory and provides the foundation of the portfolio selection model:

> I do not believe it is an exaggeration to say that, until relatively recently, the basic model of portfolio choice used in economic theory was a one-parameter model. Investors were assumed to rank portfolios by reference to one parameter only—the expected return, possibly corrected by an arbitrary "risk premium," constant and unexplained. This approach was rationalized, if at all, by assuming either subjective certainty or constant marginal utility. It is now more than a decade ago that I participated in the modest endeavor of *doubling the number of parameters of investors' probability estimates* involved in economists' analyses of asset choices.[8]

8 J. Tobin, "Comment on Borch and Feldstein," *The Review of Economic Studies*, 36 (January 1969), 14, emphasis supplied.

The two-dimensional risk-return approach underlies the portfolio choice. Essentially, an investor is assumed to be able to express his preferred trade-offs between risk and return. He might state, for example, that in a given situation he would require an increase in annual return of at least 5 percent to assume a risk increase of 2 percent. Such investor preferences, expressed in the form of indifference curves, are then matched with the actual risk-return trade-offs offered in the stock market to determine the optimal portfolio for the investor.[9] The optimal choice is thus based on the simultaneous consideration of the preferred and available risk and return aspects of securities.

The two-dimensional investment approach has a wide range of applications in addition to the optimal portfolio choice. Among the most useful is the evaluation of mutual and pension funds' performance. Briefly, the portfolio performance of such funds was traditionally evaluated by comparing the realized portfolio return (dividends plus capital gains) with an average market return (e.g., the Dow Jones index) and/or the returns on competitors' funds. Such a one-dimensional comparison (average returns only) is obviously inappropriate, since it ignores risk differentials between the evaluated portfolio and the standard with which it is compared. Omission of the risk factor is most serious when the fund's return is compared with the average return of the stock market, since the latter refers to a maximum diversified portfolio (i.e., the market portfolio) which is substantially less risky than most funds' portfolios. Hence, a higher-than-average return on the fund's portfolio does not necessarily indicate a superior performance; the difference in returns may be a mere reflection of the risk differentials. Thus, evaluation of mutual funds' performance is incomplete and even misleading when risk differentials among portfolios are not accounted for. As mentioned above, portfolio theory provides a framework for the necessary two-dimensional risk-return evaluation of fund performance.[10]

Portfolio theory assumes that future outcomes (e.g., expected returns) for each security can be estimated in the form of a probability distribution. Under certain conditions all the information contained in the probability distribution can be summarized by two parameters—the

---

[9] The number of actual portfolios available in the stock market is, of course, almost infinite. However, only a relatively small number of portfolios is *efficient*. An efficient portfolio, for a given level of expected return, is the one with the lowest dispersion of return, measured by the variance or standard deviation. The group of efficient portfolios, known as the *efficient set,* represents the optimal trade-offs between risk and return available in the market. The point of tangency between the efficient set and the investor's indifference curves denotes the optimal portfolio, or risk-return combination, for the investor. For elaboration on this optimization process, see Sharpe, *op. cit.,* Chap. 4.

[10] For a comprehensive discussion of such an evaluation procedure, see E. F. Fama, "Risk and the Evaluation of Pension Fund Performance," *Measuring the Investment Performance of Pension Funds for the Purpose of Inter-Fund Comparisons* (Park Ridge, Ill.: Bank Administration Institute, 1968), pp. 191–224.

mean and standard deviation of the distribution.[11] Stated differently, under certain circumstances an investor can perform his portfolio selection process solely on the basis of the mean and standard deviation of the returns distribution, rather than having to consider the complete probability distribution. This is known as the *mean-standard deviation model:* the mean (a central tendency measure) serves as a measure of expected return, while the standard deviation (a dispersion measure) indicates the riskiness of the portfolio by measuring the possible deviation of actual outcomes from the expected ones. The following discussion will be concerned with the mean-standard deviation model.[12]

B. The interrelationships among securities

Suppose estimates of the expected returns and standard deviations of returns are available for a set of securities; what combination (i.e., portfolio) should the investor choose? An answer to this question requires knowledge of the relationship between the means and standard deviations of individual securities and those of the portfolio. Specifically, the question is, Given the expected returns and standard deviations of returns for each security, what are the expected return and standard deviation of the portfolio?

The statistical concept of the weighted sum of random variables implies that the portfolio's expected return is simply the weighted average of the expected returns of its individual components, the weights being the proportions of the total funds invested in each security.[13] Thus, the expected return, E_p, of a portfolio comprised of n securities is [14]

$$E_p = \sum_{i=1}^{n} w_i E_i, \tag{12.1}$$

where

E_i = expected return on security i, and
w_i = proportion of the total funds invested in security i

(the n w_i's should, of course, sum to 1, i.e., $\sum_{i=1}^{n} w_i = 1$).

---

[11] These conditions are (*a*) the probability distribution of returns is a two-parameter distribution (e.g., the normal distribution), *or* (*b*) the investor's utility of consumption function is positively sloping (i.e., positive marginal utility of consumption) and concave to the origin (i.e., marginal utility decreases as consumption increases).

[12] Most of the portfolio theory literature has been developed within the framework of the mean-standard deviation model.

[13] See Appendix A for a survey of some basic statistical concepts underlying the following discussion.

[14] Expressions (12.1), (12.2), and (12.3) refer to a specific time period. A subscript denoting the time period was omitted for simplicity of exposition.

Assume that the annual expected return of security A is 15 percent and that of security B is 10 percent. The relative shares of the total funds invested in A and B are 60 percent and 40 percent, respectively. The expected return of the portfolio comprised of A and B is

$$E_p = .60 \times 15 + .40 \times 10 = 13 \text{ percent.}$$

The relationship between the standard deviations of the individual securities and the standard deviation of the portfolio's returns is somewhat more involved, since it depends on the following three elements: the standard deviations of the individual securities, their correlation coefficients, and the proportions invested. The variance (i.e., the square of the standard deviation), σ^2_p, of a portfolio comprised of two securities, A and B, is

$$\sigma^2_p = w^2_A \sigma^2_A + w^2_B \sigma^2_B + 2 w_A w_B r_{A,B} \sigma_A \sigma_B. \tag{12.2}$$

The portfolio's variance thus equals the sum of the variances of the individual securities (σ^2_A and σ^2_B), weighted by the squared proportions (w^2_A and w^2_B), plus the product of the correlation coefficient between returns of the two securities ($r_{A,B}$) and the standard deviations of returns σ_A and σ_B), weighted by twice the product of the proportions ($2w_A w_B$).[15]

Suppose a portfolio consists of two securities whose standard deviations of returns are .02 and .03 respectively, the proportions of total funds allocated to the securities are .60 and .40, and the correlation coefficient between returns of the securities is .25. The variance of the portfolio's return according to (12.2) will be

$$\begin{aligned} \sigma^2_p &= (.60)^2 \times (.02)^2 + (.40)^2 \times (.03)^2 + 2 \times .60 \times .40 \times .25 \times .02 \times .03 \\ &= .000576. \end{aligned}$$

The standard deviation of the portfolio's return is

$$\sigma_p = \sqrt{.000576} = .024.$$

In general, the variance of returns for an n-security portfolio is

$$\sigma^2_p = \sum_{i=1}^{n} w^2_i \sigma^2_i + \sum_{i=1}^{n} \sum_{\substack{j=1 \\ j \neq i}}^{n} w_i w_j r_{ij} \sigma_i \sigma_j. \tag{12.3}$$

---

[15] The covariance, $\text{cov}_{A,B}$, is often substituted in the portfolio theory literature for the correlation coefficient. The relationship between these two measures of association is

$$\text{cov}_{A,B} = r_{A,B} \sigma_A \sigma_B.$$

The covariance thus equals the product of the correlation coefficient between the securities' returns and their standard deviations of returns. Substituting the covariance into expression (12.2) yields

$$\sigma^2_p = w^2_A \sigma^2_A + w^2_B \sigma^2_B + 2w_A w_B \text{cov}_{A,B}$$

The explicit consideration of the interrelationships between security returns, measured by the correlation coefficient, r_{ij}, or by the covariance is one of the major characteristics of the portfolio model. The returns on *each pair* of securities in the portfolio may be positively correlated, uncorrelated, or negatively correlated. A positive correlation $(0 < r_{ij} \leq 1)$ indicates that a change (e.g., an increase) in the return on one security is likely to be associated with a change in the *same direction* (e.g., also an increase) in the return on the other security. For example, the returns of securities of two firms in the same industry are expected to be positively correlated, since industry-wide events will affect the returns on both securities in the same direction. Thus, an increase in demand for domestic cars, brought about by a quota on foreign cars, is expected to cause an increase in the stock returns of both General Motors and Ford companies. Returns on positively correlated securities will therefore tend to move over time in the same direction.[16] When returns on two securities are not likely to move in the same (or opposite) direction, they are said to be uncorrelated $(r_{ij} = 0)$. For example, the returns on a savings account will be uncorrelated with a stock's returns, since the former are constant over a given period while the latter will usually fluctuate.[17] Returns are negatively correlated $(-1 \leq r_{ij} < 0)$ when a change in the returns on one security is likely to be accompanied by an opposite change in the returns on the other security. Because of the strong common effects operating on all securities in the market, it seems unlikely that actual returns of securities will be substantially negatively correlated.[18]

The effect of interrelationships between security returns on the variability or riskiness of the portfolio's return should now be clear. The higher the positive correlation between the securities in the portfolio, the higher the variability of the portfolio's returns, since the returns on individual securities will tend to move in the *same* direction, thus increasing the amplitude of the portfolio's return. Using the former two-security example, suppose the correlation coefficient between the two securities is .90, rather than .25. In this case, the portfolio's standard deviation will increase from .024 to .028. When the correlations between securities' returns are low (or even negative), some securities will yield increased returns while others will yield, during the same period, decreased returns, resulting in an offsetting process which will stabilize the portfolio's returns. Thus, portfolio risk, as measured by the variability of the portfolio's return, should be related to both the variability of

16 An extreme example will clarify this point. The returns of two common stocks of the *same firm* will obviously be perfectly correlated (i.e., $r_{ij} = 1$), since any change in the returns on one security will be accompanied by an identical change in the returns on the other security.

17 The effects of price-level changes are ignored in this example.

18 More on correlation in Appendix A.

returns on the individual securities [first term on the right-hand side of (12.3)] and the interrelationships among the returns on the securities [second term on the right-hand side of (12.3)]. As will be shown below, the interrelationships among security returns play a major role in the portfolio selection decision, since they are usually the major determinant of the portfolio's risk.

C. The portfolio diversification principle

The intuitive notion of investment diversification as a mechanism for risk reduction can now be rigorously defined.[19] Expression (12.3) states that the total risk of the portfolio, as measured by its standard deviation of returns, consists of two components: the individual risk elements of each security and the correlations between returns on securities. Considering the latter component, it is clear that the overall risk of the portfolio can be reduced when investment is made in low-correlated securities such as stocks of firms in unrelated industries (e.g., food and electronics); stocks and bonds; stocks, saving accounts and cash; and securities of firms based in different countries. A mere increase in the number of securities that make up the portfolio evidently provides little advantage in risk reduction when the securities' returns remain highly correlated.[20]

It is important to note that the overall portfolio risk is mainly determined by the relationships between returns on the individual securities rather than by their individual riskiness (i.e., their standard deviation of returns). Consider expression (12.3); when the number of securities in the portfolio is increased by one, the number of terms on the right-hand side of the equation is increased by $2n - 1$, one term involving the variance of the new security (i.e., its individual riskiness), and $2n - 2$ terms involving the correlation coefficients of the new security with each of the n securities already in the portfolio. Thus, if the portfolio is comprised of a relatively large number of securities, the contribution of the variance of an additional security to the total riskiness of the portfolio is virtually swamped by the effect of the correlation coefficients between securities. It is conceivable that a security whose variance of return is very high (i.e., a highly risky security) might actually reduce the variance of a portfolio to which it is added if this security has low

---

[19] See also Appendix B for mathematical formulation.

[20] When security returns are perfectly positively correlated, the standard deviation of the portfolio will equal the weighted average of the standard deviations of the individual securities. Given the proportions invested in each security, this is the maximum value of the portfolio's standard deviation. When returns on securities are negatively correlated, it might be possible to reduce the portfolio's risk to zero, thus producing a riskless portfolio from a combination of risky securities. This is known as a "perfect hedging."

correlation coefficients with other securities in the portfolio. For example, the risk of a large portfolio consisting mainly of securities of electronic firms will probably be reduced by adding stock of a food-processing firm because of the low return correlation between the two industries. This risk reduction will occur even if the individual riskiness (i.e., standard deviation) of the food-processing firm is very high. In a large portfolio, individual riskiness of securities is therefore of secondary importance in the determination of the portfolio's risk; the relationship among returns is the determining factor.

For a given degree of return correlations, the number of securities in a portfolio will also affect the extent of risk reduction; the variance of the portfolio's return will decrease as the number of securities is increased. It can be shown that the initial rate of risk decrease is very fast, hence a substantial reduction in the variability of a portfolio's returns can be achieved with a relatively small number of securities.[21]

Risk reduction through diversification is thus affected by three factors: (*a*) the individual riskiness of each security, (*b*) the number of securities in the portfolio, and (*c*) the degree to which security returns are correlated. In a large portfolio (e.g., a portfolio consisting of fifteen to twenty securities or more), the third factor predominates.

D. The simplified "market model"

The selection process of an optimal portfolio requires the estimation of a prohibitively large number of variables. Specifically, to determine the expected return and standard deviation of an n-security portfolio, the following variables should be estimated:

	Number
Individual expected returns	n
Individual standard deviations	n
Correlation coefficients (covariances)	$(n^2 - n)/2$
Total number of estimates	$(n^2 + 3n)/2$

Thus, for a ten-security portfolio, 65 variables should be estimated; but for a one-hundred-security portfolio, a total number of 5,150 vari-

---

[21] Brealey showed that under certain conditions, a portfolio of ten stocks provides 88.5 percent of the maximum possible advantage of diversification, while a portfolio of twenty stocks provides 94.2 percent of these advantages. See *An Introduction to Risk and Return from Common Stocks* (Cambridge, Mass.: M.I.T. Press, 1969), p. 126. Note, however, that it has been estimated that the average number of stocks directly owned by individual investors is between three and four (Arthur D. Little, Inc., "Studies of the Mutual Fund Industry," Report to the Investment Company Institute, June 1967). This is obviously a small number of securities, from a diversification point of view, despite the fast decrease in risk mentioned above.

ables is required.[22] It is obvious that a model requiring the estimation of such a large number of input variables is not operational, and hence a simplified selection process should be designed.

The large number of variables required for portfolio selection is mainly caused by the correlation coefficients between pairs of security returns. Thus, of the 5,150 inputs required for a one-hundred-security portfolio, 4,950 are correlation coefficients while only 200 represent expected return and standard deviation terms. To decrease the number of correlation coefficients required, Markowitz suggested the following simplified "market model." [23] Recall that the correlation coefficients measure the degree of interrelationship (covariability) between security returns. The existence of such a relationship is mainly due to economy-wide factors operating simultaneously on all firms (e.g., changes in interest rates) and to industry-wide factors operating on firms within a given industry. If, as empirical evidence suggests, the latter effect is relatively small, it can be assumed that interrelationships between security returns result mainly from market-wide factors. Accordingly, the interrelationships *between* security returns can be described by the association of each security's return with that of the market,[24] rather than by the pairwise relationship required by the original portfolio model [the r_{ij}'s in (12.3)]. Stated differently, given a strong market effect operating on all securities, the correlation of each security with a common market index can replace the pairwise correlations between securities. Such a substitution substantially reduces the number of inputs to be estimated for portfolio selection. For example, instead of the 4,950 correlation coefficients required for the one-hundred-security portfolio, only 102 variables have to be estimated when the market return is used as a common index. These are the market's expected return, the market's standard deviation of return, and 100 measures for the relationships between each security and the market's return.[25]

[22] A consideration of all the thirteen hundred or so stocks traded on the New York Stock Exchange for possible inclusion in a portfolio requires the estimation of about 850,000 variables.

[23] Markowitz, *Portfolio Selection: Efficient Diversification of Investments, op. cit.*, pp. 96–101. The market model was later extended by W. F. Sharpe, "A Simplified Model for Portfolio Analysis," *Management Science*, 9 (January 1963), 277–93. This model is also known as the "diagonal model."

[24] The market's return refers to the average weighted return on all securities in the stock market. This return can be well approximated by general indexes, such as the Dow Jones index. For a discussion of the appropriate market index, see L. Fisher, "Some New Stock Market Indexes," *Journal of Business*, 39 (January 1966), 191–225.

[25] The use of money as a common denominator provides a clarifying analogy to the market model. Instead of having each commodity priced in terms of all other commodities (e.g., the price of one desk is six and one-half chairs, 750 beer cans, etc.), each is priced in terms of the common denominator—money. The almost infinite number of possible prices in a barter economy is reduced by the use of money to a number of prices equal to the number of commodities. The market return in the market model is thus the analogue of money in a nonbarter economy.

Operationally, the market model assumes that the return on each security is linearly related to the market return:

$$\tilde{R}_{it} = a_i + \beta_i \tilde{R}_{Mt} + \tilde{\epsilon}_{it}, \qquad (12.4)$$

where

$\tilde{R}_{it}$ = rate of return on asset i for period t,

$\tilde{R}_{Mt}$ = aggregate rate of return on all securities in the market.

The tildes in (12.4) denote that the two rates of return are random variables, that is, they are subject to a probability distribution.[26] The major assumption underlying the market model is that the sole source of interrelationship between future returns on any two securities is the effect of market-wide events reflected in the market return, $\tilde{R}_M$. The total return of a security, $\tilde{R}_i$, can thus be decomposed into two components: a general component, $\beta_i \tilde{R}_M$, which reflects the extent of common movement of security i's return with the average return on all other securities in the market, and a specific component, $a_i + \tilde{\epsilon}_{it}$, which reflects that part of the security's return that is independent of all other securities in the market.

The variability of future returns on an individual security (i.e., its riskiness) is therefore affected by two factors: the variability of the market as a whole and the variability specific to the security; the former is usually known as the "systematic risk" element and the latter as the "unsystematic risk." It can be shown that when securities are combined in a portfolio, their specific components of variability become relatively unimportant, leaving the common variability associated with general market changes as the major contributor to the portfolio's risk.[27] Thus, in a large, diversified portfolio, the unsystematic risk components of each security are practically eliminated while the systematic risk components constitute the portfolio risk. Accordingly, the coefficient β_i in (12.4), which indicates the extent to which the security's return is subject to the systematic variability of the market, measures the *contribution* of security i to the total riskiness of the portfolio. Thus, from a portfolio point of view, which is most relevant for investor decisions, β_i measures the riskiness of the security.

---

[26] The assumptions regarding the behavior of the residual term in (12.4) are similar to those of the linear regression model:

$$E(\tilde{\epsilon}_{it}) = 0 \qquad (12.4a)$$

$$\sigma(\tilde{R}_{Mt}, \tilde{\epsilon}_{it}) = 0 \qquad (12.4b)$$

$$\sigma(\tilde{\epsilon}_{it}, \tilde{\epsilon}_{jt}) = 0, \text{ for all } i \neq j. \qquad (12.4c)$$

The first assumption states that the expected value of the residual term is zero. The second assumption states that the residual is uncorrelated with the market return, while the third assumption refers to the cross-sectional independence of the residual terms.

[27] See Appendix B.

A stock's β value indicates the degree to which the return responds to general market movements. For example, when the market goes up or down 5 percent in a given day, a stock with a β of one will go up or down approximately 5 percent too.[28] A stock whose β equals one can therefore be regarded as having an average degree of systematic risk. A security with a β of two will tend to go up or down 10 percent when the market moves 5 percent; such a security may be regarded as having a higher-than-average degree of systematic risk. A security with a β of .5 will go up or down approximately 2.5 percent when the market moves 5 percent, indicating a lower-than-average degree of risk. In general, the percentage change in the price of a security in a short period of time will tend to equal its β value times the percentage change in the level of the market over that period of time.

E. The capital asset pricing model

Sharpe [29] and Lintner [30] extended portfolio theory to a capital asset pricing model intended to explain how market prices of capital assets are determined; in particular, to describe the process of security price (or return) adjustment to reflect risk differentials. The capital asset pricing model rests on the following assumptions:

1. Each investor acts on the basis of predictions (expected returns and correlation coefficients of returns) about the future outcome of securities. There is complete agreement among all investors regarding these outcomes, namely, all investors have the same set of predictions.
2. Each investor can borrow or lend at the pure (riskless) rate of interest. This rate is thus identical for both borrowing and lending, and the same for every investor.
3. All investors prefer more expected wealth to less and are risk averse.

Based on these assumptions, it can be shown that when capital markets are in equilibrium the expected return on an individual security, $E(\tilde{R}_i)$, is related to its systematic risk, β_i, in the following linear form: [31]

$$E(\tilde{R}_i) = E(\tilde{R}_0) + [E(\tilde{R}_M) - E(\tilde{R}_0)]\beta_i, \qquad (12.5)$$

[28] This is only an approximation depending on the value of the constant term, a_i.

[29] W. F. Sharpe, "Capital Asset Prices: A Theory of Market Equilibrium under Conditions of Risk," *Journal of Finance,* 19 (September 1964), 425–42.

[30] J. Lintner, "The Valuation of Risk Assets and the Selection of Risky Investments in Stock Portfolios and Capital Budgets," *Review of Economics and Statistics,* 47 (February 1965), 13–37.

[31] See, for example, Sharpe, *Portfolio Theory and Capital Markets, op. cit.,* pp. 91–96.

where

$E(\tilde{R}_0)$ = expected return on a security that is riskless in the market portfolio, i.e., a zero-β security,[32]

$E(\tilde{R}_M)$ = expected return on the market portfolio,[33]

β_i = systematic risk of security i, as defined above (12.4).

Expression (12.5) thus states that in equilibrium, a security's expected return equals the expected return of a riskless security, $E(\tilde{R}_0)$, plus a risk premium.[34] The risk premium consists of a constant, $[E(\tilde{R}_M - E(\tilde{R}_0)]$, which is the difference between the market's expected return and that of the riskless security, times the systematic risk of the security, β_i. For example, if the annual expected return on the riskless security is 6 percent, and the annual expected return on the market is 10 percent, then the expected returns on securities of different levels of systematic risk should be, according to (12.5), as follows:

β_i	Expected return $E(\tilde{R}_i)$
0.0	6%
0.5	8
1.0	10
1.5	12
2.0	14

Expression (12.5) has two major implications. First, in equilibrium, rates of return on individual securities will reflect only their systematic risk component, that is, that portion of the variability resulting from the association between the security's return and that of the market as a whole, measured by β_i. The unsystematic risk elements [e.g., $\tilde{\epsilon}_{it}$ in (12.4)] which are unrelated to the market return are not present in (12.5), since they are not expected to affect the security's return and price. Stated differently, only the systematic risk element will command a price in the form of increased rates of return. The reason is obvious: since, as mentioned above, the unsystematic risk element can be eliminated by efficient diversification, no compensation for bearing this risk will be offered in the market. However, the systematic risk element of a security, β_i, cannot be eliminated by diversification; hence in a risk-averse market, investors will demand a compensation for bearing this risk in the form of higher rates of return (and prices). Thus, in equi-

[32] Stated differently, the returns of this security are *uncorrelated* with the market return.

[33] The "market portfolio" is a portfolio comprised of all securities in the market, with the proportions invested in each security equal to the proportion of this security in the total market value of all securities.

[34] The expected return on a riskless security can usually be well approximated by the yield on short-term government bonds.

librium, the systematic risk component of a security is a complete measure of its risk; no other risk components would affect the security's return and price.

The second major implication of the capital asset pricing model is that in a market of risk-averse investors, higher risk should always be associated with higher expected return. Stated differently, investors must be paid to assume additional degrees of risk.

The assumptions underlying the capital asset pricing model are obviously restrictive and unrealistic, especially those concerned with the complete agreement among investors regarding future security outcomes (usually known as the "homogeneous expectation" assumption), and investors' ability to borrow and lend unlimited amounts at the riskless interest rate. However, the realism of a model's assumptions is usually not of great concern to the user; the major question determining the validity of a positive (descriptive) model is how well it can describe or predict a given phenomenon, such as the relationship between risk and. return in the stock market. Accordingly, we turn to empirical tests of the major implications (predictions) of the capital asset pricing model.

Attempts to test the validity of the first implication—β is a complete measure of a security's risk in an efficient portfolio—resulted in conflicting findings. Douglas [35] and Lintner [36] found an association between unsystematic risk elements and observed average returns, implying that a premium is paid for bearing unsystematic security risk. This finding is obviously inconsistent with the capital asset pricing model, expression (12.5).[37] However, Fama and Macbeth,[38] using monthly stock price data (as compared with the annual and quarterly data used by Douglas and Lintner), confirmed the model's first implication; no risk element other than the systematic risk, β, affects average stock returns.[39]

With respect to the second implication of the capital asset pricing model that higher risk levels would be associated with higher rates of

[35] G. W. Douglas, "Risk in the Equity Markets: An Empirical Appraisal of Market Efficiency," *Yale Economic Essays*, 9 (Spring 1969), 3–45.

[36] J. Lintner, "Security Prices and Risk: The Theory and a Comparative Analysis of A.T.&T. and Leading Industries," Paper presented at the Conference of Regulated Public Utilities, University of Chicago, 1965.

[37] Additional inconsistencies were reported in M. Blume and I. Friend, "A New Look at the Capital Asset Pricing Model," *The Journal of Finance*, 28 (March 1973), 19–34.

[38] E. F. Fama and J. D. Macbeth, "Risk, Return and Equilibrium: Empirical Tests," *The Journal of Political Economy*, 81 (May-June 1973), 607–36.

[39] It should be noted, however, that the Douglas and Lintner studies suffer from various statistical and data shortcomings, some of which were overcome by Fama and Macbeth. For elaboration on these shortcomings, see M. H. Miller and M. Scholes, "Rates of Return in Relation to Risk: A Re-Examination of Some Recent Findings," in *Studies in the Theory of Capital Markets*, M. C. Jensen, ed. (New York: Frederick A. Praeger, Inc., 1972), pp. 47–78.

return, the supporting empirical evidence is more consistent. Jensen [40] and Fama and Macbeth,[41] among others, found that on average there is a positive trade-off between return and risk; in periods of rising stock prices, high β stocks and portfolios have returned more than low β stocks and portfolios.

SUMMARY

Portfolio theory constitutes the most advanced and promising attempt to deal with optimal investment decisions under conditions of uncertainty. The theory therefore is of considerable interest to financial statement analysts engaged in providing information for investment decisions. This chapter focused on several basic principles and implications of the portfolio model relevant to financial analysis. The first and probably major attribute of the model is the explicit consideration of the risk element, along with the expected return, in the portfolio selection decision. The relationship between the risk and return characteristics of individual securities and those of the portfolio were then examined. It was shown that the degree of statistical association, or correlation between returns on individual securities, is the major determinant of a portfolio's risk. Principles of diversification as a means of risk reduction were also discussed, particularly the importance of investing in securities whose returns are largely uncorrelated. The "market model" was presented as an attempt to operationalize the portfolio model by reducing the number of parameters to be estimated. The chapter closed with a discussion of the capital asset pricing model designed to describe the process of security price formation in capital markets.

APPENDIX A: A REVIEW OF SOME RELEVANT STATISTICAL CONCEPTS

Expected value and variance of a random variable

A *random variable,* $\tilde{X}$, is one that is subject to a probability distribution, that is, it can take a (possibly infinite) number of values $x_1, x_2, \ldots$, with probabilities $p_1, p_2, \ldots$. Stated differently, the probability is p_i ($p_i \geqq 0$ for each i, and the sum of p_i over all i equals 1)

---

[40] M. C. Jensen, "Risk, the Pricing of Capital Assets, and the Evaluation of Investment Portfolios," *Journal of Business*, 42 (April 1969), 167–247.

[41] Fama and Macbeth, *op. cit.*

that the variable will take the value x_i. For example, the probability is .45 that next year's rate of return on a specific stock will be 10 percent.

The *expected value* of a random variable is just the mean of its probability distribution. The expected value of a discrete random variable, $\tilde{X}$ is

$$E(\tilde{X}) = \sum_{i=1}^{n} x_i p_i, \qquad (12.6)$$

where p_i is the probability that the random variable will take the value x_i. The expected value is thus the weighted average of all the possible values of $\tilde{X}$, where the probabilities are used as weights.[42]

Consider now several different random variables $\tilde{X}_1, \tilde{X}_2, \ldots, \tilde{X}_n$, such as next year's rates of return on n different stocks. The *expected value of the sum* $(\tilde{X}_1 + \tilde{X}_2 + \ldots + \tilde{X}_n)$ is just the sum of the individual expectations:

$$E(\tilde{X}_1 + \tilde{X}_2 + \ldots + \tilde{X}_n) = E(\tilde{X}_1) + E(\tilde{X}_2) + \ldots + E(\tilde{X}_n). \qquad (12.8)$$

Suppose that the random variables are weighted by the constants $w_1, w_2, \ldots, w_n$, which sum to one. The *expected value of the weighted sum* will be

$$E(w_1\tilde{X}_1 + w_2\tilde{X}_2 + \ldots + w_n\tilde{X}_n) = w_1 E(\tilde{X}_1) + w_2 E(\tilde{X}_2) + \ldots + w_n E(\tilde{X}_n). \qquad (12.9)$$

Thus the expectation of a weighted sum of the individual variables is the sum of the weighted expectations. For example, the expected return on a portfolio will equal the sum of the expectations of the individual returns, each weighted by the relative share of investment in the portfolio, w_i.

The *variance,* $\sigma^2(\tilde{X})$, of a random variable is the expectation of the squared deviations of the possible values of the variable from the mean (expected value):

$$\sigma^2(\tilde{X}) = \sum_{i=1}^{n} [x_i - E(\tilde{X})]^2 \, p_i. \qquad (12.10)$$

The variance is thus a measure for the degree of variability (dispersion) in the probability distribution of the random variable; the larger the

---

[42] When the random variable $\tilde{X}$ is continuous, its expected value is defined as

$$E(\tilde{X}) = \int_{-\infty}^{\infty} xf(x)dx, \qquad (12.7)$$

where $f(x)$ is the density function of $\tilde{X}$.

possible deviations of outcomes from the mean, the larger the variability. The *standard deviation*, $\sigma(\tilde{X})$, is the square root of the variance:

$$\sigma(\tilde{X}) = \sqrt{\sigma^2(\tilde{X})}. \qquad (12.11)$$

The *variance of a weighted sum of random variables is*

$$\sigma^2 \left(\sum_{i=1}^{n} w_i \tilde{X}_i \right) = \sum_{i=1}^{n} w_i^2 \, \sigma^2(\tilde{X}_i) + \sum_{i=1}^{n} \sum_{\substack{j=1 \\ j \neq i}}^{n} w_i w_j \, \text{cov}_{ij}. \qquad (12.12)$$

The first term on the right-hand side of (12.12) is the weighted sum of the variances of the individual variables, weighted by the squares of the weights. The second term is the weighted sum of the covariances, cov_{ij}. The computation of a portfolio's variance, expression (12.3) above, is based on (12.12).

The correlation coefficient and the covariance

The statistical tool for discovering and measuring the degree of relationship (association) between two variables is known as correlation analysis. The coefficient of correlation, r, which indicates the degree of relationship, is a number varying from $+1$, through zero, to -1. The sign indicates whether the relationship is positive (a plus sign) or negative (a minus sign) while the magnitude of the coefficient indicates the degree of association; a zero coefficient indicates absolutely no relationship between the variables while a coefficient of ± 1 indicates perfect association (positive or negative).

Suppose the variables correlated are the returns on two securities denoted by R_A and R_B. Figure 12.1 shows a scatter diagram of a perfect positive correlation ($r = 1$) where all pairs of outcomes lie along a straight upward-sloping line. In this case above-average returns on security A will *always* occur with above-average returns on security B. The returns in Figure 12.2 are also positively correlated yet not perfectly so ($0 < r < 1$) since observations are more scattered than in Figure 12.1. In this case above average returns on A are *likely* to occur with above-average returns on B. Returns in Figure 12.3 are uncorrelated ($r = 0$), since above-average returns on A may occur with above-average returns on B, as well as with below-average returns on B. Thus, there is no relationship between returns on the two securities. Figure 12.4 exhibits a case of negatively correlated returns ($-1 < r < 0$), where above-average returns on A are likely to occur with below-average returns on B. When the negative correlation is perfect, all observations will lie on a downward-sloping straight line.

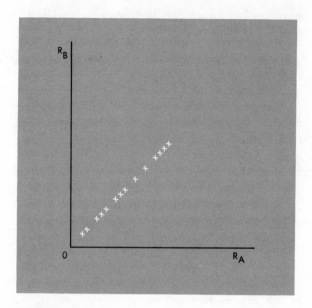

FIGURE 12.1

Perfect positive correlation of returns

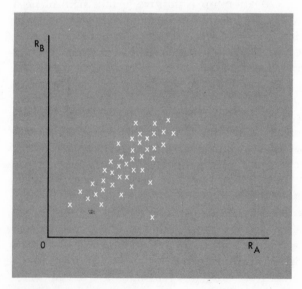

FIGURE 12.2

Positively correlated returns

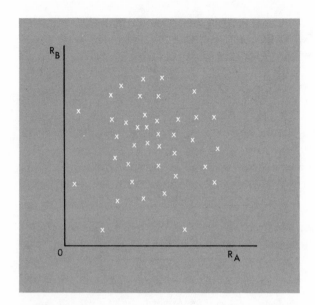

FIGURE 12.3

Uncorrelated returns

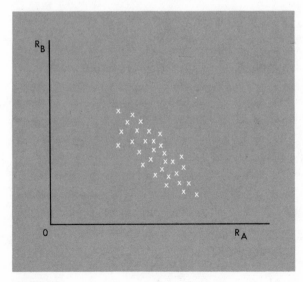

FIGURE 12.4

Negatively correlated returns

The correlation coefficient, r, between two variables X and Y is measured by the following formula:

$$r = \frac{\displaystyle\sum_{i=1}^{N} (X_i - \bar{X})(Y_i - \bar{Y})}{N\sigma_x \, \sigma_y} \tag{12.13}$$

where

$\bar{X}$ and σ_x = mean and standard deviation of X, respectively,
$\bar{Y}$ and σ_y = mean and standard deviation of Y, respectively, and
N = number of observations (e.g., possible outcomes).

Table 12.1 provides an example of the computation of the correlation coefficient for the returns of two securities.

TABLE 12.1

Basic Data for Securities A and B

Period	Returns on A R_A	Returns on B R_B	$(R_A - \bar{R}_A) \times$ $(R_B - \bar{R}_B)$
1966	4.5%	7.0%	1.5
1967	6.5	10.0	1.5
1968	5.0	8.5	0
1969	6.0	9.5	.5
1970	5.5	7.5	0
Mean, R	5.5	8.5	Total 3.5
Standard deviation, σ	1.58	2.55	

Based on the above data, the correlation coefficient is

$$r_{AB} = \frac{3.5}{5 \times 1.58 \times 2.55} = +.174.$$

The *covariance* is a measure of association closely related to the correlation coefficient:

$$\text{cov}_{AB} = r_{AB} \, \sigma_A \, \sigma_B. \tag{12.14}$$

The covariance thus equals the product of the correlation coefficient and the standard deviations of the variables. Using the data in Table 12.1, the covariance between the returns on securities A and B is

$$\text{cov}_{AB} = .174 \times 1.58 \times 2.55 = .701.$$

APPENDIX B: THE EFFECTS OF DIVERSIFICATION [43]

Recall that the variance of the portfolio's return (12.3) is

$$\sigma_p^2 = \sum_{i=1}^{N} w_i^2 \sigma_i^2 + \sum_{\substack{i=1 \\ }}^{N} \sum_{\substack{j=1 \\ i \neq j}}^{N} w_i w_j \, \mathrm{cov}_{ij},$$

where cov_{ij} = covariance between the returns on security i and j.[44] Suppose (for simplification of exposition) that equal amounts of money are invested in each of the N securities in the portfolio, that is,

$$w_i = 1/N, \quad i = 1, \ldots, N.$$

In this case, the variance of the portfolio's return is

$$\sigma_p^2 = \frac{1}{N^2} \sum_{i=1}^{N} \sigma_i^2 + \frac{1}{N^2} \sum_{\substack{i=1 \\ }}^{N} \sum_{\substack{j=1 \\ i \neq j}}^{N} \mathrm{cov}_{ij}. \qquad (12.15)$$

Suppose further that of all the N securities, security g has the largest variance of returns:

$$\sigma_g^2 = M, \quad M < \infty,$$

that is, the N variances have a finite upper bound. Accordingly, the first term on the right-hand side of (12.15) must satisfy

$$\frac{1}{N^2} \sum_{i=1}^{N} \sigma_i^2 \leq \frac{NM}{N^2} = \frac{M}{N}. \qquad (12.16)$$

This expression will obviously be smaller the larger the value of N (the number of securities), indicating that the sum of security variances will decrease as the number of securities in the portfolio increases. The *rate* of decrease will be very fast at the beginning, when few securities are incorporated into the portfolio, since the sum of the variances will be proportional to $1/\sqrt{N}$.

For a very large portfolio, the first term on the right-hand side of (12.15) will approach zero (i.e., the contribution of the individual risk of each security to the portfolio risk is negligible), so that

$$\sigma_p^2 \cong \frac{1}{N^2} \sum_{\substack{i=1 \\ }}^{N} \sum_{\substack{j=1 \\ i \neq j}}^{N} \mathrm{cov}_{ij}. \qquad (12.17)$$

[43] Adapted from E. F. Fama and M. H. Miller, *The Theory of Finance* (New York: Holt, Rinehart & Winston, Inc., 1972), pp. 253–55.

[44] The covariance is substituted for $r_{ij} \, \sigma_i \, \sigma_j$ in (12.3).

The mean of the covariances between returns of the securities in the portfolio is

$$\overline{cov}_{ij} = \frac{\displaystyle\sum_{\substack{i=1 \\ i \neq j}}^{N} \sum_{j=1}^{N} cov_{ij}}{N(N-1)}. \tag{12.18}$$

Substituting expression (12.18) into (12.17) yields

$$\sigma_p^2 \cong \frac{1}{N^2} \sum_{\substack{i=1 \\ i \neq j}}^{N} \sum_{j=1}^{N} cov_{ij} = \frac{N-1}{N^2(N-1)} \sum_{\substack{i=1 \\ i \neq j}}^{N} \sum_{j=1}^{N} cov_{ij} = \frac{N-1}{N} \overline{cov}_{ij}. \tag{12.19}$$

Expression (12.19) indicates that the variance of the portfolio's return approaches the average covariance ($\overline{cov}_{ij}$) between the returns of individual securities within the portfolio, since as the number of securities in the portfolio (N) increases the term $(N-1)/N$ approaches 1. Thus, the dispersion (risk) of the portfolio's return depends primarily on the *relationships* between the returns on the individual securities.[45] Consequently, in a large portfolio, the contribution of an individual security to the riskiness of the portfolio depends primarily on the covariability of return on that security with returns on other securities, rather than on the variance (individual riskiness) of this security.

---

[45] If returns on all N securities were independent, then the variance of the portfolio's return would be close to zero.

CHAPTER THIRTEEN

The Role of
Financial Statement Analysis
in the Portfolio Decision

It was shown in the preceding chapter that optimal portfolio decisions require dependable estimates of the risk and return characteristics of individual securities. The portfolio decision is simplified in the framework of the capital asset pricing model where the security's systematic risk, β, fully determines its equilibrium rate of return [see expression (12.5)].[1] Therefore, in the context of the capital asset pricing model, security analysis is actually confined to the estimation of systematic risk elements, that is, to the evaluation of the contribution of each security to the overall riskiness of the portfolio. The question examined in this chapter is whether financial statement analysis can assist in the optimal estimation of systematic risk measures.

MEASUREMENT ERRORS IN SYSTEMATIC RISK ESTIMATES

The systematic risk measures required for portfolio decisions cannot be directly observed in the stock market, since they reflect the *future*

---

[1] Stated differently, from expression (12.5) it is obvious that the only *firm-related* variable systematically affecting expected returns is the β value. The remaining variables on the right-hand side of (12.5), the expected return on a riskless portfolio and the expected return on the market portfolio, are general market indicators.

sensitivity (i.e., ex ante risk) of securities' rates of return to general market fluctuations. The most commonly used estimation procedure is to derive the $\hat{\beta}$ values [2] from a historical time series of rates of return:

$$R_{jt} = \hat{a}_j + \hat{\beta}_j R_{Mt} + u_{tj}, \qquad (13.1)$$

where

R_{jt} = observed rate of return on security j for period t, and
R_{Mt} = observed rate of return on the market portfolio for period t.

However, if the process that generates the security's returns is not stationary (stable) over time, the historically determined $\hat{\beta}$ values will contain serious measurement errors. In this case, the $\hat{\beta}$ will be a biased and inconsistent estimate of the "true" systematic risk, leading to nonoptimal portfolio decisions. It seems reasonable that basic changes in the firm's characteristics, such as mergers, changes in the product line, or changes in input mix, will alter the nature of the process generating the rates of return. Since such changes occur quite frequently in the life of most firms, an estimation of systematic risk based exclusively on historical returns is rather hazardous.[3]

An improvement of systematic risk estimation obviously requires knowledge about the relationship between the firm's financial and operating characteristics (e.g., capital structure, capital intensity, etc.) and its riskiness as perceived by investors. Unfortunately, this relationship is largely unknown, since there is no satisfactory model that describes risk in terms of firm variables. Therefore, the objective of financial statement analysis in this context is to determine the relationship between accounting data (reflecting firm characteristics) and risk measures. Given such a relationship, an optimal model for the estimation of systematic risk can be designed.

THE ASSOCIATION BETWEEN ACCOUNTING DATA AND SYSTEMATIC RISK

Ball and Brown investigated the association between the cross-sectional covariability (common movement) of securities' rates of return and the covariability of accounting income numbers.[4] Specifically, they

[2] The hat, ^, denotes an estimate of the "true" β value.

[3] The evidence on the stationarity of systematic risk estimates is rather inconclusive; see M. E. Blume, "On the Assessment of Risk," *The Journal of Finance*, 26 (March 1971), 1–10; and W. F. Sharpe and G. M. Cooper, "NYSE Stocks Classified by Risk," *Financial Analysts Journal*, 28 (March–April 1972), 46–56.

[4] R. Ball and P. Brown, "Portfolio Theory and Accounting," *Journal of Accounting Research*, 7 (Autumn 1969), 300–23.

correlated the following two covariability measures: (a) the covariability between a security's returns and the market return, measured by the R^2 (coefficient of multiple determination) of the market model (12.4), and (b) the covariability between the firm's accounting income and an index of aggregate income for all firms, measured by the R^2 of an *accounting market model*.[5] Ball and Brown thus measured the association between the common movement of returns on individual securities with the market return, and the comovement of individual firms' accounting income with the aggregate income of all firms.

Results, based on a sample of 261 Compustat firms, indicated a considerable degree of association between accounting and market measures of comovements:

> Comovement in the accounting income of firms appears to predict moderately well the estimated degrees of association between the returns on firms' securities and the market return. They are better predictors of the estimated systematic risks of firms. The highest product-moment (Spearman's rank order) correlation coefficient is .47 (.46) in the first case and .59 (.64) in the second. These indicate that the comovements in accounting incomes explain approximately 20–25 percent of the cross-sectional variability in (estimated) degrees of association with the market, and 35–40 percent in systematic risks.[6]

Thus, there appears to be a significant association between the systematic variability (i.e., relative to the market) of accounting income numbers and that of market returns.

Beaver, Kettler, and Scholes investigated the relationship between various accounting measures of risk suggested in the financial statement analysis literature and market-based risk measures.[7] Traditional accounting risk measures are not defined in terms of covariability of returns as are the market risk measures, yet they are supposed to indicate various risk aspects of the firm's operations. The following accounting risk measures were considered in the study:

1. *Dividend payout,* measured by cash dividends divided by earnings available for common stockholders. The rationalization for measuring risk by

---

[5] The parameters of this model were estimated by means of the following least-squares regression:

$$I_{it} = a_{1i} + a_{2i} I_{Mt} + u_{it},$$ (13.2)

where

I_{it} = accounting income for firm i in year t, and
I_{Mt} = the market index of accounting income, calculated as an average of the income in year t of all firms in the sample.

[6] Ball and Brown, *op. cit.,* p. 319.

[7] W. H. Beaver, P. Kettler, and M. Scholes, "The Association between Market Determined and Accounting Determined Risk Measures," *The Accounting Review,* 45 (October 1970), 654–82.

the dividend payout ratio rests on the well-known phenomenon of dividend stabilization; firms are usually reluctant to change drastically, and in particular to cut dividends, once a certain level has been established. Consequently, firms with a high degree of earnings volatility will probably distribute a lower percentage of earnings than more stable firms, in order to avoid the necessity of reducing dividends in trough years. The dividend payout ratio may therefore be a surrogate for management's perception of the uncertainty (unexpected volatility) of the firm's earnings.

2. *Assets growth,* measured by the annual change in total assets. High growth is sometimes achieved by investing in assets whose riskiness exceeds the firm's previous risk or the industry's average risk. Growth brought about by investment in such above-average risk projects may therefore be associated with higher levels of security risk.

3. *Leverage,* measured by the ratio of total senior securities to total assets.[8] The effect of the degree of leverage on the firm's financial risk (i.e., on the volatility of the earnings stream which accrues to common stockholders) was discussed in Chapter 2.

4. *Liquidity,* measured by the current ratio. Liquidity measures have traditionally been regarded as indicators of the probability of corporate failure. It can also be argued that liquid (current) assets are less risky than noncurrent ones. For example, cash may be regarded as a riskless asset when price-level changes are ignored. Therefore, a high current ratio may be associated with a low level of risk.

5. *Asset size,* measured by the firm's total assets. It is widely believed that large firms are less risky (more stable) than small ones.[9] As was shown in Chapter 9, empirical evidence supports this belief with respect to bankruptcy risk; the bankruptcy rate for small firms is higher than that for large firms. Firm size may therefore be negatively associated with risk.

6. *Earnings variability,* measured by the standard deviation of the earnings-price ratio. This variable is an explicit measure for earnings variability (volatility), which is believed to be positively associated with the firm's risk.

7. *Earnings covariability*—the β value in the market model (12.4) is a measure for the systematic risk of a security. It is possible to compute an analogous β value for accounting income by regressing the firm's time series of earnings on an index of average accounting earnings for the economy.[10] Such an accounting β value measures the sensitivity of the firm's earnings to changes in earnings of all other firms.[11]

---

[8] Senior securities are defined as all fixed claims to earnings (including current liabilities) that have priority over common stocks.

[9] Hymer and Pashigian, for example, found that the variance of growth rates (i.e., volatility of the firm) of large firms is smaller than that of small firms; see "Firm Size and Rate of Growth," *Journal of Political Economy,* 70 (December 1962), 556–69.

[10] This was done by Ball and Brown in "Portfolio Theory and Accounting," *op. cit.* See expression (13.2), footnote 5.

[11] By analogy to the market model, the total variability of the firm's income series is regarded as consisting of two components: a systematic component affected by economy-wide events, and a specific component associated with the unique attributes of the firm's operations.

To measure the association between accounting and market risk measure, Beaver, *et al.*, computed cross-sectional correlation coefficients between each of the seven accounting variables and the market β value for 307 Compustat firms. These correlation coefficients were computed for individual securities as well as for portfolios and are reported in Table 13.1.[12]

The following results should be noted: The signs of all the correlation coefficients are in the expected direction (except for the liquidity measures in period 2). The correlation coefficients of four variables—payout, leverage, earnings variability, and the accounting beta—are statistically significant in both periods. The degree of association is highest for the earnings variability measure. All correlation coefficients for portfolios are larger than those for individual securities. The last finding seems to be of significance, since the portfolio level is obviously more

TABLE 13.1

Contemporaneous Association between Market Determined Measure of Risk and Seven Accounting Risk Measures [a]

Variable	Period One (1947–56)		Period Two (1957–65)	
	Individual Level	Portfolio [b] Level	Individual Level	Portfolio [b] Level
Payout	−.49 (−.50)	−.79 (−.77)	−.29 (−.24)	−.50 (−.45)
Growth	.27 (.23)	.56 (.51)	.01 (.03)	.02 (.07)
Leverage	.23 (.23)	.41 (.45)	.22 (.25)	.48 (.56)
Liquidity	−.13 (−.13)	−.35 (−.44)	.05 (−.01)	.04 (−.01)
Size	−.06 (−.07)	−.09 (−.13)	−.16 (−.16)	−.30 (−.30)
Earnings Variability	.66 (.58)	.90 (.77)	.45 (.36)	.82 (.62)
Accounting Beta	.44 (.39)	.68 (.67)	.23 (.23)	.46 (.46)

Source: W. H. Beaver, P. Kettler, and M. Scholes, "The Association between Market Determined and Accounting Determined Risk Measures," *The Accounting Review*, 45 (October 1970), p. 669.

[a] Rank correlation coefficients appear in the top row, and product-moment correlations appear in parentheses in the bottom row.

[b] The portfolio correlations are based upon 61 portfolios of 5 securities each.

[12] For the technique of forming portfolios, see Beaver *et al.*, *op. cit.*, p. 669.

relevant than the individual security level for portfolio analysis. The high correlation coefficients for the earnings variability measure (.90 and .82 for the two periods, portfolio level) led the authors to conclude:

> The evidence indicates that accounting risk variables can be used to select and to rank portfolios such that the ranking has a high degree of correlation with ranking the same portfolios according to the market risk measure. The evidence is consistent with the contention that the accounting risk measures are impounded in the market risk measures.[13]

The second stage of the Beaver, *et al.*, study was concerned with the ability of accounting risk measures to *predict* market-determined risk. Specifically, accounting measures in the first period (1947–56) were used to predict the β values in the second period (1957–65). These predictions were compared with a naïve no-change forecast (i.e., the β value in the second period will equal that of the first period). Results indicated that the prediction of β values based on accounting risk variables (especially on the portfolio level) was superior to the naïve forecast.

Bildersee correlated the systematic risk of preferred stocks, as measured by the β values derived from the market model, with some traditional accounting risk measures, such as the current ratio and leverage.[14] The association was generally significant and in the expected direction. When the preferred stocks in the sample were divided into groups of high and low quality (according to stock ratings), accounting measures were found to be strongly associated with the latter group and only slightly with the former. Leverage was the variable most strongly associated with the preferred stock β values ($R^2 = .627$ for the total sample, and R^2's of .037 and .664 for the high- and low-quality subgroups, respectively).[15] The various accounting variables combined into a linear regression model explained (in terms of R^2) about 64 percent of the cross-sectional variability of β values for the total sample, and about 70 percent of the β variability for the low-quality preferred stocks.

Gonedes also examined the association between market-based and accounting-based estimates of systematic risk.[16] The former (i.e., β values) were derived from the market model, while the latter were derived from

[13] Beaver, *et al.*, *op. cit.*, p. 670.

[14] J. Bildersee, "Risk and Return on Preferred Stocks: An Application of Portfolio Theory" (Ph.D. dissertation, Graduate School of Business, University of Chicago, 1971), Chap. 6.

[15] Note that Bildersee's leverage variable is not a pure accounting measure, since he used the market value of common and preferred stock in its determination.

[16] N. J. Gonedes, "Evidence on the Information Content of Accounting Numbers: Accounting-Based and Market-Based Estimates of Systematic Risk," *Journal of Financial and Quantitative Analysis*, 8 (June 1973), 407–43.

the accounting analogue of the market model proposed by Ball and Brown. Using a sample of ninety-nine Compustat firms, Gonedes found a statistically significant correlation between the market-based and accounting-based β values when the accounting income numbers were transformed to first differences (i.e, income at time t minus income for the preceding period, $t - 1$). However, when the untransformed (absolute) income numbers were used to compute the accounting β values, the relationship between the risk measures was found to be statistically insignificant. The latter finding is inconsistent with Beaver, *et al.*'s, results (bottom row in Table 13.1) which indicated a significant correlation between the accounting and market β values. This inconsistency might, of course, result from sample differences between the two studies, yet Gonedes suggests another explanation. Beaver, *et al.*'s, accounting β's were obtained from *deflated* income numbers, that is, the accounting earnings used in the regression were divided by stock prices.[17] The β coefficient of the market model is, of course, also a function of stock market prices. Hence, the strong association reported by Beaver, *et al.*, might reflect, at least partially, the fact that both risk estimates incorporate market prices. However, Gonedes's accounting β's were derived from pure accounting variables—net income divided by total assets—thus avoiding the possibility of spurious correlation.

Breen and Lerner regressed cross-sectional β values for several hundred Compustat firms on the following seven financial variables: the debt to equity ratio, the debt to equity ratio squared, a measure of earnings growth, a measure of the stability of earnings growth, the size of the firm, the dividend payout ratio, and the number of shares traded.[18] The regression coefficients of the stability of earnings growth, size, payout, earnings growth rate, and number of shares traded had the expected sign and were statistically significant in the majority of the regressions. However, the coefficients of multiple determination, R^2, were in most cases rather low (ranging from .058 to .540), indicating the absence of important explanatory variables from the regression equations.

FIRM CHARACTERISTICS UNDERLYING RISK MEASURES

The empirical findings presented in the preceding section suggest an association between financial statement variables and market-determined measures of systematic risk. However, the main shortcoming of these findings is the absence of a conceptual justification for the financial

17 For details on computation, see Beaver, *et al.*, *op. cit.*, p. 666.

18 W. J. Breen and E. M. Lerner, "Corporate Financial Strategies and Market Measures of Risk and Return," *The Journal of Finance*, 28 (May 1973), 339–51.

variables that were correlated with market risk measures. Here, as in many other areas of financial analysis research, the empirical investigation was basically a "fishing expedition": a large number of financial variables were correlated in various statistical forms with systematic risk measures, yielding in some cases significant correlations. The problem with such a methodological approach is that given sufficient resources, the researcher is eventually bound to find some significant correlations. However, results of such research are difficult to generalize (e.g., they will usually change from sample to sample), and no real insight is gained into the investigated process. In particular, the above-mentioned studies failed to identify the basic firm characteristics that determine the risk of common stocks. Such an identification process should obviously be based on a theoretical investigation of the operational and financial processes affecting the firm's risk. Following are some examples.

Lev hypothesized that the firm's operating leverage, that is, the ratio of fixed to variable operating costs, is a determinant of the firm's degree of risk.[19] Consider two hypothetical firms which are identical in all respects (industry, size, etc.) except the operating leverage. The periodic net earnings, x_{jt}, of these firms will be

$$x_{jt} = (pQ)_{jt} - (vQ)_{jt} - F_{jt}, \qquad j = 1, 2 \qquad (13.3)$$

where

p_{jt} = average price per unit of firm j's product in period t,
Q_{jt} = number of units sold,
v_{jt} = average variable costs per unit, and
F_{jt} = total fixed costs in period t.

Differentiating expression (13.3) with respect to Q_{jt} yields:

$$x'_{jt} = p_{jt} - v_{jt}. \qquad (13.4)$$

The term involving the fixed costs, F_{jt}, vanishes, since, by definition, these costs are unaffected by demand fluctuations within a specified range. The derivative of earnings with respect to demand, x'_{jt}, thus equals the difference between the average product price and the variable costs, which is known as the "contribution margin." Suppose firm 1 has a higher operating leverage (i.e., it is more capital intensive) than firm 2. Accordingly, the variable costs per unit of firm 1 will be lower than those of firm 2, that is, $v_{1t} < v_{2t}$. Therefore, from (13.4) $x'_{1t} > x'_{2t}$, namely, the earnings volatility of firm 1, induced by demand fluctuations, will be larger than that of firm 2. And, in general, the higher the operating

19 B. Lev, "On the Association between Operating Leverage and Risk," *Journal of Financial and Quantitative Analysis* (June 1974).

leverage (i.e., capital intensity), the higher the earnings volatility with respect to demand fluctuations.

Lev went on to show analytically that earnings volatility (affected by operating leverage) is directly related to both the overall and the systematic risk (β value) of common stocks.[20] This hypothesis was tested on a sample of firms in three industries: electric utilities, steel manufacturers, and oil producers. Results indicated a statistically significant association between operating leverage and risk; both the overall and systematic common stock risk measures were found to be positively associated with the degree of operating leverage. Thus, the capital intensiveness characteristic of the firm's production process seems to be a determinant of its common stock risk.

Hamada linked the Modigliani and Miller capital structure hypothesis with the portfolio theory capital asset pricing model.[21] In particular, he investigated the relationship between the firm's financial risk, as measured by its capital structure (leverage), and the common stock systematic risk (β value). Such a relationship is implied by the Modigliani and Miller hypothesis; systematic risk of levered firms in a given risk class should vary with their leverage. Empirical results were found to support this hypothesis—leverage, measured by market rather than book values, accounted for about 21 to 24 percent of the systematic risk variability of the common stocks in the sample (304 firms). In addition, a long-run measure of leverage, based on twenty-year data, performed more successfully than annual leverage measures in the explanation of β values. Hamada therefore concluded that corporate leverage counts considerably in the determination of common stock systematic risk.

Another attempt to investigate the operational determinants of stock risk measures was made by Lev and Kunitzky drawing upon organization theories of firm behavior.[22] Specifically, various organizational theorists, notably Thompson, and Cyert and March, hypothesized that firms attempt to avoid environmental uncertainty by stabilizing (smoothing) their input and output flows.[23] Thus, for example, inventories are maintained in order to absorb unexpected fluctuations in the supply of raw materials and in the demand for the firm's products; on-the-job training programs provide a constant labor force largely

---

[20] Overall risk was defined as the standard deviation of monthly stock returns over a specified period.

[21] R. S. Hamada, "The Effect of the Firm's Capital Structure on the Systematic Risk of Common Stocks," *The Journal of Finance*, 27 (May 1972), 435–52.

[22] B. Lev and S. Kunitzky, "On the Association between Smoothing Measures and the Risk of Common Stocks," *The Accounting Review* (April, 1974).

[23] J. D. Thompson, *Organizations in Action* (New York: McGraw-Hill Book Company, 1967). R. M. Cyert and J. G. March, *A Behavioral Theory of the Firm* (Englewood Cliffs, N.J.: Prentice-Hall, Inc., 1963).

independent of labor market changes; vertical mergers decrease supply and demand dependence; and peak-load pricing policies are intended to smooth out peak and trough demand differentials. If these hypotheses are valid, then the degree of stability of the firm's input (e.g., raw material purchases) and output (e.g., sales) series should be associated with its level of risk and hence with the riskiness of its common stock. The larger the stability of operations, the smaller the risk.

This hypothesis was tested by Lev and Kunitzky on a sample of 260 Compustat firms. Stability (smoothness) measures were defined for various series, such as production, sales, capital expenditures, and earnings, and then cross-sectionally related by a regression analysis to common stock overall and systematic risk measures. Results indicated a statistically significant association between the extent of stability of production, sales, capital expenditures, earnings, and dividends, and both market-determined risk measures. These findings are therefore consistent with the hypothesis that firms can decrease operational risk by stabilizing their input and output flows.

EVALUATION OF EVIDENCE

The question posed in this chapter was, To what extent can financial statement data improve the estimation of the common stock risk measures required for portfolio decisions? The first set of evidence concerned the association between financial statement variables and systematic risk measures (β values). Results indicate that such an association indeed exists, particularly between measures indicating income variability (or comovement with aggregate income) and systematic common stock risk.

However, association between accounting-determined and market-determined risk measures does not necessarily imply that financial statement data are useful for portfolio decisions. First, the prediction of future risk measures rather than contemporaneous association is the main concern of the analyst, and results regarding the predictive power of financial data are almost nonexistent.[24] Second, and more important, given the probability of serious measurement errors in conventionally estimated risk measures (i.e., those exclusively based on historical price series), the analyst's objective should be to *improve* upon such risk estimates rather than to explain or predict them. Again, the findings on contemporaneous association are, at best, an initial step in the search for optimal risk estimation.

[24] Recall that Beaver, *et al.*, performed such a prediction test, albeit a very limited one.

Optimal estimation of risk obviously requires knowledge of the firm's operating and financial characteristics that determine its level of risk. Such knowledge is unfortunately meager; investment (portfolio) theory has not been satisfactorily integrated with the economic theory of the firm (e.g., production theory) and with corporate finance (e.g., capital budgeting). The studies presented in the preceding section provide some relevant information; operating leverage, financial leverage, and the stability of input and output series appear to be among the determinants of a firm's risk. However, much more has to be known about the determinants of securities' risk before the usefulness of financial statement data for portfolio decisions can be comprehensively examined.

SUMMARY

An optimal estimation of common stock systematic risk (β value) is a fundamental requirement of the portfolio selection model. Conventionally measured β values, based on historical stock prices, probably contain serious measurement errors and hence deviate from the "true" ex ante risk measures required for portfolio decisions. The question raised in this chapter was whether financial statement data can improve the estimation of systematic risk. Available evidence offers only a tentative answer; various accounting-based risk measures were found to be significantly associated with conventionally measured β values, suggesting the possible usefulness of financial statement data for risk estimation. However, no direct evidence on the ability of accounting data to improve conventional risk estimates is currently available.

CHAPTER FOURTEEN

Efficient
Capital Markets

An efficient capital market is defined as one in which security prices always fully reflect all publicly available information concerning the securities traded. Such a market is efficient in the sense that it properly fulfills the primary role of a capital market—the optimal allocation of resources. Empirical evidence strongly indicates that large capital markets, such as the New York Stock Exchange, are indeed efficient according to the above definition.

The major implications of capital markets efficiency are (a) security prices will adjust rapidly and in an unbiased manner to any new information released to the public, and (b) price changes in efficient markets will behave over time as a random walk, that is, in a patternless manner. These implications have a far-reaching effect on security analysis. Some widely used methods, such as the various chartist techniques, are useless in efficient markets, while other analytical methods should be substantially modified. Indeed, the theory of efficient capital markets may well have changed the course of security analysis. The present chapter provides a discussion of the efficient capital markets theory, the relevant empirical evidence, and the implications for security analysis. The next chapter will examine the role of financial statement analysis in efficient capital markets.

RANDOM WALKS IN THE STOCK MARKET

A common belief among security analysts is that history tends to repeat itself, at least as far as the stock market is concerned. Such a belief implies that past series of security prices contain useful information for the prediction of future prices because general patterns will be repeated at regular intervals. Charts and diagrams of stock price behavior appear to support this belief; such graphs seem to exhibit systematic trends and patterns, thereby suggesting that knowledge of past price behavior can be used to predict the future. The alleged systematic trends and patterns in security prices underlie the various chart techniques used by financial analysts.[1]

Roberts was among the first to question the existence of systematic patterns in stock prices.[2] He demonstrated that a series of cumulating *random* numbers, which are obviously free of any systematic patterns, may closely resemble actual stock price series. Figure 14.1 shows that the *levels* of simulated random numbers reveal the well-known head-and-shoulders formation of real stock prices, which is exhibited in Figure 14.2. However, *changes* in the random numbers shown in Figure 14.3 naturally do not exhibit any pattern, as is the case with actual stock price changes in Figure 14.4. Roberts therefore concluded that the "patterns" observed in stock prices may be as illusory as those generated by random numbers and hence of no use for prediction purposes.

The hypothesis regarding the random behavior of stock price changes was soon put to extensive empirical testing.[3] Osborne[4] found a close resemblance between the behavior of stock price changes and the random movement of small particles suspended in a solution, which is known to physicists as "Brownian motion." Granger and Morgenstern,[5] Moore,[6] and Fama[7] provided substantial empirical support for the

[1] For elaboration on chartist methods, see B. Graham, D. L. Dodd, and S. Cottle, *Security Analysis*, 4th ed. (Hightstown, N.J.: McGraw-Hill Book Company, 1962), pp. 713–16.

[2] H. V. Roberts, "Stock Market 'Patterns' and Financial Analysis: Methodological Suggestions," *The Journal of Finance*, 14 (March 1959), 1–10.

[3] The earliest evidence on the random behavior of prices (in the Paris commodity exchange) was provided by L. Bachelier in *Théorie de la Spéculation* (Paris: Gauthier-Vilars, 1900).

[4] M. F. M. Osborne, "Brownian Motion in the Stock Market," *Operations Research*, 7 (March–April 1959), 145–73.

[5] C. W. J. Granger and O. Morgenstern, "Spectral Analysis of New York Stock Market Prices," *Kyklos*, 16 (1963), 1–27.

[6] A. B. Moore, "Some Characteristics of Changes in Common Stocks," in *The Random Character of Stock Market Prices*, P. H. Cootner, ed. (Cambridge, Mass.: M.I.T. Press, 1964), pp. 139–61.

[7] E. F. Fama, "The Behavior of Stock Market Prices," *Journal of Business*, 38 (January 1965), 34–105.

random walk hypothesis; using statistical tests of dependence between successive stock price changes (e.g., serial correlation and runs analyses), they found generally insignificant departures from randomness. Empirical evidence thus suggested that stock price changes behave in a random manner, namely, that successive changes are practically independent over time. The random or patternless behavior of stock price changes implies, of course, that efforts to predict future prices from historical series are as useful as the prediction of future outcomes of coin tosses from observed outcomes. Accordingly, the various chartist methods and mechanical trading rules, based on the belief in systematic stock price patterns, appear to be useless efforts.

FROM RANDOM WALKS TO EFFICIENT CAPITAL MARKETS

In the late sixties, research emphasis shifted from the statistical properties of stock price changes to an investigation of the stock market economic characteristics that bring about the random walk phenomenon. This shift led to the development of the efficient capital markets theory. An efficient capital market is defined as one in which prices always fully reflect all publicly available information concerning the securities traded. This implies that in an efficient capital market, security prices will adjust *instantaneously* and in an *unbiased* manner to any new information released to the market. Such a market is efficient in the sense that it properly fulfills the primary role of a capital market—the optimal allocation of resources. Specifically, a necessary condition for optimal resource allocation is that market prices always provide accurate signals for investor choices. This will be the case when security prices fully reflect all publicly available information relevant to the prediction of future outcomes (e.g., dividend payments, price changes, etc.). Capital, in such a market, will continuously flow to the most profitable investments resulting in an optimal resource allocation.[8]

The sufficient conditions for market efficiency are (*a*) no transaction costs in trading securities, (*b*) available information is costless to all market participants, and (*c*) all investors agree on the implications of available information for current prices and distributions of future

---

[8] The practical implications of market efficiency for stock trading, derived from the "fair game" model, are further discussed in the Appendix.

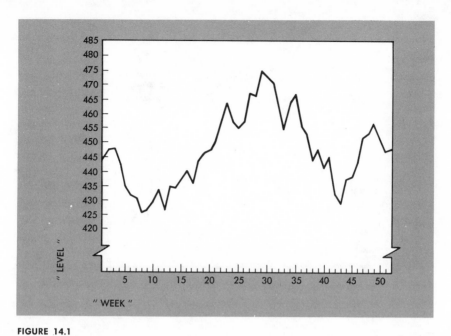

FIGURE 14.1

Simulated market levels (random numbers) for 52 weeks

Source: H. V. Roberts, "Stock Market 'Patterns' and Financial Analysis: Methodological Suggestions," *The Journal of Finance,* 14 (March 1959), 5.

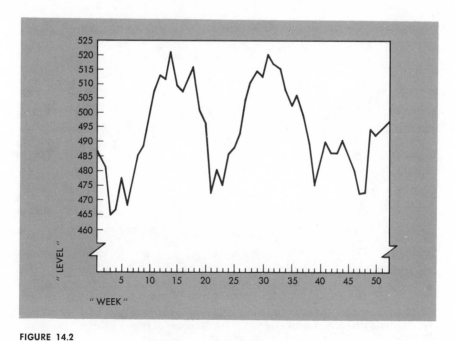

FIGURE 14.2

Actual Friday closing levels, December 30, 1955–December 28, 1956, Dow Jones Industrial Index

Source: Roberts, *The Journal of Finance,* p. 6.

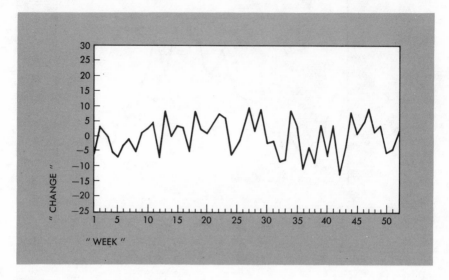

FIGURE 14.3

Simulated market changes (random numbers) for 52 weeks

Source: Roberts, *The Journal of Finance*, p. 5.

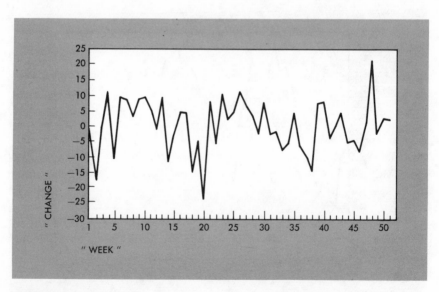

FIGURE 14.4

Actual changes from Friday to Friday (closing) January 6, 1956–December 28, 1956, Dow Jones Industrial Index

Source: Roberts, *The Journal of Finance*, p. 5.

prices of each security. Samuelson[9] and Mandelbrot[10] proved that under such market conditions security prices will behave randomly, or to put it more accurately, will follow a martingale process.[11]

A heuristic interpretation of the Samuelson-Mandelbrot proof follows. The first two sufficient conditions for market efficiency—no transaction costs and free information—assure that strong competition prevails among investors. These competitive forces, in addition to the agreement among investors regarding the implication of new information (the third condition), will cause prices to adjust instantaneously and in an unbiased manner to new information. This can be seen more clearly in an *inefficient* market where the above conditions do not hold. Suppose, for example, that information indicating a future increase in the earnings of a specific firm (e.g., resulting from the development of a new product) is very costly to obtain and, once obtained, is kept secret by a small group of investors (i.e., information does not flow freely in the market). The investors who obtain the information first will naturally capitalize on it by purchasing the firm's stocks. This will result in an initial price increase which will be followed by further increases as more and more investors become aware of the new favorable information. Consequently, during the adjustment period, prices will not fully reflect the information, and moreover, price changes will be dependent over time due to the series of successive increases. However, if investors could obtain the favorable information without cost and agree on its implications, *prompt* action (i.e., stock purchase) would be taken, resulting in an instantaneous price change and an unbiased reflection of the information in the stock's price. Competition among investors, brought about by costless information and trading and the agreement among investors regarding the implications of new information, will thus result in efficient capital markets where prices adjust instantaneously to new information and hence no dependencies in stock price changes exist.[12]

The theory of efficient capital markets may thus provide an explanation for the observed random behavior of stock price changes. However, the sufficient conditions of market efficiency listed above are rather restrictive and undoubtedly unrealistic; transactions costs do

[9] P. A. Samuelson, "Proof That Properly Anticipated Prices Fluctuate Randomly," *Industrial Management Review*, 6 (Spring 1965), 41–49.

[10] B. Mandelbrot, "Forecasts of Future Prices, Unbiased Markets, and Martingale Models," *Journal of Business, Security Prices: A Supplement,* 39 (January 1966), 242–55.

[11] A martingale process was defined in Chapter 8.

[12] Unless, of course, there are dependencies in the information flow to the market, e.g., good news tends to follow good news.

exist in capital markets, information is obviously not freely available to all participants, and investors do not necessarily agree on all the implications of information for current and future prices. Nevertheless, as Fama argued, real capital markets may still be reasonably efficient:

> Fortunately, these conditions are sufficient for market efficiency, but not necessary. For example, as long as transactors take account of all available information, even large transaction costs that inhibit the flow of transactions do not in themselves imply that when transactions do take place, prices will not "fully reflect" available information. Similarly (and speaking, as above, somewhat loosely), the market may be efficient if "sufficient numbers" of investors have ready access to available information. And disagreement among investors about the implications of given information does not in itself imply market inefficiency unless there are investors who can consistently make better evaluations of available information than are implicit in market prices.[13]

Thus, as with any positive (descriptive) model, the fact that the underlying assumptions violate some real-life conditions is not a sufficient reason to reject the model. Despite the unrealistic assumptions, the predictions of the model can still fit reasonably well observed phenomena. For example, although actual successive price changes may not be strictly independent, as in perfectly efficient capital markets, the extent of dependence may still be so small as to render any mechanical trading rule practically useless (especially when transaction costs are accounted for). The question whether the efficient markets model reasonably describes phenomena in real capital markets is therefore empirical and cannot be settled on a priori grounds.

THE EVIDENCE

The large number of empirical studies concerning the theory of efficient capital markets can be classified into three categories: [14]

> . . . weak form tests in which the information subset of interest is just past price (or return) histories. Most of the results here come from the random walk literature. When extensive tests seemed to support the efficiency hypothesis at this level, attention was turned to semi-strong form tests in which the concern is the speed of price adjustment to other obviously publicly available information (e.g., announcements of stock splits,

[13] E. F. Fama, "Efficient Capital Markets: A Review of Theory and Empirical Work," *The Journal of Finance*, 25 (May 1970), 387–88.
[14] This section draws on the comprehensive survey article by Fama, *ibid.*, pp. 383–417.

annual reports, new security issues, etc.). Finally, *strong form* tests in which the concern is whether any investor or groups (e.g., management of mutual funds) have monopolistic access to any information relevant for the formation of prices.[15]

All empirical studies have therefore been concerned with whether prices fully reflect particular subsets of available information. The main results of these studies are briefly summarized below.[16]

1. Weak-form tests. These tests were concerned with two major issues: the extent of dependence of successive price changes, and the profitability of trading systems. Research referring to the first issue relied on common statistical tools such as serial correlation and runs analyses to determine the degree of dependence of successive price changes. Tests were conducted on stock and commodity prices in the United States, France, and Britain. Results confirming the random walk hypothesis were consistent: The extent of dependence in successive price changes was generally found to be negligible, so that the price series seemed to be well approximated by a random walk.[17] Regarding the second issue—trading systems—research concentrated mainly on the profitability of various filter techniques.[18] Obviously, the use of a filter rule will be profitable only if successive price changes are dependent. For example, if a large price increase is followed by further increases more often than by decreases (the alleged psychological effect in stock markets), then buying the stock after the first increase will, on average, yield abnormal gains. Such positive dependency will, of course, occur only when the market does not react instantaneously, that is, when prices adjust *gradually* to new information. In efficient markets, however, the filter technique cannot be expected to consistently outperform a simple buy-and-hold strategy. Results of empirical tests examining a large number of filters indicated that when transaction costs were accounted for, the filter technique did not outperform a buy-and-hold strategy. Thus the weak-form statistical tests, as well as trading system tests, generally uphold the efficient capital markets theory.

---

[15] *Ibid.,* p. 388.

[16] Because of the large number of studies involved, no attempt will be made to reference specific articles. A bibliographical list is provided by Fama, *ibid.*

[17] For some slight exceptions, see Fama, *ibid.,* p. 394.

[18] A typical *x* percent filter rule would be as follows: If the closing price of a particular stock increases by at least *x* percent, buy the stock and hold until the price decreases by at least *x* percent from the highest price following the purchase. At this time, simultaneously sell the holding and go short. Maintain the short position until the daily closing price rises at least *x* percent above a subsequent low. At this time cover the short position and go long. Price movements of less than *x* percent in either direction should be ignored.

2. Semi-strong-form tests. These tests examined whether current prices fully reflect all available information, that is, they focused on the *speed* of price adjustment to new information. Each test was concerned with the speed of price adjustment to a specific kind of event. Among the events tested were stock splits, annual earnings announcements, large secondary offerings of common stock (i.e., large underwritten sales of existing common stocks by individuals and institutions), and new issues of stocks. Evidence from these tests generally indicated a quick price adjustment process and thus confirmed the efficient markets theory. However, since only a few events were examined, the scope of the semi-strong evidence of market efficiency is as yet somewhat restricted.

3. Strong-form tests. These tests were concerned with the question whether there are individuals having access to information that is not generally available and therefore not fully reflected in security prices (i.e., monopoly power on information). The few tests conducted in this area point to the existence of such individuals. Specifically, specialists (floor traders) on stock exchanges have access to lists of unexecuted buy-and-sell limit orders (the "specialist's book"). This information is not available to the general public and, as evidence indicates, is probably turned to profit by the specialists. As expected, corporate officers were found to have monopolistic access to information about their firms. However, the group of floor traders is rather restricted, and corporate officers are prohibited from exploiting information about their firms. Therefore, the practical impact of the monopolistic power of these individuals seems rather limited. Of greater importance is the question whether managers of mutual funds possess, as they often claim, information unknown to the general public. Accordingly, several empirical studies concerned with the performance of mutual funds attempted to establish:

> . . . (a) whether in general fund managers seem to have access to special information which allows them to generate "abnormal" expected returns, and (b) whether some funds are better at uncovering such special information than others.[19]

Results regarding both questions were unfavorable to mutual funds' management. The unimpressive performance of these funds, when portfolio risk was accounted for, suggested that fund managers do not have access to information that is not fully reflected in security prices, or, alternatively, that they do not use such information for the benefit of fund shareholders.

---

[19] Fama, "Efficient Capital Markets," *op. cit.,* p. 410.

It can be concluded therefore that the empirical evidence, especially of the weak-form and semi-strong-form tests, generally supports the efficient capital markets theory.[20] Thus, despite various market imperfections (e.g., transaction costs), stock prices generally appear to reflect publicly available information and adjust rapidly to new information.

IMPLICATIONS FOR SECURITY ANALYSIS

It has been argued that the efficient capital markets theory implies the uselessness of security analysis. Specifically, when security price changes behave randomly, then no technique or analytical tool can be expected to *systematically* yield above-average returns. The apparent inconsistency between this alleged implication and the fact that so many security analysts (about eleven thousand) are currently employed by financial institutions led many to regard the efficient markets theory with a mixture of disbelief and amusement. However, a careful consideration of the theory and the underlying economic process indicates no inconsistency with profitable security analysis. In fact, security analysis may not only be useful in efficient capital markets—it is *essential* to market efficiency:

> There is a curious paradox. In order for the [efficient markets] hypothesis to be true, it is necessary for many investors to disbelieve it. That is, market prices will promptly and fully reflect what is knowable about the companies whose shares are traded only if investors seek to earn superior returns, make conscientious and competent efforts to learn about the companies whose securities are traded, and analyze relevant information promptly and perceptively. If that effort were abandoned, the efficiency of the market would diminish rapidly.[21]

Thus, the efficient capital markets theory cannot imply the uselessness of security analysis, since the continuous efforts of analysts are a major factor in bringing about market efficiency. However, the efficient capital markets theory does suggest important areas for change and improvement in security analysis.

The random walk behavior of security price changes clearly implies the uselessness of the various chartist methods and mechanical trading rules (e.g., the filter techniques), which are based on the assump-

[20] For a discussion of some noncorroborative evidence, see D. Downes and T. R. Dyckman, "A Critical Look at the Efficient Market Empirical Research Literature as It Relates to Accounting Information," *The Accounting Review*, 48 (April 1973), 300–17.

[21] J. H. Lorie and M. T. Hamilton, *The Stock Market, Theories and Evidence* (Homewood, Ill.: Richard D. Irwin, Inc., 1973), p. 98.

tion that price changes are substantially dependent over time. With respect to other forms of security analysis, usually known as the fundamental or intrinsic value methods, the situation is more involved. The fundamental approach to security analysis assumes that each security at any point in time has an intrinsic value (i.e., equilibrium price) depending mainly on the earnings prospects of the firm issuing the security. Through a careful study of various accounting and nonaccounting factors, such as management's quality and the outlook for the industry and the economy, the analyst is supposed to be able to determine whether the actual price of the security deviates from its intrinsic value. If prices tend to move toward intrinsic values, then knowledge of such deviations can be used to produce above-average gains (i.e., buy when the price is below intrinsic values and sell, or even go short, when the price is above intrinsic values).[22]

Note that fundamental analysis, unlike the chartist methods and mechanical trading rules, is not restricted to the information contained in the historical price series. Indeed, the major objective of the analyst's investigation is to obtain information that is as yet unknown to the general public. Experience gained by concentration on specific industries, connections with corporate officers, and unique analytical tools (e.g., a successful earnings prediction model) might uncover such information. The usefulness of such inside information in producing above-average gains is clearly consistent with the efficient capital markets theory, which refers only to publicly available information.[23]

While security analysis conducted in efficient capital markets might be financially rewarding, it clearly must be substantially different from conventional textbook recipes. First, it is very unlikely that an analytical method that proves useful in uncovering inside information will continue to be so over the long run. Extensive use of the method in investment decisions will soon result in market prices reflecting the value of information provided by the method and thereby gradually decrease its usefulness. As with any competitive market, gains from a new discovery or invention are usually short-lived; nevertheless, such gains can be very large. Accordingly, well-known and "proved" analytical tools, such as those suggested in security analysis texts or offered to the public by investment houses, are probably useless by the time they are published; originality, secrecy, and prompt action are conditions for successful security analysis. Second, having completed the analysis, the investor must determine whether the information uncovered is really inside information, that is, not already impounded in the security's price; in other words, the investor must ascertain that his assessment of the

---

[22] For elaboration on the fundamental approach to security analysis, see Graham, Dodd, and Cottle, *op. cit.*, pp. 434–49.

[23] See Appendix for a rigorous definition of available and inside information.

security's future outcomes differs from that of the market. Thus, an optimistic forecast regarding the future earnings of a company is not by itself a justification for purchasing its stock; it is necessary that the forecast be significantly more optimistic than that of the market as a whole. Therefore, the major conditions of successful security analysis in efficient capital markets are a profound understanding of the impact of firm and economy-wide events on security prices, originality and secrecy in developing analytical tools, and alertness in using them. Obviously, the analyst's task in efficient markets is not an easy one.

SUMMARY

Stock prices in efficient capital markets fully reflect all publicly available information and adjust rapidly and in an unbiased manner to new information. Extensive empirical evidence generally upholds the efficient markets theory for large stock exchanges. The implications of market efficiency for security analysis are far reaching. Chartist methods and trading rules that are exclusively based on the assumption of dependencies in stock price time-series are probably useless. Fundamental analysis might be financially rewarding in efficient capital markets only if inside information could be systematically uncovered, and even then the gains from a specific method would probably accrue for a relatively short period. Successful security analysis therefore requires constant originality, ingenuity, and alertness.

APPENDIX: THE "FAIR GAME" MODEL

An efficient capital market was defined above as one in which security prices fully reflect all publicly available information.[24] This somewhat abstract definition can be operationally interpreted (i.e., an interpretation that lends itself to empirical testing) in terms of the following "fair game" model. The fact that security prices fully reflect all available information implies that price behavior will be such that any speculation based on the information impounded in historical prices will be a fair game, that is, the expected profit to the speculator will be zero. Stated differently, no above-average gains can be expected by trading in efficient markets unless access is available to inside information.[25] The fair game model is a direct implication of efficient markets theory, since if speculation turns out not to be a fair game (i.e., the expected profit to the

[24] This Appendix draws on Fama, "Efficient Capital Markets," *op. cit.*

[25] Inside information is defined as that information to which the market would react if it were available (e.g., the exact content of a forthcoming financial report.)

speculator is positive), then security prices cannot have reflected all available information. In particular, prices do not reflect the information that enabled the speculator to obtain the above-average gains. This interpretation of the efficient markets concept in terms of the fair game model has the important advantage of providing the researcher with testable hypotheses. For example, if prices behave in such a way that speculation based on available information is a fair game, then the success of any trading system (e.g., filter rules) based on past price data is obviously ruled out. Tests of the performance of trading systems could therefore be used to verify the efficient markets theory.

To make the efficient markets theory empirically testable, the process of security price formation must be specified. A well-known class of such processes is the "expected return" theories which postulate that, conditional on some relevant information set, the equilibrium expected return on a security is a function of its risk.[26] The various expected return theories can generally be described as follows:

$$E(\tilde{P}_{j,t+1}|\Phi_t) = [1 + E(\tilde{r}_{j,t+1}|\Phi_t)]P_{jt}, \qquad (14.1)$$

where

E = expected value operator,
P_{jt} = price of security j at the end of period t,
$\tilde{r}_{j,t+1}$ = the return (in percentages) on security j during period $t + 1$, and
Φ_t = the set of information that is assumed to be "fully reflected" in the price at time t.

The tildes indicate that $\tilde{P}_{j,t+1}$ and $\tilde{r}_{j,t+1}$ are random variables at t. The value of the equilibrium expected return $E(\tilde{r}_{j,t+1}|\Phi_t)$, estimated on the basis of the available information, Φ_t, will be determined by the particular expected return model used. However, expression (14.1) implies that no matter which expected return model is assumed to apply, the information represented by Φ_t is fully utilized in determining equilibrium expected returns. This then is the sense in which the available information, Φ_t, is said to be fully reflected in the price, P_{jt}.

The assumption that expected returns impound the information set, Φ_t, rules out the possibility of gaining above-average profits (i.e., returns in excess of equilibrium expected returns) from trading systems based solely on the information in Φ_t. To prove this let $x_{j,t+1}$ be the excess market value of security j at the end of $t + 1$ over the expected

---

[26] See, for example, the capital asset pricing model (Chapter 12), which states that in equilibrium the expected return on a security will equal the pure (riskless) interest rate plus a risk premium which is a function of the security's systematic risk (β value).

value of this security projected at time t on the basis of the information Φ_t:

$$x_{j,t+1} = P_{j,t+1} - E(\tilde{P}_{j,t+1}|\Phi_t). \tag{14.2}$$

Then, by definition:

$$E(\tilde{x}_{j,t+1}|\Phi_t) = 0, \tag{14.3}$$

namely, the sequence $\{x_{jt}\}$ is a "fair game" with respect to the information sequence $\{\Phi_t\}$. Expression (14.3) thus states that when the information Φ_t is fully utilized in the formation of equilibrium market prices, the expected profits from any trading system based on this information cannot be in excess of the equilibrium expected returns (i.e., those earned by a simple buy-and-hold policy). All such trading systems are therefore "fair games."

CHAPTER FIFTEEN

The Role of
Financial Statement Analysis
in Efficient Capital Markets

The role of financial statement analysis in efficient capital markets will be examined in this chapter from both the positive and normative points of view. The positive point of view is concerned with whether information currently provided in financial statements is used in the process of investment decision making, while the normative point of view is concerned with how this information ought to be used by investors. Although financial analysis is normatively oriented, the positive aspect is of importance because market efficiency implies, among other things, that investors will act upon any relevant information and ignore all irrelevant data. Accordingly, if investors were found to disregard financial data, it would suggest the irrelevance of the accounting information system. However, if results indicated that financial data were used by investors, efforts should be made to increase the benefits of the data and/or decrease their cost. Thus, as with most economic issues, both the positive and normative aspects of financial analysis are to a large extent interdependent and therefore have to be investigated simultaneously.

The following section deals with the question whether investors use financial statement data. Next, the effect of changes in accounting measurement techniques on investor decisions is examined. This question bears directly upon market efficiency, since in efficient markets accounting changes would not be expected to systematically affect security prices. The chapter closes with a discussion of the optimal use of financial statement analysis in efficient capital markets.

DO INVESTORS ACT UPON PUBLISHED FINANCIAL DATA?

The belief in the relevance of financial data for investment decision making is, naturally, shared by most accountants:

> Accounting reports provide the information by which millions of investors judge corporate investment performance and by reference to which they make investment decisions. Every day, decisions concerning the allocation of resources of vast magnitude are made on the basis of accounting information.[1]

The widespread publication of accounting information (e.g., earnings reports) in the financial media, and the extensive regulation concerning the form and content of financial reports (e.g., the SEC rules), indicate that many nonaccountants also subscribe to the view that financial information is extensively used by investors.

However, skeptics argue that financial statements are by no means the only source of information concerning the firm's economic situation. Specifically, investors have ready access to various dependable sources of nonaccounting information, such as industry production statistics, data on unfilled orders, and the national accounts, which might also be relevant for assessing the firm's future course. At the extreme, it is sometimes argued that because of the historical nature of accounting data and the possible manipulation of results allowed by generally accepted accounting principles, financial data are of little or no use to investors.[2] These conflicting views on the usefulness of financial data motivated a series of studies concerned with the extent of investors' use of financial data.

Empirical evidence strongly indicates that stock price fluctuations are closely related to accounting earnings changes. Niederhoffer and Regan, for example, found that earnings changes were the most important factor separating the best- from the worst-performing stocks in 1970.[3] Specifically, out of the fifty NYSE stocks with the largest capital gains in

---

1 American Accounting Association, "Report of the Committee on Establishment of an Accounting Commission," *The Accounting Review*, 46 (July 1971), 610.

2 See references in Chapter 6, footnotes 1–4.

3 V. Niederhoffer and P. J. Regan, "Earnings Changes, Analysts' Forecasts, and Stock Prices," *The Financial Analysts Journal*, 28 (May–June 1972), 65–71.

1970 (range: 37 to 125 percent), forty-five registered earnings increases. However, out of the fifty stocks with the largest losses (range: −49 to −78 percent) only four had earnings increases. Furthermore, twenty of the top fifty stocks recorded earnings gains of at least 25 percent, whereas all but six of the bottom fifty suffered earnings declines in excess of 25 percent. Based on these and adidtional findings, the authors concluded that ". . . by all measurements and time spans, profits held the key to superior or inferior stock performance." [4]

However, it should be noted that a contemporaneous association between changes in stock prices and earnings does not directly indicate the *extent* of investors' use of financial data. It can be argued, for example, that investors obtain most of the information from nonaccounting sources (e.g., analysts' predictions). Moreover, association between two variables does not indicate the direction of causation. To focus on the effect of financial information on investor behavior, it is necessary to refine the analysis by concentrating on the *timing* of information release and eliminating the possible effects of nonaccounting information sources.

Ball and Brown used the efficient markets framework to examine the amount of information contained in published annual net income numbers.[5]

> Recent developments in capital theory provide justification for selecting the behavior of security prices as an operational test of usefulness [of income numbers]. An impressive body of theory supports the proposition that capital markets are both efficient and unbiased in that if information is useful in forming capital asset prices, then the market will adjust asset prices to that information quickly [and] changes in security prices will reflect the flow of information to the market. *An observed revision of stock prices associated with the release of the income report would thus provide evidence that the information reflected in income numbers is useful.*[6]

The major problem involved in determining the information content of a financial report is to identify the portion of the total information that was already *expected* by investors prior to the information release. Obviously, only the *unexpected* part of the total information would be relevant to the market. For example, if investors could perfectly predict the content of the next financial statement, then the released report would not convey relevant information except for confirming investors' expecta-

---

[4] *Ibid.*, p. 71. This conclusion is consistent with the findings of J. W. Ashley, "Stock Prices and Changes in Earnings and Dividends: Some Empirical Results," *Journal of Political Economy*, 70 (February 1962), 82–85.

[5] R. Ball and P. Brown, "An Empirical Evaluation of Accounting Income Numbers," *Journal of Accounting Research*, 6 (Autumn 1968), 159–78.

[6] *Ibid.*, pp. 160–61, emphasis supplied.

tions.[7] Thus, the larger the discrepancy between the expected and actual financial outcomes, the larger the amount of information provided by the report.

The first stage of Ball and Brown's analysis involved a determination of the market's expectation regarding the firm's earnings. Since this expectation could not be directly observed, some general prediction model had to be used to provide the expectations. The prediction model used was based on their previous findings that a substantial part of a firm's earnings variability is associated with the variability of aggregate earnings of all firms.[8] A conditional prediction of a firm's earnings can, therefore, be made on the basis of aggregate earnings and the past relationship between the earnings of the specific firm and those of all other firms. The amount of new information is measured by the difference between actual and predicted earnings (i.e., the prediction error).

Operationally, the information content of income numbers was estimated by means of the following least-squares regression:

$$\Delta I_{j,t-\tau} = \hat{a}_{1jt} + \hat{a}_{2jt}\,\Delta M_{j,t-\tau} + \hat{u}_{j,t-\tau},\ \tau = 1, 2, \ldots, t - 1, \qquad (15.1)$$

where

$$\Delta I_{j,t-\tau} = \text{actual change in firm } j\text{'s income, and}$$
$$\Delta M_{j,t-\tau} = \text{change in the average income of all firms.}$$

The regression residual, $\hat{u}_{jt}$, is equal to the unexpected income change (i.e., the forecast error):

$$\hat{u}_{jt} = \Delta I_{jt} - \Delta \hat{I}_{jt}, \qquad (15.2)$$

where $\Delta \hat{I}_{jt} =$ the expected change in firm j's income derived from (15.1). The sign of the unexpected income change, $\hat{u}_{jt}$, was used in determining the value of the incremental information content of the income number. Specifically, a positive $\hat{u}_{jt}$ was defined as "good news," since the actual change in the firm's earnings was larger than the expected one. Accordingly, a negative $\hat{u}_{jt}$ was defined as "bad news," and a zero residual as "no news." It was hypothesized that if the released income figure contained new information not yet impounded in the price, then "good news" ($\hat{u}_{jt} > 0$) would trigger an increase in the firm's stock price, since investors, upon receiving the new information, would revise upward their previous assessment of the stock's profitability; accordingly, "bad news"

---

[7] It should be noted that the confirmation of expectations might also affect investor behavior. Any expectation is associated with some degree of uncertainty which is resolved by the confirming information. This confirmation effect would, of course, not be reflected in Ball and Brown's results.

[8] See R. Ball and P. Brown, "Some Preliminary Findings on the Association between the Earnings of a Firm, Its Industry and the Economy," *Empirical Research in Accounting: Selected Studies, 1967,* Supplement to Vol. 5, *Journal of Accounting Research,* 55–77.

$(\hat{u}_{jt} < 0)$ would trigger a decrease in the stock price; and "no news" $(\hat{u}_{jt} = 0)$ would have no effect on the price, since the market's expectation already impounded in the price was confirmed by the released income number. Thus, the extent of association between income forecast errors and stock price changes would indicate to what extent the information conveyed by the annual income numbers was new and relevant to investors. However, instead of considering total stock price changes, Ball and Brown extracted the portion of the change that reflected a general movement in the market.[9] Thus, attention was confined to the price change specific to the stock considered.

The upper panel of Figure 15.1 shows the average price behavior for the "good news" cases, that is, the stocks for which actual earnings were larger than expected. The lower panel shows the price behavior of the stocks experiencing "bad news." In both cases, the examined period covered twelve months prior to the income announcement (month 0), and six months subsequent to it. It is evident that price behavior conforms to the hypothesis stated above; in the cases in which actual earnings were above expectations there was a continuous price increase up to the announcement month. When actual earnings were below expectations, the price decreased continuously. Some slight price adjustments continued for as long as two months after the announcement of the income figure (month 0). Results thus indicated that unexpected income changes are associated with specific stock price movements.

With respect to the information content of the income number, Ball and Brown found that about 50 percent or more of all the information about an individual firm that becomes available during the year is captured in that year's income number. However, most of this information was anticipated by the market before the income figure was released: Figure 15.1 shows that, on average, only 10–15 percent of the price adjustment took place in the month of income announcement (month 0). This finding may be explained by the fact that a substantial part of the relevant accounting information leaked to the market before the formal release of the annual income number by more timely media such as interim reports and statements by company officials.[10] However, despite the

---

[9] This was done by focusing on the "market model" residuals, ϵ_{it} in (12.4). The residual analysis was discussed earlier in Chapter 3.

[10] Similar results were obtained by using the same method on Australian data; see P. Brown, "The Impact of the Annual Net Profit Report on the Stock Market," *The Australian Accountant*, 40 (July 1970), 277–83. Australian annual reports were found to have a somewhat larger information content than their U.S. counterparts (20–25 percent of the total annual adjustment as compared with 10–15 percent for U.S. firms), probably because interim reports are released in Australia only once a year as compared with the three quarterly reports conventionally released in the U.S. The ostensibly smaller leakage of earnings information in Australia is probably responsible for the larger information content of the annual income numbers.

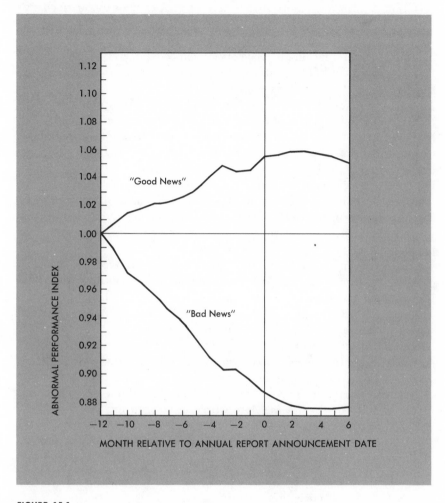

FIGURE 15.1

The price behavior of stocks experiencing
"good" and "bad" income news

Source: R. Ball and P. Brown, "An Empirical Evaluation of Accounting Income Numbers," *Journal of Accounting Research*, 6 (Autumn 1968), 169.

leakage, it seems that the release of income figures provides relevant information to investors and triggers portfolio rearrangements.

Ball and Brown's analysis also provided some estimates of the extra profit that could have been made by predicting whether the published income figure would be above or below market expectations. The annual stock price appreciation of companies experiencing above-expectation earnings was more than 7 percent greater than the price change that could be attributed to general market effects. Over the year, the stocks of companies with disappointing earnings fell almost 10 percent below the level that might have been expected merely from general market movements. Thus, ability to predict the *direction* of earnings changes would have paid handsomely.

Ball and Brown's study was based on various assumptions, the most restrictive of which is probably the specific expectations model used. Test results obviously depend on the assumption that investors' expectations of future earnings are formed by the prediction model (15.1); other prediction models might have yielded different results. Given the rather imperfect knowledge regarding the formation of investors' expectations, it would be desirable to examine the effect of financial data on investor decisions *independently* of a specific prediction model. Such an approach was taken by Beaver who investigated the effect of earnings announcements on stock prices and volume of trade.[11]

Relevant financial information was defined by Beaver as that which changes investors' expectations.[12] When such expectations regarding future outcomes of the firm (e.g., profits, growth, etc.) change, investors will react by rearranging their portfolios.[13] Accordingly, if a financial statement conveys relevant information to investors (i.e., changes their expectations), an unusually large volume of transactions in the firm's shares, at and subsequent to the release of information, should be observed. It is, therefore, possible to determine whether financial statements convey information to investors by comparing the volume of transactions in the vicinity of the release date with the volume for the rest of the year.[14]

Beaver's sample consisted of 143 firms (mainly in the food-process-

---

[11] W. H. Beaver, "The Information Content of Annual Earnings Announcements," *Empirical Research in Accounting: Selected Studies, 1968*, Supplement to Vol. 6, *Journal of Accounting Research*, 67–92.

[12] Recall that this definition of information was also used by Ball and Brown. The source of the definition is the mathematical theory of information (communication), which measures the amount of information conveyed by a message as a function of the change in the receiver's prior expectations with respect to a given event. For elaboration, see C. E. Shannon and W. Weaver, *The Mathematical Theory of Communication* (Urbana, Ill.: The University of Illinois Press, 1964).

[13] The change in expectation must, of course, be sufficiently large to compensate for the transaction costs involved in portfolio rearrangement.

[14] Beaver examined both *volume* and *price* reaction to the new information: "An important distinction between the price and volume tests is that the former reflects changes in the expectations of the market as a whole while the latter reflects changes in the expectations of individual investors. A piece of information may be neutral in the sense of not changing the expectations of the market as a whole but it may greatly alter the expectations of individuals. In this situation, there would be no price reaction, but there would be shifts in portfolio positions reflected in the volume." (Beaver, *op. cit.*, p. 69.)

ing and textile industries) which released their earnings figures during the years 1961 through 1965. A total of 506 earnings announcements were available. Since informational effect was examined, the crucial factor was the date on which the released information *first* became known to the public. This date was assumed to be the day in which the earnings announcement appeared in the *Wall Street Journal*. The week that included this day was defined as "week 0." The average volume of transactions in this week was then compared with the weekly average volume for eight weeks before "week 0" and eight weeks after it to determine the informational effect of the earnings announcement. Results of this comparison for the total sample are presented in Figure 15.2. A strong volume reaction in "week 0" is evident; the average volume in this week was 33 percent larger than the average volume during the nonreport period (i.e., the sixteen weeks excluding "week 0"), and it is by far the largest volume observed during the seventeen weeks examined. It therefore appears that

> Investors do shift portfolio positions at the time of the earnings announcements, and this shift is consistent with the contention that earnings reports have information content. . . . The investor response appears to be very rapid, for almost all of the above-normal activity occurs during week 0.[15]

Investor reaction to the publication of financial data was corroborated by other researchers. Brown and Kennelly, using the residual analysis technique, found that quarterly earnings-per-share reports convey new and useful information to the market.[16] May, using a combination of Beaver's and Ball and Brown's techniques, confirmed the association between quarterly earnings announcements and stock price changes.[17] Martin constructed a model based on accounting variables to explain the variability in earnings-price ratios.[18] The relatively high coefficients of

[15] *Ibid.*, p. 74. It is interesting to note that when Beaver's method was replicated on Israeli data, no significant investor reaction to earnings announcements was noticed. This lack of reaction can probably be ascribed to the long delay in financial statement publication in Israel (an average of about six months for the sample) and to capital market inefficiences. See B. Lev and B. Yahalomi, "The Effects of Corporate Financial Statements on the Israeli Stock Exchange," *Management International Review* (1972/2–3), 145–50.

[16] P. Brown and J. W. Kennelly, "The Informational Content of Quarterly Earnings: An Extension and Some Further Evidence," *Journal of Business,* 45 (July 1972), 403–15.

[17] R. G. May, "The Influence of Quarterly Earnings Announcements on Investor Decisions as Reflected in Common Stock Price Changes," *Empirical Research in Accounting: Selected Studies, 1971,* Supplement to Vol. 9, *Journal of Accountng Research,* 119–63.

[18] A. Martin, "An Empirical Test of the Relevance of Accounting Information for Investment Decisions," *Empirical Research in Accounting: Selected Studies, 1971,* Supplement to Vol. 9, *Journal of Accounting Research,* 1–31.

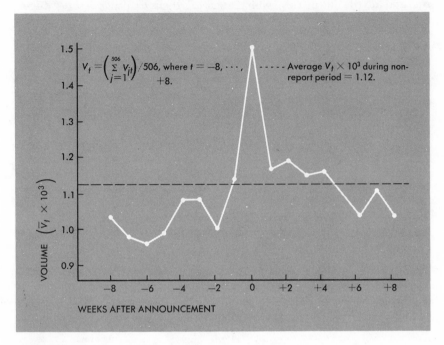

FIGURE 15.2

*Weekly volume of stock trade around the income
announcement week*

> *Source:* W. H. Beaver, "The Information Content of Annual Earnings Announcements," *Empirical Research in Accounting: Selected Studies, 1968,* Supplement to Vol. 6, *Journal of Accounting Research,* 89.

multiple determination, R^2's (generally larger than .60), were interpreted to indicate that accounting information is useful for investment decision making. Kiger corroborated earlier findings by reporting that interim reports were used by investors, particularly to predict annual income.[19]

Summarizing, the evidence presented in this section indicates that the information conveyed by financial statements is useful to investors.[20] Investor reaction to the announcement of financial data was apparent in all the studies mentioned above. It should be noted that the estimates of the marginal usefulness of financial data, particularly Ball and Brown's 10–15 percent, are probably conservative. First, most studies focused only

[19] J. E. Kiger, "An Empirical Investigation of NYSE Volume and Price Reactions to the Announcement of Quarterly Earnings," *Journal of Accounting Research,* 10 (Spring 1972), 113–28.

[20] For a different interpretation of some of this evidence, see G. J. Benston, "Required Disclosure and the Stock Market: An Evaluation of the Securities Exchange Act of 1934," *The American Economic Review,* 63 (March 1973), 137–40.

on investor reaction to the income number announcement, thereby ignoring the possible informational value of other financial statement items. Second, the studies by Ball and Brown and by Beaver examined the effect of annual earnings announcements. Given that most firms publish quarterly reports, it seems reasonable to assume that a substantial portion of the information contained in the annual report has already been conveyed to investors by the more timely quarterly reports.[21] Accordingly, financial statement data (both quarterly and annual) might be more useful to investors than indicated by the above studies.

THE EFFECT OF CHANGES IN ACCOUNTING TECHNIQUES ON INVESTOR DECISIONS

Generally accepted accounting procedures (e.g., the various inventory valuation methods) allow a firm to exercise considerable control over the published financial results. Consequently, a firm's economic condition may be reported in several different ways.[22] A question of major importance to both management and analysts is whether investor decisions can be affected by a mere change in accounting technique, given that the firm's underlying economic situation is unchanged.[23] If such an effect exists, as is widely believed,[24] it is clearly inconsistent with market efficiency, since changes in accounting techniques and their effect on financial results are usually specified in the financial statements, thus enabling astute investors to "see through the numbers" and correctly price securities. Therefore, in efficient capital markets, firms would not be able to systematically affect stock prices by merely manipulating accounting techniques; only real economic changes would affect investor decisions. An empirical investigation into the market impact of accounting changes, besides the obvious interest to financial analysts and accountants, would thus provide an indirect test of market efficiency.

The early research concerning the possible effects of alternative accounting methods on investor decisions was conducted in the form of

21 Note that the findings concerning the predictive power of quarterly reports, discussed in Chapter 8, corroborate this assumption.

22 This subject was elaborated on in Chapter 6.

23 For a survey of trends in accounting technique changes, see P. Frishkoff, "Some Recent Trends in Accounting Changes," *Journal of Accounting Research, 8* (Spring 1970), 141–44.

24 This belief is also shared by nonaccountants, as evidenced by the following statement cited from "Profits: The Big Bath," *Newsweek,* July 27, 1970, p. 54: "The subject of accounting is one calculated to glaze the eyes of most warm-blooded mortals, but the games that astute businessmen play under the cover of the auditor's art are ignored by laymen, particularly the nation's 30.9 million stockholders, at considerable peril."

experimental and simulation studies. Jensen, by means of questionnaires sent to security analysts, examined the effects of alternative depreciation and inventory methods on investment decisions.[25] Results indicated that different accounting techniques did affect the opinions of analysts, primarily through the impact on earnings-per-share figures. Dyckman, in a series of studies, presented participants with two (and later three) sets of identical financial statements, except for inventory valuation methods (LIFO vs. FIFO). [26] Results were somewhat conflicting: In both the first and third studies, participants' decisions were affected by the specific inventory valuation method, while results of the second study indicated that participants were indifferent to the method used. Bruns also examined the effect of inventory valuation methods on a sample of businessmen and students.[27] Results indicated that the accounting variations did not affect pricing, advertising, and production decisions. Barrett examined the effect of various recording methods of intercorporate investment and concluded that the accounting method did not influence the judgment of financial analysts as long as sufficient information was given in footnotes.[28]

Turning to simulation studies, Bonini found that under given conditions, a firm using the LIFO inventory method tends to generate more profits than a firm using the average cost inventory method.[29] He reasoned that the LIFO method increases the variability of profits over time, as compared with the average cost method, and hence stimulates more attention and pressures by managers toward higher profits. Brigham simulated the effects of alternative depreciation and tax-accounting methods on utility rates and earnings.[30] Results indicated that profits under flow-through and normalized tax-accounting methods were generally

[25] R. E. Jensen, "An Experimental Design for Study of Effects of Accounting Variations in Decision Making," *Journal of Accounting Research*, 4 (Autumn 1966), 224–38.

[26] T. R. Dyckman, "On the Investment Decision," *The Accounting Review*, 39 (April 1964), 285–95; Dyckman, "The Effects of Alternative Accounting Techniques on Certain Management Decisions," *Journal of Accounting Research*, 2 (Spring 1964), 91–107; Dyckman, "On the Effects of Earnings-Trend, Size and Inventory Valuation Procedures in Evaluating a Business Firm," in *Research in Accounting Measurement*, R. K. Jaedicke, Y. Ijiri, and O. Nielsen, eds. (American Accounting Association, 1966), pp. 175–85.

[27] W. J. Bruns, Jr., "Inventory Valuation and Management Decisions," *The Accounting Review*, 40 (April 1965), 345–57.

[28] M. E. Barrett, "Accounting for Intercorporate Investments: A Behavioral Field Experiment," *Empirical Research in Accounting: Selected Studies, 1971*, Supplement to Vol. 9, *Journal of Accounting Research*, 50–65.

[29] C. P. Bonini, *Simulation of Information and Decision Systems in the Firm* (Englewood Cliffs, N.J.: Prentice-Hall, Inc., 1963).

[30] E. F. Brigham, "The Effects of Alternative Depreciation Policies on Reported Profits," *The Accounting Review*, 43 (January 1968), 46–61.

comparable. Comisky and Mlynarczyk found that various differences among accounting methods yield smaller actual variations in income than those predicted by financial analysts.[31] Greenball examined the question whether certain accounting methods generate earnings estimates that are more useful to investors than those generated by other accounting methods.[32] Using a simulation experiment which can be viewed as a common stock investment game, he concluded that (*a*) the performance of the three accounting approaches to valuation was ranked as follows: current operating profit, historical cost, and business profit; (*b*) absorption and direct costing method performed about equally; and (*c*) investors using accounting data, regardless of their limitations, were better off than those who ignored the data.

Any attempt to generalize the aforementioned results is obviously a frustrating task, since (*a*) the findings are, to some extent, inconsistent, and (*b*) the usefulness of questionnaire and simulation studies for investigating positive economic problems is somewhat questionable, as argued by Jensen:

> In a sense I used these pages as a medium for venting my long-standing criticism of game studies of human behavior, and in particular, business game studies of "business" behavior. Such studies are merely studies of how people play a simple game, and in general have no proven bearing on how the same people behave in real situations where more complex goals, penalties, and human interactions make life a different game in a different ball park played under different rules.[33]

We turn, therefore, to empirical tests of the possible effects of alternative accounting techniques on investor decisions.

One of the earliest attempts to relate alternative accounting methods to security prices was by O'Donnell who examined the effect of alternative depreciation and tax-accounting methods on the price-earnings ratios of twenty-five electric utilities.[34] Specifically, he divided the sample into two classes: (*a*) firms that used accelerated depreciation (as permitted by the 1954 Code) for tax purposes and straight-line for financial reporting, and (*b*) firms that used accelerated depreciation for tax purposes but

[31] E. E. Comisky and F. A. Mlynarczyk, "Recognition of Income by Finance Companies," *The Accounting Review*, 43 (April 1968), 248–56.

[32] M. N. Greenball, "Evaluation of the Usefulness to Investors of Different Accounting Estimators of Earnings: A Simulation Approach," *Empirical Research in Accounting: Selected Studies, 1968*, Supplement to Vol. 6, *Journal of Accounting Research*, 27–58.

[33] R. E. Jensen, discussion of T. J. Mock, "Comparative Values of Information Structures," *Empirical Research in Accounting: Selected Studies, 1969*, Supplement to Vol. 7, *Journal of Accounting Research*, 180.

[34] J. L. O'Donnell, "Relationships between Reported Earnings and Stock Prices in the Electric Utility Industry," *The Accounting Review*, 40 (January 1965), 135–43.

"normalized" their reported earnings.[35] Other things being equal, the reported earnings of firms in group *a* will be higher than those in group *b*. The trends in the average price-earnings ratios for the two subsamples were then compared to find whether the market regards the income figures resulting from different accounting procedures as reflecting real economic differences. O'Donnell concluded that investors were not fooled by the accounting differences:

> . . . it is clear that investors in electric utility stocks do not blindly accept reported earnings. They make their own estimates of business income and price the securities accordingly. It follows that raising earnings by altering accounting procedures will not necessarily result, even in the short run, in higher stock prices.[36]

In a follow-up study, O'Donnell used a somewhat larger sample (fifty-six firms) of electrical utilities.[37] His earlier results were confirmed: Investors tended to regard the higher earnings of firms that did not defer the tax savings (group *a*) as inferior to the normalized earnings.

Summers, using a sample of twenty-three airlines, reported that investors were indifferent to alternative accounting methods of interperiod tax allocation, investment credit, and funds-flow statements.[38] He concluded that each accounting treatment probably provided investors with the necessary information for unbiased security pricing.

Staubus examined the association between several earnings measures and the discounted values (for various holding periods) of common stocks.[39] The earnings measures were (*a*) net earnings as reported by the firms; (*b*) current flows (i.e., net earnings plus depreciation, depletion, and amortization expenses); and (*c*) net recurring fund-flows, defined as the firm's earnings computed on a cash basis. These variables were correlated with the sum of discounted future net cash receipts (dividends plus terminal value) from the stock. Based on correlation coefficients, current flows were found to be more closely associated with discounted stock values ($r^2 = .762$) than reported earnings ($r^2 = .730$). Fund-flows had the

---

[35] Specifically, they reduced current earnings by the tax savings resulting from using accelerated rather than straight-line depreciation. This deduction is credited to a deferred liability account. For elaboration, see APB Opinion No. 11, "Accounting for Income Taxes" (New York: American Institute of Certified Public Accountants, December 1967).

[36] O'Donnell, *op. cit.*, p. 141.

[37] J. L. O'Donnell, "Further Observations on Reported Earnings and Stock Prices," *The Accounting Review*, 43 (July 1968), 549–53.

[38] E. L. Summers, "Observation of Effects of Using Alternative Reporting Practices," *The Accounting Review*, 43 (April 1968), 257–65.

[39] G. J. Staubus, "The Association of Financial Accounting Variables with Common Stock Values," *The Accounting Review*, 40 (January 1965), 119–34.

lowest correlation coefficient of the three earnings measures ($r^2 = .627$). These results led Staubus to conclude:

> The apparent failure of earnings to show closer association with discounted stock values than did current flows clearly implies that investors are better off relying on "earnings before depreciation" than on the traditional concept of net income.[40]

However, it seems doubtful whether the slight difference in the squared correlation coefficients (.762 vs. .730) warrants such a strong conclusion. Considering the relatively small sample (forty-five firms), such a difference may well arise from random sampling errors.

Mlynarczyk examined the effect of alternative accounting methods for income taxes on electric utility stock prices.[41] Specifically:

> Did investors distinguish between deferred tax accounting (normalizing) and flow-through tax accounting in valuing the earnings of companies in the electric utility industry in the period 1957–61? [42]

A stock valuation model was formulated and linear regressions were run on cross-sectional data of the ninety-five firms in the sample. Results indicated that normalizing companies enjoyed a premium in price over the flow-through companies, that is, investors seemed to adjust upward to the lower profits of the normalizing companies. These premiums amounted to 10 percent, 9 percent, and 7 percent in 1959, 1960, and 1961, respectively. Based on these findings, Mlynarczyk concluded that:

> . . . it appears that if alternative accounting measures having major impact on reported profits are few in number (in this case, one), and if the alternatives are communicated in the reporting process, investors are able to adjust for the measuring variations.[43]

Gonedes investigated the effect of two accounting measurement procedures (alternative investment credit amortization and interperiod tax allocation), and a reporting procedure (the presentation of funds-flow statement in annual reports), on the firm's cost of equity capital.[44]

40 *Ibid.*, p. 129.

41 F. A. Mlynarczyk, Jr., "An Empirical Study of Accounting Methods and Stock Prices," *Empirical Research in Accounting: Selected Studies, 1969*, Supplement to Vol. 7, *Journal of Accounting Research,* 63–89.

42 *Ibid.*, p. 70. Recall that this problem was earlier examined by O'Donnell.

43 *Ibid.*, p. 76. It should be noted that the evidence bears only upon the correct *direction* of adjustment. Whether the *extent* of adjustment was appropriate is still an open question (e.g., it might be that investors overadjust or underadjust the earnings of flow-through firms).

44 N. J. Gonedes, "The Significance of Selected Accounting Procedures: A Statistical Test," *Empirical Research in Accounting: Selected Studies, 1969*, Supplement to Vol. 7, *Journal of Accounting Research,* 90–123.

He used a conventional model in which the price of common stocks is determined by the discounted value of expected dividends. A linear regression analysis on cross sections of sixty-one industrial firms resulted in some evidence of a relationship between the accounting procedures and the cost of equity capital. However, this relationship was rather weak; for example, out of the nine regression coefficients of the accounting variables, only four were statistically significant.

Although the preceding empirical results seem, in general, to support the contention that investors are able to "see through the numbers," no definite conclusions can be drawn because of various methodological deficiencies in these studies; the samples were in most cases small and nonrandom, no control groups of firms were used, and most important, the studies failed to account for important nonaccounting factors affecting stock prices, particularly general market movements. These deficiencies were, to some extent, removed in the following studies.

Kaplan and Roll, using a sample of about 350 firms, examined the effect of differences in accounting methods relating to the investment tax credit (i.e., considering the tax savings as current income vs. spreading the savings over the life of the project) and to depreciation (straight-line vs. accelerated).[45] The residual analysis method, based on Sharpe's market model, was used to account for general stock price and interest rate movements. Results generally indicated that accounting changes did not have a statistically significant effect on stock prices.[46]

Ball also used the residual analysis to investigate the price effect of various changes in accounting techniques, such as inventory and depreciation methods and subsidiary accounting.[47] His analysis was novel in various respects, particularly in the use of a cross-sectional rather than a time-series market model and the adjustment for changes over time in the sample's average degree of systematic risk. Results again indicated that the accounting changes had no effect on market prices.

Can the market be fooled by changes in financial results through manipulation of accounting techniques, or are investors able to see

[45] R. S. Kaplan and R. Roll, "Investor Evaluation of Accounting Information: Some Empirical Evidence," *Journal of Business*, 45 (April 1972), 225-57.

[46] It should be noted, however, that a temporary effect on stock prices was discernible for the investment credit case: "Securities of firms that increased reported earnings by adopting the flow-through method of accounting for the investment credit [i.e., recognized currently the whole tax savings] experienced abnormally good times in the ten weeks surrounding their earnings announcement. . . . The proportion of securities with individually positive cumulative returns rises more than 14 percent from 0.416 in week 25 to 0.562 in week 36. This is a significant movement in security prices, and its coincidence with increased accounting earnings is highly suggestive of a positive relation." (*Ibid.*, p. 240.)

[47] R. Ball, "Changes in Accounting Techniques and Stock Prices," *Empirical Research in Accounting: Selected Studies, 1972*, Supplement to Vol. 10, *Journal of Accounting Research*.

through the numbers? Empirical evidence generally indicates that accounting changes had no significant effect on stock prices, implying that investors are able to recognize economic reality despite the different reporting modes. However, a qualification is warranted here; in a few cases, accounting changes seemed to have some effect on stock prices.[48] Whether such effects are systematic and of economic importance is yet to be determined.

FINANCIAL ANALYSIS IN EFFICIENT MARKETS

The evidence presented in this and the preceding chapter indicated that (*a*) large capital markets are efficient in the sense that security prices generally reflect all publicly available information, (*b*) financial statement information is used in investment decision making, and (*c*) investors are able in most cases to distinguish between real economic changes and changes in financial data resulting from the use of different accounting techniques. This evidence has important implications for financial statement analysis.[49]

Evidence indicates that some of the information contained in corporate financial statements is unexpected by investors, that is, is not impounded in security prices at the time of information release. In addition it was found that investors react to the unexpected information once it becomes known. This suggests that a major objective of financial analysis should be the *prediction* of future financial results. For example, Ball and Brown estimated that knowledge of the sign of the earnings forecast error (i.e., whether the news will be "good" or "bad") twelve months before the earnings announcement would yield an above-average return of about 8.5 percent. Analysts' efforts should therefore be directed toward the development of financial data prediction models. As outlined in Chapter 8, models concerned with earnings prediction would probably be based

[48] Recall Kaplan and Roll's finding regarding the effect of the investment tax credit method mentioned above. Some effect of changes in depreciation methods on stock prices was noted by T. R. Archibald in "Stock Market Reaction to the Depreciation Switch-Back," *The Accounting Review*, 47 (January 1972), 22–30. Baskin reported an effect of exception to the accounting consistency rule on stock prices in "The Communicative Effectiveness of Consistency Exception," *The Accounting Review*, 47 (January 1972), 38–51.

[49] Some implications for accountants and regulatory bodies (e.g., the SEC) can be found in N. J. Gonedes, "Efficient Capital Markets and External Accounting," *The Accounting Review*, 47 (January 1972), 11–21; R. G. May and G. L. Sundem, "Cost of Information and Security Prices: Market Association Tests for Accounting Policy Decisions," *The Accounting Review*, 48 (January 1973), 80–94; and George J. Benston, *op. cit.*

on interim report information, expected future events (e.g., the introduction of a new product), and industry- and economy-wide indicators. Or, as indicated in Chapter 13, models concerned with estimates of future risk changes would be based on the relevant firm characteristics, such as operational and financial leverage, and sales and production stability.

The importance of predicting future financial outcomes is emphasized by the fast adjustment of security prices in efficient markets to new information. Little is to be gained from acting upon financial information after its release to the general public. Action should be taken on the basis of predictions rather than on available information. Thus, for example, a financial report announcing record earnings should not necessarily trigger a purchase of the firm's securities, since the favorable information will already be reflected in increased prices. Rather, this information should be used as an input to a prediction model concerned with future outcomes. The orientation of financial statement analysis should therefore shift from the traditional examination designed to identify undervalued or overvalued stocks to the development and use of prediction models.

Recall the conclusion in the preceding chapter that in efficient capital markets, security prices will impound not only all publicly available financial information but also the value of all known analytical tools. Thus, any prediction model or method of financial analysis that becomes publicly known will quickly lose its usefulness because the value of the derived information (e.g., predictions) will already be reflected in security prices. Analytical tools are therefore self-destructive in efficient markets unless kept secret, and even then their useful life is relatively short. Therefore, ingenuity, originality, and secrecy are necessary conditions for successful financial analysis. Efforts should be continually made to design new models and tools and to obtain access to new information sources. In short, the objective is to transform publicly available information to inside information by the application of original tools and techniques.

It should be noted that in real capital markets the cost of processing information is by no means negligible. Given this cost, it might be that various information sources are generally available, yet because of the high processing costs the value of information is not fully reflected in security prices. Suppose, for example, that demographic census data on trends in population growth are relevant for the prediction of earnings growth rates. Suppose further that the cost of processing this information is currently higher than the expected benefits. Consequently, investors would ignore such information and hence its value would not be impounded in security prices. However, if a financial analyst succeeded in sufficiently reducing the information-processing cost, he would obviously be rewarded by above-average gains. Accordingly, an important objective of financial statement analysis is the reduction of information-processing costs. Tools, such as decomposition measures which efficiently scan large data files to detect unusual phenomena, should be developed to decrease processing costs. Here again the objective is to transform publicly available information (which is not reflected in stock prices) to inside information.

Analysis of historical financial data might also be useful in defining "corporate personality," that is, in determining whether a consistent set of behavior patterns exists which might be used to predict management response to environmental changes (e.g., credit tightening). The existence of a stable corporate personality is frequently argued by organizational behaviorists, and some preliminary evidence indicates that accounting data may be useful in defining such corporate personality.[50]

It should be noted that a substantial portion of the financial analyst's activities is performed outside the confines of efficient capital markets. Many investment decisions are concerned with partnerships or privately owned firms whose equities are not traded in stock markets. Investments are frequently made in foreign countries, particularly developing ones, where capital markets are largely inefficient. In such cases the role of financial analysis will not be restricted to the development of prediction models or to the uncovering of inside information. The objective will be close to the traditional "intrinsic value" evaluation. Conventional tools, such as ratio analysis, will be used to arrive at a fair value of the enterprise examined, based on its past performance and future prospects.

Finally, note that the preceding discussion was exclusively concerned with financial analysis for investment in corporate equities (e.g., common stock). However, analysts are engaged in various other activities which are not directly related to equity investments and hence extend beyond the confines of the efficient capital markets model; for example: credit analysis for bank-lending decisions, where the main objective is to estimate the probability of the applicant's default; analyses of financial reports for collective-bargaining purposes, where the objective is to estimate the relationship between changes in employee productivity and wages; or financial analysis of public utility accounts to justify a case for rate changes.

SUMMARY

The role of financial statement analysis in efficient capital markets was discussed above. Two empirical questions were examined in this

50 See G. H. Sorter, S. Becker, R. Archibald, and W. H. Beaver, "Accounting and Financial Measures as Indicators of Corporate Personality—Some Empirical Evidence," in *Research in Accounting Measurement,* R. K. Jaedicke, Y. Ijiri, and O. Nielsen, eds. (American Accounting Association, 1966), pp. 200–10.

context: (*a*) Do investors currently use financial statement information in their investment decisions? and (*b*) Are such decisions affected by changes in the accounting techniques employed by firms? Empirical evidence seems to provide an affirmative answer to the first question; all the studies presented indicated some investor reaction to the release of financial information. The evidence regarding the second question is somewhat less conclusive; while investors generally appeared to be able to "see through the numbers," there were a few cases in which changes in accounting methods seemed to affect security prices.

Discussion then turned from an examination of investor behavior to the normative aspects of financial statement analysis. Specifically, the implications of the efficient capital markets model for optimal financial analysis were examined. It was concluded that financial analysis in efficient markets should mainly be (*a*) oriented toward the prediction of future financial results and (*b*) aimed at decreasing the cost of information processing.

CHAPTER SIXTEEN

Synthesis

In the first chapter of this book it was asserted that a new approach to financial statement analysis is emerging. Numerous aspects of this approach were subsequently discussed and various models and empirical findings presented. The time has come to evaluate the state of financial statement analysis and to outline the desired course for future progress. The following conclusions and observations will be classified according to the three main groups involved in financial statement analysis: the information processors—financial analysts, the information suppliers—accountants, and those in charge of future progress—researchers.

CONCLUSIONS FOR FINANCIAL ANALYSTS

Given the evidence on capital markets efficiency (Chapter 14), it seems appropriate to envisage the analyst as operating most of the time in a competitive environment where new and less costly information sources are constantly sought, and where prices react rapidly to the release of new information. Competition generally prevails even beyond the confines of the stock markets. For example, bank financial analysts, engaged in the provision of information for lending decisions, compete for new information (e.g., on firms in need of financing) with analysts of other banks, analysts of insurance companies, investment houses, and so forth. The highly competitive nature of the environment in which analysts generally operate calls for the design of financial statement information systems possessing the following characteristics: (*a*) capability for an efficient (i.e., least cost) handling of mass data (e.g., firms' published reports, reports to regulatory agencies, industry- and economy-wide statistics, etc.); (*b*) ability to provide data and answer queries in a short time, that is, a "quick response" system; and (*c*) generality and flexibility—the former characteristic refers to the ability of the information system to handle diverse requests without substantial modifications, while the latter refers to a system that, when necessary, can be modified at low cost. To satisfy the preceding three requirements, financial statement analysis must be modified as follows.

Formalization of financial analysis. Traditional financial analysis is mainly concerned with the provision of data on the historical economic situation of the firm. Measures were thus developed to indicate the firm's past and present profitability, liquidity, and operational efficiency. Estimates of future outcomes required for decision making are derived from this information in a rather informal manner, based largely on the analyst's judgment and intuition. However, the modern approach views the prediction of future outcomes as an integral part of the formal financial analysis. Accordingly, the computation of financial indicators (e.g., ratios) constitutes the preliminary stage of the formal analysis rather than the final stage as was traditionally the case. This shift in emphasis is significant; it requires that analysts' efforts be directed to the development of formal models intended to explain and predict economic phenomena such as earnings growth, bond ratings, financial failure, and mergers. Model construction and verification should therefore replace the traditional emphasis on the development of new ratios. Numerous examples of such models were provided in Part II of the book, and despite various shortcomings they provide a general framework within which improved models can be developed. This new approach should also be combined with a shift from the traditional univariate financial analysis (i.e., the examination of ratios independently of one another) to a multivariate analysis where several indicators are simultaneously considered for the explanation and prediction of business phenomena.

The future course of financial statement analysis will thus be characterized by a gradual incorporation in the formal evaluation process of decision fragments that were hitherto treated either intuitively or heuristically.[1] Such a development is, of course, in line with the progress of decision and information sciences toward a continuous substitution of formal models for heuristic, intuitive problem solving.

Incorporation of nonaccounting information. The importance of nonaccounting information for the explanation and prediction of business phenomena was repeatedly demonstrated in the preceding chapters. Financial statement information is constrained by accounting conventions to reflect in a specific manner a limited set of events, thereby providing only a portion of the decision-relevant information. Various kinds of nonaccounting information are obviously relevant for decision making, for example, firm age and location for bankruptcy prediction, changes in market share, load factors, and employee absenteeism for performance evaluation, bond subordination status for the prediction of bond ratings, the outlook for the industry and the economy for earnings prediction, and so forth. Modern financial analysis will thus experience an increased use of nonaccounting data in financial models.[2]

Stock market data, reflecting the aggregate assessment of investors regarding future outcomes of securities, constitute an important source of information for financial analysts. For example, changes in price-earnings ratios indicating the growth prospects of the firm may be usefully incorporated in bankruptcy and bond ratings prediction models. The residual analysis, discussed in Chapter 3, may be used to identify the occurrence of firm-specific events. Changes in bond risk premiums might indicate changes in the riskiness of the firm. Increased use should therefore be made of stock market data in the construction of financial models.

Unconventional form of variables. Traditional financial analysis is almost exclusively based on ratio-type variables. Since it has been shown above (Chapter 5) that ratios are rather restricted indicators of economic phenomena, increased use should be made of unconventional forms of financial indicators. Of special promise are the measures indicating dynamic aspects of the firm's behavior, such as earnings variability over time (used in the prediction of risk premium, Chapter 10), smoothing measures of financial statement items (correlated with systematic

---

[1] The alert observer of the professional literature (e.g., *Financial Analysts Journal*) will recognize an increasing trend toward model construction and formalization of the investment analysis process.

[2] During the process of a shift in emphasis, there is always the danger of overshooting; in this case, the increased use of nonaccounting data might lead some enthusiasts to ignore the basic financial statement data. This might have occurred in the Penn-Central bankruptcy, as argued in R. F. Murray, "Lessons for Financial Analysis," *Journal of Finance*, 26 (May 1971), 327–32.

risk, Chapter 13), and the decomposition measures (Chapter 4) indicating changes in financial statement structures.

The analyst should also experiment with various transformations of the original variables intended to yield improved predictive results. Thus, for example, a logarithmic transformation of financial ratios will in most cases decrease their positive skewness (Chapter 5), resulting in a smaller degree of violation of the least-squares regression assumptions. The use of first differences of the examined variables rather than their absolute values will under certain circumstances decrease variable misspecification. Ideally, of course, the form of variables and the transformations required will be dictated by the theory underlying the investigated phenomenon.

Statistical considerations. Analysts following the new approach should pay increased attention to the statistical properties of financial measures and models. For example, the high degree of contemporaneous correlation among ratios implies that a few carefully selected ratios (three or four in most cases) will convey most of the information contained in financial statements. However, it should be recalled that the ratio correlation might adversely affect the precision of regression estimates (see the discussion of multicollinearity in Chapter 5).

The appropriate standard of ratio evaluation is still a problematic issue. Is the industry reference the relevant one? If so, should the industry mean, median, or other measures of central tendency be used for comparative purposes? More basically, why should the investigated firm be compared with the average or typical firm in its industry rather than with the most successful one? No adequate answers are available to these questions. It should be noted, however, that the industry-average standard of comparison, traditionally a cornerstone of financial analysis, plays a relatively minor role in a multivariate analysis. For example, in a multiple regression model, it is usually possible to account for industry effects by a dummy variable, rather than by an individual comparison of each ratio with the industry mean. The major statistical problem facing an analyst is that of model specification, that is, the appropriate choice of explanatory variables, relative weights, and mathematical form of the model (Chapter 5).

Accounting considerations. The allegations concerning the irrelevance of financial statement data because of the inconsistencies between accounting and economic valuation principles were shown to be exaggerated (Chapter 6). The economic principles of income measurement and asset valuation are ill defined in a world of uncertainty and hence cannot serve at present as guidelines for financial reporting. However, various modifications of, and additions to, currently published financial data are of substantial importance to financial analysts, in particular the modification of historical income and asset values to reflect current asset prices, the publication of nonaccounting statistics and operational data, and the disclosure of management's budgets and forecasts. Until such data are generally reported, the analyst must secure them from the firm.

The adverse effects of the leeway allowed by generally accepted accounting principles were also shown to be somewhat exaggerated (Chapter 6). In most cases the information needed to convert (at least approximately) the financial results from one accounting method to another is provided in the financial statement. For example, firms are now required to disclose in a footnote the obligation under lease contracts, thereby allowing the analyst to adjust the balance sheet figures to reflect appropriately the lease obligation. When the information required to adjust the reported results is not provided in the financial statement, the analyst must obtain it directly from the firm.

Operating in efficient markets. The conditions of capital markets efficiency suggest substantial changes in the behavior of financial analysts. Most important, analytical tools and techniques cannot be adopted from books, articles, or financial institutions; they must be original and developed specifically for a given purpose. In efficient markets, the value of *published* models and information-processing systems is already impounded in security prices, and therefore their usefulness to analysts is questionable. The importance of available models, such as those presented in the preceding chapters, is twofold: they further understanding of the investigated phenomena (e.g., bond risk premiums), and they provide a framework within which original models can be developed. Available tools and techniques of financial analysis should therefore be considered as a starting point in model construction.

However, originality and ingenuity are not sufficient conditions for success in efficient markets. Secrecy and prompt action are at least as important. Given the self-destructive nature of financial models (i.e., once they become publicly known their usefulness diminishes rapidly), they should be kept in secret and the decisions recommended by the models should be promptly executed. Traditional financial statement analysis is obviously unfitted for operation in efficient capital markets.

CONCLUSIONS FOR ACCOUNTANTS

Most accountants apparently do not yet fully realize that the usefulness of financial statement analysis is the major test for the value of their product. Stated differently, the justification for the rather heavy private and social cost of the elaborate financial accounting system maintained by business enterprises lies in the ability of financial state-ment analysis to improve users' decision making. Accordingly, it is appropriate to examine various financial accounting issues and con-troversies from the viewpoint of financial statement analysis.

The usefulness of new reporting modes. Accounting progress is characterized by advances of new kinds and forms of financial reporting. Quarterly data, fund statements, and segmented reports of diversified companies provide some recent examples. The accounting literature is replete with a priori and rather inconclusive arguments regarding such reporting suggestions. Given that the main purpose of financial account-ing is to improve decision making, the merits of suggested reporting modes should be evaluated within the framework of financial statement analysis. Specifically, the suggested information should be incorporated in financial models to examine whether the resulting decisions are superior to those reached without this information. Thus, for example, the usefulness of interim reports was investigated by examining the im-provement in the prediction of annual earnings brought about by the quarterly earnings figures (Chapter 8). Recall, however, that a complete evaluation of an information system requires a specification of the deci-sion model for which the information is used. Predictability is not a sufficient criterion for selecting information systems (Chapter 7). Thus, the evaluation of new accounting reporting modes requires the specifica-tion of users' decision models. A promising framework for the evaluation of accounting information is provided by the portfolio model (Chapters 12–13), which is the most advanced and well-specified investment deci-sion model currently available.[3] Thus, alternative accounting informa-tion systems for investment decisions can be ranked according to their success in selecting portfolios. Obviously, the portfolio model is not the only framework for evaluating accounting information.

Standardization of accounting principles. A long-standing contro-versy among accountants and users of financial statement information concerns the effects of the leeway allowed by generally accepted account-ing principles of income measurement and asset valuation (Chapter 6). Evidence suggests, with some exceptions (see Chapter 15), that users are in most cases able to recognize the firm's economic situation despite different reporting modes. There is no evidence of systematic effects of changes in accounting techniques on investor decisions. However, such evidence does not imply that there is no need for increased standardization of accounting principles. Even if investors were per-

---

[3] For elaboration on the use of financial decision models for the evaluation of accounting information, see W. H. Beaver, "The Behavior of Security Prices and Its Implications for Accounting Research," Report of the Committee on Research Meth-odology in Accounting, *The Accounting Review*, Supplement to Vol. 47 (1972), 407–37.

fectly able to recognize and adjust for any differences in accounting techniques, they would obviously incur costs in the adjustment process. These information-processing costs imposed on society might be decreased by a standardization of accounting techniques. A complete analysis of the accounting standardization problem therefore requires the consideration of welfare economic issues weighing social and private benefits against costs. Until such a comprehensive analysis is made, accountants are advised to use the following rule of thumb for financial reporting purposes. Where users' adjustment costs in converting one form of information to another are negligible (e.g., the various methods of reporting the investment tax credit or computing earnings-per-share), there is no need to enforce standardization. Full disclosure of the information would suffice. However, where users' adjustment costs are substantial (e.g., the various methods of recording mergers), increased standardization is called for. Such cost considerations would be appropriate for regulatory bodies, such as the SEC and the AICPA, in deciding upon the standardization problem.

Competition in the information market. Accountants should realize that various information sources, in addition to accounting, compete for the privilege of being used by decision makers. In efficient capital markets, the failure of one source to provide efficiently the relevant information paves the way for other sources to fulfill the need. Users will select the most relevant and efficient information systems, ignoring redundant and expensive information. Accordingly, one test for the usefuless of an information system, accounting in our context, is to observe whether investors react (i.e., trade securities) upon the release of the information. Various important accounting issues, such as the relative advantages of alternative measurement principles or the effectiveness of statutory requirements (e.g., the SEC rules), can be investigated by examining investor reactions.[4] For example, the usefulness of disclosing earnings forecasts can be examined by observing (on a sample of firms that currently report this information) the effect of such disclosure on investor behavior.[5]

Many questions related to the role of accounting in the information market are still unanswered and deserve accountants' attention: (*a*) When information (e.g., on the firms' future plans) is not disclosed

---

[4] For elaboration on this issue, see *ibid.;* and N. J. Gonedes, "Efficient Capital Markets and External Accounting," *The Accounting Review,* 47 (January 1972), 11–21. For some reservations on the usefulness of market tests for accounting policy decisions, see R. G. May and G. L. Sundem, "Cost of Information and Security Prices: Market Association Tests for Accounting Policy Decisions," *The Accounting Review,* 48 (January 1973), 80–94.

[5] The techniques of such analysis (e.g., the residual method) were discussed in Chapter 15.

to the general public, some individuals might obtain it and earn above-average returns at the expense of all other investors. The question then is, What social costs are imposed on the public by accounting rules that permit nondisclosure of information (e.g., the withholding of data on current prices)? (*b*) What is the comparative advantage of accountants in providing any type of information? To answer this question, the alternative sources of information should be specified and the costs associated with each source determined. (*c*) What is the proper role of regulatory bodies, such as the SEC and AICPA?

CONCLUSIONS FOR RESEARCHERS

It was stated in the Introduction (Chapter 1) that the major objective of the new approach to financial statement analysis is to construct formal information systems integrally related to decision makers' models. It is clear that this objective has not yet been fully attained. Various financial models have been developed and presented above, but they still do not constitute a unified and verified financial statement information system. Given the short history of the modern approach to financial analysis, this failure can readily be understood. However, maturity calls for a change; crude financial models can no longer be accepted, conflicting results should be satisfactorily explained, and a coordinated research effort should replace the sporadic bursts of the past. Following is a more specific outline of the major deficiencies of current research and some suggestions for improvement.

Theory construction. The major deficiency of current research lies in the inadequacy of the models used. In most cases it appears that researchers, having defined their objective, embark on a "fishing expedition" which consists of indiscriminately experimenting with a large number of variables and mathematical models. Consequently, results are usually of an *ad hoc* nature and difficult to generalize. The bankruptcy prediction models (Chapter 9) provide a case in point. Because of the different mathematical models, samples, and statistical designs used in the various studies, it is impossible to compare results and determine the relative performance of the models suggested. Clearly, no substantial progress can be achieved without a consolidation of available research.

The inadequate models currently employed are generally a symptom of the lack of a theory underlying the phenomenon examined. Consider again the bankruptcy prediction example; a well-defined theory of corporate failure would have guided researchers in the choice of explanatory variables and mathematical structure, that is, in the model specification, thereby allowing comparability and continuity of research efforts. Future research in financial analysis should therefore be based on more solid theoretical grounds. In some areas, relatively well-specified theories already exist. For example, the portfolio theory (Chapter 12) specifies the informational requirements of the optimal portfolio selection process. Researchers can take off from this stage and investigate the optimal ways of providing the required information. In areas where adequate theories do not exist (e.g., corporate bankruptcy, the process generating corporate earnings, etc.), research efforts should be concentrated on theory construction. Researchers in financial analysis should thus invade the areas of economics, finance, accounting, sociology, and so forth, and participate in the formation of the required models.

Decision model specification. The discussion in Chapter 7 indicated that a complete evaluation of financial statement information systems requires a specification of the decision model for which the information is requested. Different decision models, and in particular different utility functions, will require different sets of information. Accordingly, evaluation of financial models by their predictive power (as was done in the interim reports studies, Chapter 8), is insufficient. A direct and explicit specification of the decision maker's value criterion in the development and verification of financial models is inescapable. In a few cases, the researcher might have some information on the user's utility function. In most cases, however, such information will not be available, and the researcher might experiment with various general, plausible forms of utility functions. Sometimes it might be desirable to settle for a less than complete ordering of information systems. For example, the "informativeness" concept advanced by Blackwell and others [6] allows a partial ordering of information systems which is effective in the presence of all conceivable preference structures.[7]

Statistical deficiences. Most current empirical studies in financial analysis suffer from statistical deficiencies. Following are a few of the most common.

Sample sizes, which used to be rather small a decade ago, are now impressive and usually consist of several hundred firms. This change was made possible by the advent of mass data banks in the form of computer

[6] D. Blackwell, "Equivalent Comparison of Experiments," *Annals of Mathematical Statistics,* 24 (June 1953), 265–72; and J. Marschak and K. Miyasawa, "Economic Comparability of Information Systems," *International Economic Review,* 9 (June 1968), 137–74.

[7] For elaboration on model specification, and in particular on the problem of the value criterion specification, see N. H. Hakansson, "Empirical Research in Accounting 1960–70: An Appraisal," in *Accounting Research 1960–1970: A Critical Evaluation,* N. Dopuch and L. Revsine, eds. (University of Illinois, Center for International Education and Research in Accounting, 1973), pp. 137–73.

tapes (e.g., the Compustat and the CRSP tapes). However, the availability of such tapes is a mixed blessing. First, the population included in the tapes is usually biased; the Compustat tape, for example, contains large, successful firms that have gone public. Results of studies based exclusively on such sources are therefore biased and difficult to generalize. Second, mass data sources are usually riddled with errors and omissions generally ignored by researchers. Preventive steps, such as a quality control check of the data (on a sample basis, of course) and the use of measures insensitive to extreme errors (e.g., the median), should be taken.

Statistical analysis is too frequently dominated by convenience. Ordinary least-squares regressions are almost exclusively used by researchers to explain and predict phenomena, without due attention to satisfying the model's underlying assumptions (e.g., linearity, homoscedasticity, etc.). In most cases, researchers do not allow the reader to judge for himself the adequacy of estimation; important measures and data, such as the F-statistics, the Von Neumann ratio, the variance-covariance matrix, and the residuals plot, are not reported in the study.

The use of the calibrated samples technique (discussed in Chapter 9) is still not widespread. Prediction models are often developed and tested on the same set of data, without due attention to the inherent bias. To eliminate this bias, the model should be tested on a hold-out sample.

The classic statistical tests of significance are usually applied in a crude and inflexible manner. For example, if the regression coefficients do not meet the .05 significance level, the hypothesis is flatly rejected. Given that financial statement analysis deals with decision making, it would seem more appropriate to substitute the Bayesian approach to inference for the classical tests of significance. Specifically, allowance should be made for prior evidence bearing upon the subject investigated, and the estimation of confidence intervals should replace the conventional inflexible null hypothesis tests.

A FINAL NOTE

We have come full circle. The presentation of the new approach to financial statement analysis was opened in Chapter 1 by outlining the failure of the traditional approach to keep pace with developments in economics and finance. The various characteristics of the new approach were then presented and evaluated throughout the book. However, the synthesis in this chapter suggests that in many respects this new approach is still in its embryonic stage. Thus, while the right course of development for financial statement analysis has been found, there is still a long way to go.

Index